STORYTELLING Activities Kit

Ready-to-Use Techniques, Lessons & Listening Cassettes for Early Childhood

By Jerilynn Changar, Ph.D.,

and Annette Harrison, Master Storyteller

Illustrations by Shelley Dieterichs

**THE CENTER FOR APPLIED
RESEARCH IN EDUCATION**
West Nyack, New York 10995

© 1992 *by*

THE CENTER FOR APPLIED
RESEARCH IN EDUCATION

West Nyack, NY

10 9 8 7 6 5 4 3 2

ISBN 0-87628-869-7

THE CENTER FOR APPLIED RESEARCH
IN EDUCATION
West Nyack, NY 10994
A Simon & Schuster Company

On the World Wide Web at http://www.phdirect.com

Printed in the United States of America

This book is dedicated
to Al and Earl
for their patience, support, and love.

Special thanks to:

Marilyn Phillips for her research assistance;

Sandy Levy for her expert recording and production of the cassette tapes, as well as her composition of the music;

Ruthilde Kronberg for her loving assistance in helping Annette create some of the stories;

Diane Davenport for her work as the musical consultant;

Stacy Washburn, Alice Joseph, and **Rosalyn Glaser,** our Early Childhood Consultants;

Sheila Onuska, our patient and thorough editor; and

Jon Pingree, Jason Guthrie Barton, and **Lora Davenport** for their clerical assistance.

ABOUT THE AUTHORS

JERILYNN CHANGAR, PH.D., has been an art educator for 29 years. She taught art education and gifted education in public schools for 14 years. For 8 years, she worked at CEMREL, Inc., as a curriculum developer and coordinator in aesthetic education and related areas, where she developed and published a variety of K–12 educational materials and conducted numerous workshops locally and nationally. Since 1986, she has been an independent consultant working on a variety of research and evaluation projects. Her teaching and workshop presentations focus on visual arts, including their relationship to children's literature and creative writing. She is currently an Assistant Professor at Southern Illinois University at Edwardsville.

ANNETTE HARRISON is a master storyteller and educator with a national and international reputation. For 14 years she has delighted audiences throughout the United States and Argentina with her "story theatre," which entertains and educates at the same time. The educational value of storytelling and how it can enhance the already existing classroom curriculum is a key element of her teacher workshops. Annette has a B.S. degree and taught in the Baltimore Public Schools early in her career. She has produced three successful storytelling cassette tapes that are recognized by NAPPS (the National Association for the Preservation and Perpetuation of Storytelling). Annette is currently the costar of *Gator Tales,* a children's television program using storytelling as a vehicle to teach self-esteem and personal responsibility.

ABOUT THIS RESOURCE

The *Storytelling Activities Kit* will encourage and assist you as a teacher, librarian, or caretaker of children ages 3–7 to tell stories and to integrate storytelling into your basic curriculum.

Storytelling is an essential component of literacy development and plays an important role in the young child's learning environment. Storytelling is a very effective means of communication. Fran Stallings speaks of this particular quality in *The National Storytelling Journal:* Spring/Summer 1988 article, "The Web of Silence: Storytelling's Power to Hypnotize."

> Stories in themselves have a special power. They compel us to "hear and attend and listen" in a way that other forms of speech do not. Public speakers, from pulpit to politics, know how an anecdote can make an audience's ears perk up.
>
> Master teachers use stories to help students absorb, understand, and remember effortlessly.

Ken Goodman in *What's Whole in Whole Language?* (Heinemann Educational Books, Inc., New Hampshire, 1986) states:

> Narratives and poetry can so completely represent the experience of the writer that readers or listeners feel the same emotions, as if the actual experience were theirs. In fiction, language can actually create experience.

The *Storytelling Activities Kit* will provide you with stories and correlated activities that offer easy and comfortable language experiences for young children, allowing you to bring storytelling magic and a sense of wonder into your classroom. The activities and the suggestions for storytelling will stimulate a learning climate that enhances oral and written communication and encourages development of other language skills.

UNIQUE AND USEFUL FEATURES

1. Simple techniques for storytelling, specifically for young children ages 3 to 7.
2. Interdisciplinary activities that relate the stories to current early childhood curriculum concepts.
3. A comprehensive multimedia resource—complete with 12 of the 24 stories on cassettes—that can be used as is or as the beginning for a total curriculum for "Teaching Through Storytelling."

This kit is designed to help children develop story awareness and build a foundation for literacy development. Specific skills developed through the use of storytelling in the classroom are:

- using the senses to develop visual imagery
- differentiating reality from fantasy
- making comparisons
- identifying concepts
- noting details
- identifying patterns and rhythms
- seeing connections such as cause and effect relationships
- making predictions
- problem solving

Each story is followed by a set of activities and reproducible worksheets using the whole language approach to extend and expand the story experience.

Each activity is designed to increase the child's growing knowledge of print, sound, and writing. The activities are organized according to basic content areas of preschool and primary education programs, making connections for the teacher between story content and form and the early childhood education curriculum.

The multisensory activities are designed to:

- develop students' self-esteem
- develop an appreciation for children's literature
- enhance language skills such as speaking, writing, listening, and reading
- develop creative problem-solving skills
- develop fine motor skills
- develop imagination

Story elements are presented and elaborated on through activities based on the visual arts, writing, story building, sound and movement, creative drama, and other expressive experiences. The activities provide structure and guidance for the students. Since young children need cues to assist in story building, suggestions are provided for how to give the students story cues. The intent is to enhance the students' and the teacher's skills in:

1. storytelling
2. integrating arts activities into the basic curriculum
3. building a repertoire of stories from oral and literary traditions that can be used in a spontaneous way at appropriate educational moments

4. teaching through storytelling using stories from folklore, children's literature, and life experiences

An essential goal of this book is to help children to learn through storytelling that words are something to play with, and something to help us share experiences and feelings in a pleasurable way. As a result, children will experience literary and expressive experiences as an integral part of their learning.

Jerilynn Changar
Annette Harrison

STORIES ON THE
STORYTELLING ACTIVITIES KIT'S
CASSETTES

Tape 1, Side A

"The Little Pine Tree"

"The Boy Who Cried Wolf"

"Grandpa's Enormous Turnip"

Tape 1, Side B

"The Snow Parlor"

"The Shoemaker and the Elves"

"The Nervous Little Hare"

Tape 2, Side A

"The Loom Pa Pas"

"The Worry Bundles"

"The Lion and the Mouse"

Tape 2, Side B

"The Three Pigs"

"Why the Sun and Moon Live in the Sky"

"Hamburger, Hamburger on a Bun"

The original music was composed by Sandra M. Levy. The recording was produced at Smith/Lee Production Studio, St. Louis, Missouri.

CONTENTS

1

Let's Talk About Storytelling

Storytelling is one of the oldest forms of communication. Throughout time, people used the oral tradition to share the simplest of events along with their most important and meaningful experiences. Stories are the lessons of life containing the oral history of a culture's beliefs and values. As we repeat the telling of events we develop a memory of the past which comes alive and connects us with the future. Storytelling is a most successful method for linking the past with the future, and teaching us about universal concepts and important events throughout history. Storytelling is a natural and important tool for teaching and learning in our classrooms.

Sharing stories is a natural means of communication. Arriving home from school, we relive the events of the day and tell our family and friends a story about a special experience with a child or how we solved a difficult problem. When we come home from a vacation and we share a particularly meaningful event with our students, we are telling a story. We continually tell stories. Storytelling is a meaningful and integral part of our lives. We tell stories to communicate ideas and feelings, joyous and sad events, lessons to be learned, and insights into ourselves and others. Each and every one of us is a storyteller.

As the storyteller you create drama in miniature—you supply the setting, introduce the characters, even speak for them, and narrate the story—you do it all. It can be a tiny little play/story such as "The Three Bears" lasting only five minutes; yet it can have the same dramatic impact for a young child as going to the theatre. Storytelling evokes imagery as magnificent as the finest book illustrations and brings the same dramatic joy and feelings of wonder and magic as the theatre. It introduces children to patterns of language and extends their vocabulary.

Storytelling is not just a listening experience; it is an interactive participatory process where the children can assist in the telling of the story and help solve the problems of the characters as the plot unfolds. For example: When telling "The Three Bears," the baby's porridge is all gone, the teller can turn to the children and say, "What should they do? Baby Bear does not have any porridge." The children can then respond with suggestions for the bears such as, "Mama Bear should make more porridge," or "Papa and Mama can share what they have," or "They can eat the berries they picked in the forest." The possibilities are unlimited as long as the flow and pace of the story are not lost.

Through this kind of active-listening process the children become involved with the story and identify with the characters. They learn empathy for others; they come to recognize that they are not alone with their feelings and that loneliness, fear, love, anger, joy, and so forth are universal. Storytelling enriches self-concept as children identify with the emotional and intellectual experiences of the characters. By participating in the adventures of the story they discover that they can also win the prize, solve the problem, have self-worth, have a place in their family, be a special person with unique talents, and recognize others in the world with similar feelings. In addition, the story is told by their very own teacher whom they already love and trust—a person who can lead them to seek out stories as a source of pleasure throughout their lives.

> It is a time of closeness, intimacy, complete trust in what is shared—a time of wonder and remembering. (Sawyer, 1942, p. 183)

At this point you might ask, "What is the difference between telling and reading a story?" There is something magical about telling without the book. Some of the differences are:

1. Your eyes are not on the words, they are on the listeners. You are looking into their eyes and they feel the story is just for them.
2. Your hands are free for movement, for expression and for drawing the children into the story.
3. There are no pictures, so the children have to use their imagination.
4. A special bonding and trust develop between you and the children. Some say the audience and the storyteller begin to breathe in the same rhythm and their hearts beat in unison.

(Of course, reading to children is also essential and we encourage you to read, read, read!)

When you begin to tell stories, it's easier to tell a story you already know. If you are ready to begin and you would like to try telling "The Three Bears" to your students, a bare-bones version of this well-known story and an outline are placed at the end of Chapter 2

Reference:

Sawyer, Ruth. *The Way of the Storyteller,* Viking Press, New York, 1962.

HOW TO USE THIS KIT

A Whole Language Approach

This kit is intended to fit right in with your language curriculum. It uses the multisensory approach of whole language and is linked to the themes and concepts of early childhood education. It should be compatible with your language, reading, and art curriculum while simultaneously making connections with science and social studies concepts. The contents of the kit and how to use them are described below.

The Cassettes

The cassettes bring the storyteller into your classroom. Each chapter has one recorded story to be used as it is for listening or to help you to learn the story for telling. The written text of the second story is included for you to tell or read. There is also an outline of the taped story for you to use if you choose to tell the story.

The Lessons

Each chapter has two fully developed lessons relating to the key concepts in the chapter and the specific content of each story. There is a variety of activities in each lesson. You will want to read over each set of activities and select or adapt the ones that make the most sense for your classroom.

Age Appropriateness

The activities are designed for ages 3 to 7. In some instances activities can be used with simple modification for any age level.

Additional Stories and Activities (* indicates tellable tales)

Additional stories are included in each chapter. A brief description of two or three stories is provided. The books may be borrowed from your library and the stories learned for telling or you may read them to the children. If the children can read, you may want to put the books in the story center. There are suggested activities for some of the additional stories and a short list of other relevant stories.

The Worksheets

The worksheets are included at the end of each story as companions to the activities. Not all activities have worksheets. In many instances they are included as a supplement. Encourage the students' imagination and creativity. Do not use the worksheets for coloring or filling in the blanks. The creations of very young children may not be recognizable by adult standards. Ask the children to tell you a story about their creations. This is an essential component of the storytelling process.

The Story Center

A story center is a place where children can retell the story they just experienced; can read other versions of the story and/or stories related to the same concept; and/or can create a new story.

1. You can use an already established play center.
2. After a story is told, set up some props for re-enactment. For example:
    a. Set up three chairs in a row, three bowls on a table, a red cap or hood, granny glasses, a lace cap, Three Little Pigs puppets.
    b. Have the students create some of the props: finger puppets, a house made out of sticks, a house of bricks, or a portrait of the Bear family.
3. Have some copies of the book available. In the case of a folktale such as "The Three Bears" or "The Three Little Pigs," you can have several different versions.
4. Put together a class book of drawings of the stories by the students and laminate it. Leave it in the center.

5. Make a puzzle out of a drawing of the three bears, the three pigs, and so forth.

6. Have a listening area where children can listen to story tapes. Perhaps you can tape the story and they can listen to it, over and over again.

7. Have other books related to the theme for them to look at.

8. Set up a recording area where they can tape their very own version of the story.

9. Have paper, crayons, and markers available so that students can draw their own version of the story.

10. Keep boxes of clothes, shoes, hats, and masks, so they can become the characters of the story. Include a variety of scarves for children to use for improvisation and creative movement.

11. Set up a Word Box (for older students). Put in new words they learned from the story. Let them pick one, look it up in the dictionary, use it in a sentence, and draw a picture of it.

A story can be shared at any time. You may want to tie stories in as they fit with your curriculum. You may share the story one day, do activities for several days, and then share the story again. Remember, children like to hear stories over and over again.

Do not feel that this kit is not for you even if you haven't reached a confidence level that allows you to do your own telling. Use the cassettes as your teller and read the additional stories as you desire. Many times you and the children can retell the story together, a technique that reinforces the concepts and gets them involved in role playing. You may want to document the whole process with photographs. Children love to see pictures of themselves and the photographs can be used to make the whole experience come alive again. Remember to pick and choose the activities and suggestions that you are comfortable with and that make sense for your setting.

THE LESSON FORMAT

Each chapter includes one complete story on tape, one written story, a story synopsis for the taped story, two complete lessons related to the key concept, a list of additional activities in abbreviated form, and a list of additional stories some of which are summarized with abbreviated activity descriptors. Each lesson has the following parts:

PART I: THE STORY EXPERIENCE

    1. ABOUT THE STORY (OR THE STORY)
    2. KEY CONCEPTS AND THEMES AND/OR UNIVERSAL IDEAS
    3. SUGGESTED COMPANION(S)
    4. PREPARATION
    5. PREPARATION FOR VISUALIZATION
    6. LISTEN TO THE STORY
    7. FOLLOW-UP DISCUSSION QUESTIONS

PART II: THE ACTIVITY

    1. OBJECTIVE
    2. INTRODUCTION
    3. MATERIALS
    4. PROCEDURE
    5. LANGUAGE DEVELOPMENT
    6. EXTENSIONS

The following section will provide a description of each component of the lesson.

Part I: The Story Experience

1. About the Story

The text of the story or a story summary.

2. Key Concepts and Themes and/or Universal Ideas

The universal idea or underlying theme of the story. This concept should be the guide, the central focus and the unifying theme for the activities. It is important to extend the story in a meaningful way. Without careful thought, it is easy to relate activities to story experiences in a superficial way.

3. Suggested Companion(s)

Toys, objects, visuals, or whatever items might relate to the story and stimulate the students' imagination (i.e., a teddy bear or a small rocking chair for "The Three Bears").

4. Preparation

Questions or statements that set the stage for the children.

5. Preparation for Visualization

A brief visualization activity (five minutes maximum) where you ask the children to close their eyes or sit quietly as you talk them through an imaginary experience related to the content or theme of the story that helps personalize the experience.

6. Listen to the Story

7. Follow-up Discussion

Suggested questions based on higher order thinking skills so you can help the children process the story.

Part II: The Activity

1. Objective

A statement of specific learning objectives.

2. Introduction

A brief overview of the activity.

3. Materials

Materials needed for the lesson. There are many materials suggested. Do not let the list inhibit your creativity. Use what is available in your school or classroom.

4. Procedure

The steps involved in doing the activity. This section takes you through each step of the activity, specifying what you need to do in the process of introduction and what the children are to do.

5. Language Development

Ideas which emphasize language development and the whole language approach to reading and writing.

6. Extensions

Additional ideas to extend the activity.

And now, if you are ready to develop your skills as a storyteller, as we hope you are, turn to Chapter 2 for tips and preparation for telling. For additional, up-to-date information about storytelling, a great resource is the National Association for the Preservation and Perpetuation of Storytelling (NAPPS).

2

Telling the Tale

THE STORYTELLER'S TOOLS

Each of you has the essential tools needed to be an effective storyteller: voice, natural gestures and movement, a sense of timing, good eye contact, and expressiveness. It's how you use them that makes the difference. To be a successful storyteller with young children there are three important characteristics you need—energy, enthusiasm, and playfulness. So learn your story and go for it. A teacher who wants to share stories in the classroom does not need professional training, only some good guidelines and practice, practice, practice. STOP AND THINK, YOU DO IT ALL THE TIME! The response from the children—their visible enchantment—will spur you on to tell more and more stories.

A. Yourself

1. Voice

When you begin storytelling, you will be surprised by the range of your voice and its many different tonal qualities.

    a. You can make your voice loud and soft. You can use a loud voice to portray a powerful character or to depict a dramatic moment. A soft, intimate voice can be used to draw the children into the story. It can also be used during the tender, loving parts of the story.

b. You can make your voice high or low or full or thin and vary your pitch according to the character who is speaking or the situation. When you tell stories you will naturally increase the range of your voice. Children love it when, as the storyteller, you cackle like a witch, whisper, snore, hiss, bark, cry, and so on.

c. Use your voice for sound effects: knocking on the door, creaky floors, the sounds of a train or airplane, or the swish of water.

d. Use your voice to express emotion such as when Baby Bear sees his broken chair.

2. Natural Gestures and Movement

a. Most of your gestures and movements will be unplanned and will happen naturally. When you portray Papa Bear, you will unconsciously raise yourself up to your fullest height. As Baby Bear you'll round your shoulders and try to become as small as you can. Relax and trust your instincts, don't force it, let it happen.

    b. Be aware that too much movement or too sudden a movement takes away from the storyline. Emphasize the *most* important parts of the story with gestures.

3. Sense of Timing

Your timing will improve with telling. Remember to speak slowly and let every word be important. Give the children time to listen and develop their own visual images. Pauses are just as important as narrative and are good for dramatic effect. You also want to make your endings clear. You might want to say something like, "And that is the end of my story."

4. Eye Contact

By making good eye contact with each child, you begin to connect the children with you and the story. Your goal is for each child to feel as if the story is especially for him or her. Eye contact helps to draw the child into the story, making the experience intimate and personal.

5. Expressiveness

Allow your body, face, eyes, and words to come alive and enhance your storytelling. Let what you feel inside shine through to your audience.

B. How to Pick a Story

Even though as a teacher of young children you are already familiar with children's books, there are some differences between selecting a story for telling and one for reading. The following guidelines will assist you in selecting stories for telling:

1. You need to pick a story that immediately gets the attention of young children. The stories in this kit have this quality. Notice that the stories relate to young children's lives; they have quick action, a simple plot, strong characters, and humor; they evoke emotions and stimulate the senses.

2. You may want to share a story you love or a story that touches you.

3. Look for:

    a. a simple plot, with each incident related to the plot
    b. quick action
    c. well-defined characters
    d. vivid word pictures
    e. events children can relate to
    f. repetition
    g. action that maintains suspense and quickly builds to a climax
    h. an ending that resolves the conflict and leaves the listener feeling satisfied

C. Where to Find a Story

This may seem obvious, but storytellers are repeatedly asked this question. Here are some suggestions:

1. Most preschool classrooms overflow with books. Pick one of your favorites.

2. Go to the library or bookstore. Children's librarians are very helpful. Tell them the concept or subject. They will lead you.

3. Seek out other resources such as teachers, storytellers, librarians, and bibliographies.

4. Search your memory for your favorite childhood stories, stories that have been in your family, or your own children's favorite stories. Use your own private bookshelves. You'll be surprised at what you find and the memories you rekindle.

5. True stories are powerful. You can turn a true event into a tellable tale.

D. How to Find the Time

Although storytelling is an important part of an early childhood curriculum, it is only one part of a very busy program. You may be asking yourself, "How do I find the time to learn a story?" The more you do it, the easier it becomes. Here are some tips that may help you.

1. Put your story on a cassette. Listen to it in the car, while doing household chores, and while taking a bath.

2. Keep the written story with you at all times. Whip it out while waiting in lines, in the doctor's office, or at any other time you are waiting for something to happen.

3. Practice your story out loud while preparing dinner, driving the car pool, or taking a shower.

4. Read the story before you fall asleep at night.

5. Try the story out on anyone you can find, the dog or cat, the parrot who will tell it back, your kids, a spouse, or anyone who will listen. Have fun with it.

E. How to Get Ready for the Telling

1. Read the story many times. At the very least, read it out loud twice. Until you hear it with your own voice it is not your story. Once it's yours, it's yours forever.

2. Reduce it down to a few sentences. What is the key concept, the essence of the story, or the main idea?

3. Discover the setting by using your senses. Include your setting in the telling. Write down everything you know or can create about the setting. Can you draw a map of your setting? Can you smell the fresh flowers or the soup cooking? Can you see the path through the forest or the little mouse hiding? Can you touch the golden hair of the princess or the water from the pond? Can you feel the soft, wet, or furry kitten? What can you hear? The creaky floors, the baby crying, or the birds singing. How does it sound? Scary, sad, cheerful. Is there something to taste? Porridge, raindrops, or lollipops. How might it taste? Sweet, fresh, or salty. Can you describe the setting so that your listener can actually be there?

4. Discover the characters. Write down the name of each main character on a separate piece of paper. Describe each of them using all your senses. Get into their skin

and look at the world through their eyes. Create dialogue between characters so that you can get to know them. As the characters speak to each other, you'll get to know them, their thoughts and feelings, the sound of their voices, and who they are.

5. Make an outline of your plot. In order to see the story and the way it unfolds, make an outline that reveals the plot. At a single glance you should be able to see the whole story. A good way to do this is to divide the story into scenes. The first scene is usually introductory. You set the stage and meet the characters. Here is where you engage the listeners and bring them into the story. The middle of the story usually introduces the conflict or the problem. The crisis usually occurs as a result of the conflict or as the problem intensifies. The end of the story comes together as the characters solve the problem. (See an example of a plot outline at the end of this chapter.)

Now that your story is outlined you can fill it in and make it as detailed as you wish. Include any important words, verses, rhythms, rhymes, and dialogue that you want to remember. Do not memorize the story verbatim. Rely on your own language.

It is important to know your plot well. Then you won't draw a blank or lose the flow of the story. Then you can be playful and improvisational and not have to worry about the exact words.

F. Decisions

Select those that meet your needs.

1. Decide on verses, rhythms, rhymes, chants and/or movements to teach the children so they can participate in the story.
2. Decide how your characters are going to be introduced. They can be introduced with body gestures, different voices, simple props, or by using one of the children as the character. Do you want to put on a scarf to introduce Mama Bear? Do you want to skip around as Goldilocks? Do you want to strut like Papa Bear?
3. Decide where the dialogue fits in. If there isn't any, create it where you think it will add interest and insight into the character. An example would be a conversation between Goldilocks and her mother before her adventure in the forest or between Mama and Papa Bear as she prepares the porridge.

4. Decide if you are going to use any special voices such as a croaking frog, a cackling witch, or a barking dog. Are you going to use sounds like a creaking floor, falling rain, whistling wind? What about voices for Papa Bear, Mama Bear, and Baby Bear?

5. Decide if you are going to use props such as puppets, pictures, a story bag, hats, and so on. Will you set up three chairs for "The Three Bears"?

6. Decide if you are going to use any of the children in the story. Are you going to pick a Goldilocks to act out her part?

7. Decide if you are going to let the children create parts of the story. Supply some words? Ideas? Become the characters? Solve the problem? As you become a more experienced storyteller this will become a natural part of your storytelling with young children. An example would be tasting the porridge with Goldilocks, or asking some questions such as, "How can the three bears keep Goldilocks from coming back?" or "How can they become friends with Goldilocks?"

We have provided you with many suggestions but we realize that much storytelling is just on-the-job training and doing what comes naturally. Pick and choose the ideas that you find most helpful.

"You Don't Need Experience, but Experience Is the Best Teacher."
(McKissack, Patricia and Kronberg, Ruthilde. *A Piece of the Wind and Other Stories to Tell*, Harper & Row, New York, 1990.)

PRACTICE TELLING "THE THREE BEARS"

PROPS: Three chairs sitting in a row.

[Start with an intimate voice to draw the children into the story. Use gestures to show BIG, MIDDLE SIZE, and SMALL.]

Once upon a time there were three bears. They lived in their very own house deep in the forest. There was Papa Bear, a great big bear; Mama Bear, a middle-sized bear; and Baby Bear, a wee little bear. Each of the bears had its own bowl for porridge: a big bowl for Papa Bear, a middle-sized bowl for Mama Bear, and a wee little bowl for Baby Bear.

They each had a chair to sit in: a big chair for Papa Bear, a middle-sized chair for Mama Bear, and a wee little rocking chair for Baby Bear. There were three beds to sleep in: a big bed for Papa Bear, a middle-sized bed for Mama Bear, and a wee little bed for Baby Bear.

[You and the children can stir the porridge with Mama Bear. Act out TOO HOT with face, voice, and gestures. Pantomime with the children—put on jackets, zip them up, and pull on hats and gloves.]

One day Mama Bear made porridge for breakfast and poured some into the three bowls. Papa Bear tasted the porridge and said, "This porridge is too hot. Let's take a walk in the forest." And so they did.

[As Goldilocks walks through the forest, have the children sing, la la la la la. Let the children taste the porridge with you. Let them gesture and make faces with you.]

A little girl named Goldilocks was walking through the forest and saw this snug little house nestled in the trees. She looked in the window, then peeked through the keyhole, but no one was there. She tried the latch and the door was not locked so she walked right in. She saw the three bowls of porridge on the kitchen table. It smelled so good and Goldilocks was hungry. She walked over to the big bowl of porridge and tasted it, but it was toooo HOT. Then she tasted the porridge in the middle-sized bowl; it was toooo COLD. Then she tasted the porridge in the wee little bowl and it was JUST RIGHT. So she ate it all up.

[Sit on each one of the chairs and have an exaggerated reaction each time.]

Now Goldilocks looked in the parlor and saw three chairs. She sat down in Papa Bear's big chair, but it was toooo HARD. Then she sat in Mama Bear's middle-sized chair, but it was toooo SOFT. So she tried Baby Bear's wee little rocking chair and it was JUST RIGHT. ROCKITY, ROCKITY, ROCKITY, BOOM! The bottom fell out and it broke into many pieces.

[Sit on the beds and have an exaggerated reaction each time. You might want to embellish your reaction for baby's bed. Talk about his quilt and his stuffed animals. Pantomime falling asleep.]

Goldilocks walked upstairs to the three bears' bedroom. First she laid down on Papa Bear's big bed, but it was toooo HIGH at the head for her. Mama Bear's middle-sized bed was toooo HIGH at the foot for her. But Baby Bear's wee little bed was not toooo HIGH at the head and not toooo HIGH at the foot, it was JUST RIGHT. She covered herself with Baby Bear's wee little quilt and fell fast asleep.

[Use three different voices and have the children participate with you. You might allow them to say their part themselves.]

The three bears finished their walk and came home for breakfast. When Papa Bear saw the spoon that Goldilocks left in his porridge, he said in a great big voice, "SOMEBODY HAS BEEN TASTING MY PORRIDGE." Goldilocks had left the spoon in Mama Bear's middle-sized bowl of porridge, too. Mama Bear said in a middle-sized voice, "SOMEBODY HAS BEEN TASTING MY PORRIDGE." Then Baby Bear looked at his wee little bowl and said in his wee little voice, "Somebody has been tasting my porridge and has eaten it all up." And Baby Bear began to cry.

[Have everyone cry with Baby Bear. They love to see you pretend to cry.]

The three bears walked into the parlor. Papa Bear saw the cushion was not straight in his big chair and he said in a great big voice, "SOMEBODY HAS BEEN SITTING IN MY CHAIR." Mama saw the cushion was squashed down in her middle-sized chair and she said in her middle-sized voice, "SOMEBODY HAS BEEN SITTING IN MY CHAIR." Then Baby Bear looked at his chair and said in a wee little voice, "Somebody has been sitting in my chair and broke it to pieces." And Baby Bear began to cry.

[Let the children tell this part with you. Example: And Mama Bear said, _____. Act out Goldilocks sleeping. Open your eyes, look around with surprise and run with your hands moving quickly on your knees. Run. Run. Run all the way home.]

The three bears went into their bedroom. Papa Bear noticed that his pillow was out of place in his big bed and he said in a great big voice, "SOMEBODY HAS BEEN SLEEPING IN MY BED." Mama Bear noticed that the blanket was wrinkled on her middle-sized bed and she said in her middle-sized voice, "SOMEBODY HAS BEEN SLEEPING IN MY BED." Then Baby Bear looked at his wee little bed and said in his wee little voice, "Somebody has been sleeping in my bed and there she is." Goldilocks woke up, opened her eyes and saw the three bears. As quickly as she could, she rolled off the bed, ran to the open window and jumped down. She ran into the forest never to be seen by the three bears ever again.

Preparation for Telling

Now you are ready to share the story with the children. You can (1) tell the story, (2) play the cassette, or (3) read the story aloud. Included in this section are some ideas on how to prepare the children for the story experience by using some visualization techniques for active listening.

Tips for Telling

Visualization

Sometimes in our technological society children find it difficult to conjure up images and use their imagination as a story is told. They have been bombarded with images on television and video games which leave little room for their own imagination to take over. The following exercises will assist you in helping them to get in touch with their ability to use their imaginations and visualize the word pictures created by the story. Use the exercises as time allows.

    A. Creating the Mood This should only take five minutes. If there is not enough time for this or the children are too young, just get them settled and tell them to close their eyes or sit quietly.

1. Make sure the children have plenty of room to stretch out and be comfortable.
2. Have them take off any constricting clothing.
3. Dim the lights.
4. "I'm going to take you on a journey inside your head. Instead of using your eyes to look out, we're going to close your eyes and look in. Before we begin, clear your mind of everything that is in it. Pretend that you're taking your hands and pushing all your thoughts away. Take a slow, deep breath. While I count to three, breathe in. One, two, three. While I count to three, let it out. One, two, three. Now let's try it again. (Repeat the same thing several times. Count slowly.)
5. "Now put your two hands on your ribs, take a deep breath, fill your lungs with air. Feel how much air you can hold. Now slowly let it out. Imagine the balloon as it floats around and the air is slowly coming out. Let's do it again. Are you feeling more relaxed?
6. "Now it's time for the journey. Imagine yourself wandering through the forest hungry and tired. It's early morning and you've had no breakfast and the air is cold and damp. The sunlight is coming through the trees and the animals are scurrying to and fro. What animals do you see? Do you hear the birds singing and the leaves moving in the wind? The leaves have just begun to turn and you see wonderful colors. What colors do you

see? Oh, look, there's a wonderful little house. What does it look like? Can you see the smoke coming out of the chimney? Can you smell the porridge? Oh, look, there's a window; you can walk up to the house and look in. What do you see? Now slowly open your eyes. It's time to listen. I'm going to tell you a story about the Three Bears."

B. Involving the Student in Active Listening

1. Ask a question that relates to the child's life and makes a connection with the story. For example, "Do you ever take a walk in the woods with your mom or dad? Do you have a special chair where you sit in your house? Do you ever have oatmeal for breakfast?" Let the response lead you into the story.

2. Prior to beginning the story you need to prepare the children for participation. For example, "I'm not going to be telling the story alone. We're going to be telling the story together. When it's time to knock on the door, we will do it together. Let's practice together. KNOCK! KNOCK! KNOCK!" Another example is as Goldilocks tries out the rocking chair, everyone pretends to rock. "Let's pretend to rock. As we rock we will say, 'Rockity, Rockity, Boom!' " If there is a chant or repetition, teach it to the children before you start the story so that they can join in. It's the anticipation of playing their part that helps to keep their focus on the story.

3. Another way to include the children in the telling is to stop the story at a suspenseful moment, look directly into their eyes and say, "What do you think happens now? What would you do?" For example, when the three bears walk into the bedroom, you would stop and say, "And what do you think they saw?"

These are some ways to involve the child actively in the storytelling process to show them that this is a participatory event. Following these tips allows for playfulness and creativity within the storytelling structure.

> The unacted story has not been played in; it's an empty structure. The process is incomplete. (Paley, Vivian Gussin, *The Boy Who Would Be a Helicopter: The Uses of Storytelling in the Classroom.* Harvard University Press, Cambridge, Mass., 1990.)

Now you are ready to jump into storytelling. Remember you have the tapes, the printed stories, and yourself as the storyteller. Gather up all of your playfulness, enthusiasm and energy, and have a great time with the children. Here is "The Three Bears" outline if you wish to use it.

"The Three Bears" Summary

I. Introduction to the Setting and Characters

   A. Deep in the forest lived three bears.

      1. Papa Bear—a great big bear with a BIG VOICE

      2. Mama Bear—a medium-size bear with a medium-size voice

      3. Baby Bear—a wee little bear, with a teeny, teeny voice

   B. Each bear had its own things.

      1. Bowls for porridge

      2. Chairs

      3. Beds

   C. One day Mama Bear made porridge.

      1. Papa Bear—"It's TOO HOT! Let's take a walk in the forest."

      2. So they did.

II. The Arrival of Goldilocks

   A. Goldilocks was walking through the forest and saw the house.

      1. Looked in the window

      2. Peeked through the keyhole

      3. Tried the latch and walked in

   B. She tasted the porridge.

      1. Big bowl—"TOO HOT"

      2. Medium-size bowl—"TOO COLD"

      3. Wee little bowl—"JUST RIGHT"—she ate it all up

   C. She sat on chairs in the parlor.

      1. Big chair—"TOO HARD"

      2. Medium-size chair—"TOO SOFT"

      3. Wee little chair—"JUST RIGHT"
        Rockity, Rockity, BOOM.

   D. She tried out the beds.

      1. Big bed—"Too high at head."

      2. Medium-size bed—"Too high at the foot."

      3. Wee little bed—"JUST RIGHT"—she fell asleep

III. The Bears return

   A. They looked in their bowls.

      1. Papa Bear—"Somebody has been tasting my porridge."

2. Mama Bear—"Somebody has been tasting my porridge."

3. Wee Baby Bear—"Somebody has been tasting my porridge and has eaten it all up!"

B. They looked in the parlor.

1. Papa Bear—"Somebody has been sitting in my chair."

2. Mama Bear—"Somebody has been sitting in my chair."

3. Wee Baby Bear—"Somebody has been sitting in my chair and broke it to pieces!"

C. They went into the bedroom.

1. Papa Bear—"Someone has been sleeping in my bed."

2. Mama Bear—"Someone has been sleeping in my bed."

3. Wee Baby Bear—"Someone has been sleeping in my bed and there she is!"

D. Goldilocks woke up and saw the bears.

1. Rolled off the bed

2. Jumped out the window

3. Ran into the forest, never to be seen again

3
All About Me

THE LITTLE PINE TREE
Adapted from an old German Folktale

About the Story

"The Little Pine Tree" is a story about a small pine tree who was not satisfied with who he was and wanted to be different. But each time his wish was granted and he became a tree with a new set of leaves, his enchantment was short-lived. He discovered that the life of each tree was far from perfect: golden leaves get stolen, glass leaves break, and colored leaves fall. The pattern continued until the little pine tree realized that he, too, was special and valuable in his own right. He then decided that being himself was a good thing to be.

Key Concepts and Themes and/or Universal Ideas

At times children and adults have a tendency to concentrate on their limitations instead of their strengths and wish they were someone else. One goal of education is to enable students to appreciate and accept themselves and become the best person they can possibly be. In addition we need not only to appreciate our own strengths and abilities but to revel in someone else's and share in their talents and special qualities. The inclusion of educational experiences which enhance self-esteem and build on children's strengths and self-concept is an essential component of a young child's growth experience.

Suggested Companion(s)

a small live pine tree and/or something with a pine scent

Preparation

Prior to hearing the story, ask students, "When you look in the mirror, do you ever wish that you looked different? Keep that in mind as we take an imaginary trip through the forest." For ages three to four start with the imaginary trip.

Preparation for Visualization

Tell the Children:

Before we hear the story, we are going to take an imaginary trip through the forest. Close your eyes. See the color green. When you see the color green, open your eyes. Close your eyes and picture a pine needle or pine needles. When you see the pine needles, open your eyes. Close your eyes again and picture a pine tree. Open your eyes. Now close your eyes and imagine that you are the pine tree. You feel the wind on your branches. You feel the warm sun, the cool air, the dampness of the ground where your feet, your roots, grow into the ground. You feel your branches, which are your arms, reaching to the sun, and the dew sparkling on your nose. Open your eyes. What did you find in the forest? What did the earth feel like? How did it feel to be a tree?

[If you can, go outside.]

Feel the earth. Smell the earth. What is it like to be in the forest? Hug a tree. What does it feel like to be a tree? Smell the leaves. If there is a pine tree, look closely. How do pine trees look and smell different from other trees?

[Go back inside.]

Sit down and pretend you are the pine tree as you hear the story. Close your eyes and imagine what it would be like to be a pine tree. Now open your eyes and I'm going to tell you a story.

Listen to the Story (Tape 1, Side A)

Follow-up Discussion Questions

1. What did you see?
2. What stands out most in your mind?
3. What was your favorite part of the story?
4. Did you ever want to be someone else? Tell us about it. (older children)

ACTIVITY ONE: EXPLORING FEELINGS

Objectives

—To identify different feelings expressed in the story

Introduction

This activity has two parts. Part One is an art activity where the children will use the worksheets to make sad and happy faces on trees. This activity is designed so that all children can easily become involved.

Part Two includes the retelling of the story so that the children will use the sad and happy trees to identify feelings in the story. The story should be retold by the teacher and children together. If you used the tape the first time, do the retelling with the children without the tape.

Materials

Sad and Happy worksheets

wax or oil crayons, markers

pre-cut trees (younger children)

Sequencing worksheet

Procedure

1. Children will complete the worksheets individually making a happy tree and happy picture of themselves on one, and a sad tree and a sad picture of themselves on the other. Younger children can paste pre-cut shapes to create faces on the trees and for their own faces. Older children can use wax or oil crayons or markers to create a sad or happy face.

2. Retell the story. When you ask, "How is the pine tree feeling?" ask all the children to hold up the worksheet with the appropriate face.

Teacher begins:

"Once upon a time there lived a little Pine Tree who lived in a big forest. He had beautiful green pine needles and a sturdy little trunk—but he would look down at himself and say, 'Yuck. I don't like me the way I am.'" (Ask the children to hold up the face to show how he feels.) " 'I wish I could be big and tall like the Oak Tree, or bear fruit like the Apple Tree, or just be like all the other trees in the forest and have leaves that change colors.'" Ask the children, "What happened next? Let's act it out. Who wants to be the pine tree and who wants to be the angel of the trees?" (The angel of the trees comes down and gives the pine tree his choice of leaves.) "Now how is the pine tree feeling? What kind of leaves does he choose?" (golden leaves) "What happens to the golden leaves? Let's act it out. Who wants to be the man and who wants to be the tree? How is the tree feeling now?" Continue the story this way. Have them hold up the appropriate feeling at the right time and continue to involve the children in the narration and the dramatization of the story.

3. After retelling the story, ask the children when they feel happy or sad. For example: How do you feel when

   —it is your birthday?

   —a puppy licks your face?

   —you get two scoops of ice cream?

   —your mother yells at you?

   —you get a new toy?

   —you have to go to bed early?

   Add your own examples.

Language Development

1. Use the sequencing worksheet. Have the children create a picture of the appropriate tree in each box. Let them take the worksheet home to retell the story to their family.

2. Identify different kinds of trees. Look in the school yard, the park, or your yard at home. What kinds of trees do you see? Are they different or the same? Are the leaves different or the same? Do they have pine needles? Are the pine needles different colors or are they the same? Do the trees have berries? Can you eat them or will they make you sick? Do the trees give you shade from the hot sun? How big is the tree? Can you hug the tree? Do your hands meet or is the tree too big? If you jump up, can you touch one of the branches? Do the branches touch the sky? If trees are accessible, have the children look at them every day for a week. Do the trees look the same on a sunny day as they do on a cloudy day? Have the children look at the trees each day and tell you everything they see. Put the words on index cards. Give the children the cards with their own words. If they can read them, have them read them back to you. As the week goes on, they should see more and more. Keep putting the words on the cards. On one day have them look at the trees and then paint the trees on 18″ by 24″ paper. Use tempera paint. Have the older children write some of their words on their pictures.

3. Ask the children if they can tell you a story about their trees. Do the story as a group story. Start the story:

> Once there was a very sad tree because he had no clothes. So he talked to his friends the clouds and they said they would help him get some clothes. He looked at the other trees and their clothes were green and orange and yellow and red. He really wanted to look like them. He asked the trees if they could help him. What did they do?

As the group creates the story you can record it. At a later time have the children act it out, recreate, and embellish the story.

Extension

Have the children draw the part of the story that made them happy or the part that made them sad. Encourage the children to talk about their pictures.

ACTIVITY TWO: THE TREE I'D LIKE TO BE!

Objectives

- —To develop body awareness and a positive self-concept
- —To be able to compare and contrast similarities and differences
- —To develop visual expression
- —To enhance self-expression

Introduction

This activity has three parts. In Part One the students will create a self-portrait. In Part Two they will make a life-size body and decorate it as the tree they'd like to be. In Part Three they tell a story about something that happened to them as if they were a tree. They can tell their story to the other boys and girls or into a tape recorder.

The purpose of this activity is for the child to empathize with the Little Pine Tree and feel what it would be like to become a tree. After exploring your immediate environment or a nearby park and looking at trees, bring in pictures and ask the children which is their favorite kind of tree and what makes it special. Ask if they could be any tree, what kind they would be. Compare the child's body parts to the tree (arms to branches, legs and torso to trunk, leaves to hair or clothes, trees breathe air like we do, and so on).

Materials

Part One: Crayons and round paper plates
Part Two: Large butcher paper, kraft paper, scissors, a variety of colored construction paper, paste or glue sticks
Part Three: Writing materials and possibly a tape recorder
Extensions: ME Buttons worksheet

Procedure

Part One

Give each child a paper plate and some crayons. If a mirror is available, have them look at their faces and locate their different features. Have the children (older children) draw a picture of themselves (self-portraits), adding as much detail as possible. Have the children talk about their picture. For younger children pre-cut some geometric shapes and guide them through pasting the appropriate shapes for each feature on their paper plates. Have the children tear construction paper and paste it on the plates for hair.

Part Two

Compare the child's body to the tree. Give each child a piece of tan, brown, or black kraft paper that is a little larger than body size. Have the children do this with a partner. Have the children take turns lying down on the paper while their partner draws their shape. You will have to do it for the younger ones and help them cut out the bodies. The children should lie down with their legs together and their arms spread out like branches. After the bodies are cut out, have the children tear leaves out of construction paper in any colors they want. Attach the head and display the bodies around the room.

Once the trees are hanging up, encourage the children to add some other things to the trees—acorns on oak trees; fruits on fruit trees; nests, birds and squirrels on all trees; pine cones on pine trees; coconuts on palm trees; monkeys on palm trees; bananas on banana trees; flowers on flowering trees.

Part Three

Older children can tell their own story. The story can begin, "It was a cold day in the forest and snow began to fall . . ." or "The children were having a picnic in the forest and they came up to me and said . . ." or "It was a spooky Halloween night and . . ." or "I woke up one morning with icicles on my branches . . ." or "A woodcutter came into the forest . . ." or "It was the hottest day of the year . . ." or do your own thing.

Language Development

1. What does it feel like to be a tree? Each child says "It feels like _____ to be a tree." Write them all on chart paper.
2. Create a poem about being a tree. You might want to share the poem *Trees* by Joyce Kilmer.
3. Create a play about living in the forest.

Extensions

1. Create the dance of the trees. The life-size trees can be tied to the children's bodies (without the heads) and they can use them as costumes if you wish. How does the tree move in the wind, when it rains, as it grows, when you shake it, when the leaves fall, and so on.
2. Compare and contrast how the trees are alike and different.
3. Students can use the worksheet with the I'M SPECIAL and the I LIKE ME BUTTONS to create self-portraits to wear proudly. Your school may have a button-making machine where you can make real buttons.
4. The song "Mail Myself to You" would lend itself to reinforcing self-concept and self-esteem. The song could be acted out so that each child would demonstrate his/her unique contributions to the world. The song is available in *The Woody Guthrie Songbook,* published by Grosset and Dunlap. It has also been recorded by several singers including Woody Guthrie.

STORY SUMMARY

I. Introduction to characters and setting

   A. A long time ago, there lived a beautiful Pine Tree.

      1. He had beautiful pine needles, sturdy little trunk, could reach out his branches, his pine smell filled the forest

      2. He looked down at himself, "YECH! I don't like me at all. I'd like to be:

         a. "Big and tall like the Oak Tree."

         b. "Able to bear fruit."

         c. "Just like all the other trees with leaves that change colors."

   B. Angel of the trees

      1. "What's wrong, little Pine Tree?"

      2. "Even you call me little," says the Pine Tree.

      3. "If you could choose leaves, what would you choose?"

II. The Pine Tree gets new leaves.

   A. I want golden leaves.

      1. Oak tree: "You'll be sorry!"

      2. Next day he had golden leaves that glistened.

      3. A man came with a ladder and sack and picked every single golden leaf.

   B. I want glass leaves. I'll be beautiful and make music, too.

      1. Oak tree: "You'll be sorry!"

      2. Next day he had glass leaves that could catch raindrops.

      3. Gentle winds blew and he made twinkling sounds.

      4. Gusty fall winds broke his leaves.

   C. I want to be like all the other trees in the forest and have leaves that change colors.

      1. Angel said, "You'll lose your leaves." "Not me, I'm special."

      2. Oak tree: "You'll be sorry."

      3. All the trees began to change colors: Pine Tree, too.

      4. Fall season came. All the trees began to lose leaves. BUT NOT THE PINE TREE, he held on to his.

      5. A winter snow came and finally his leaves fell one at a time to the ground.

III. Pine Tree becomes himself AGAIN.

   A. "I've been so foolish; I wish I could be myself again."

1. "First I wanted golden leaves, someone came and took them."
2. "Then I wanted glass leaves, everyone knows that glass breaks."
3. "They told me I'd lose my leaves, I just didn't believe them."
4. "I WISH I could be myself AGAIN."
5. The Angel of the trees was listening.
   a. Very next day, he was himself again.
   b. Oak tree: "You are beautiful just the way you are."
6. He was so happy just being HIMSELF!

Look at me!
Look at my
Tree!
We are as
sad as we
can be!

Activity One, Procedure #1

**All About Me
Worksheet**

Look at me!
Look at my
Tree!
We are as
happy as
can be!

Activity One, Procedure #1

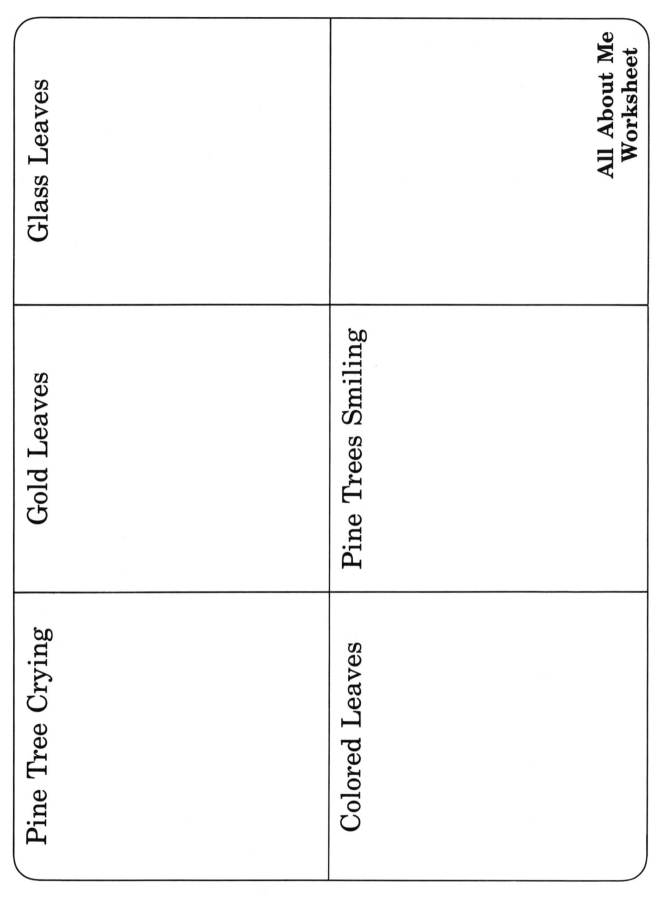

Pine Tree Crying	Gold Leaves	Glass Leaves
Colored Leaves	Pine Trees Smiling	All About Me Worksheet

Activity One, Language Development #1

I Like Being Me!

I'm Special!

Activity Two, Extensions #3

THE DIRTY BOY
By Robert Kavet*

The Story

This is a story about a little boy who just hated to take baths. So he just didn't.

In time the dirt got so thick that no one liked the dirty little boy. People would point at him and say, "Look at that dirty little boy." *[Pantomime pointing.]*

His mother, his father, everyone pleaded with him to wash his hands, wash his face, his neck, his ears. But he wouldn't because he just didn't like soap or water.

Then came summer and something remarkable happened. All kinds of things started growing on the little boy. Beautiful flowers grew out of the dirt on his head—red roses, yellow daisies, blue asters. *[Use hand gestures to show the flowers growing.]*

Carrots grew out of his ears, tomatoes around his arms, potatoes from under his nails, even strawberries on his feet. *[Make big exaggerated gestures.]*

Then everyone said, "My, look at that pretty garden," or "Isn't it beautiful," and "Smell those flowers!" He wasn't much of a boy, but he certainly was a great vegetable patch and flower garden.

His mother and father were very proud of him and took him to flower shows and garden club meetings. But they missed their little boy. He couldn't ride his bike. He couldn't play ball. He couldn't skate.

Certain things bothered him. The butterflies were all right, but the bees were frightening. *[Listeners can buz-z-z.]*

He didn't mind the sprinkling or weed pulling. *[Pantomime pulling up weeds from your head.]* But the fertilizer and bug killer bothered him.

One day toward the end of summer the flowers wilted and the vegetables died. And again he

36

looked just like a dirty little boy, so dirty that no one knew who he was.

Then suddenly one day a rain storm washed all the dirt away. *[All together you and the listeners can pretend to take a shower in the rain.]*

Everyone was happy to see him again. He didn't mind washing or taking baths anymore. It felt good to be clean.

When people asked where he had been, his mother and father said that he had been away on a farm. But he knew better. *[Pause.]* The farm had been on him.

The Dirty Boy by Robert Kavet, © 1971, by Carolrhoda Books, Inc., 241 First Avenue North, Minneapolis, MN 55401. Reprinted by permission of the publisher.

Key Concepts and Themes and/or Universal Ideas

This is a simple story that reminds children that there are certain things such as taking a bath, brushing our teeth, and eating healthy foods, that we must do to stay healthy and that the alternatives can be much worse. It also reminds them that certain activities are not as unpleasant as they may initially appear to be.

Suggested Companion(s)

bathtub toys
vegetables and flowers growing in containers (and/or pictures)
soap and washcloth
miniature bathtub

Preparation for Visualization

Tell the Children:

Before hearing the story we are going to close our eyes and pretend that we are SOOOO dirty that vegetables start growing out of our head. Just imagine that a vegetable is slowly growing out of your ear. Now do we all know what a vegetable is? Is it a carrot, broccoli, or a string bean? Is it your most favorite vegetable or least favorite vegetable? What does it feel like as it slowly begins to grow? Does it tickle? Does it hurt? Your mom always told you if you don't take a bath, potatoes will grow out of your ears. What do you think your mom will say as she sees the vegetables growing out of your ear? What do you think your friends will say?

Listen to the Story

Follow-up Discussion Questions

1. What part of the story did you like best?
2. Do you like to take a bath?
3. Do you think the little boy was happy being dirty?
4. What do you think your friends would say if flowers and vegetables were growing out of your head?
5. What's the most fun about taking a bath?
6. What's the worst part of taking a bath?
7. What are some things that you have to do that seem worse than they actually are when you do them?

ACTIVITY ONE: DIRTY LITTLE CHILDREN

Objectives

- To develop visual expression
- To develop language skills
- To encourage dramatic play
- To encourage good health habits

Introduction

The children will create their own self-portraits with vegetables and/or flowers growing out of their heads. Children can role-play the parents and the child arguing about taking a bath.

Materials

paper bags that can fit over the children's heads

large white or tan paper plates

crayons, markers, or construction paper

scissors

paste or glue

Procedure

1. Children will first discuss whether they like to take a bath or not and what it feels like to be dirty. They can brainstorm about what vegetables and/or flowers could grow out of their head. Make a list on the board. You can also find pictures in magazines.

2. Younger children can be given pre-cut flowers and vegetables or magazine pictures to be glued to a paper plate. The plate will represent their head and they can draw in their face. They can glue on the flowers and the vegetables.

3. The older children can be given a paper bag that can be put over their head like a mask. Help them cut out the eyes and mouth and then decorate their face with markers, crayons, or cut paper. Remind them that they haven't taken a bath and their faces are dirty. Then give the children construction paper and have them cut out flowers and vegetables to paste on their bag.

4. The children can role-play the parents and the child. The parents are to try and convince the child to take a bath, telling all the reasons why. The child will resist, telling all the reasons for not wanting to take a bath. You can stop them and turn to the class and say, "How can we solve this problem?"

Language Development

1. When the children complete the initial activities, have them write or dictate a story titled "It's Fun to Be Dirty" or "Fun in the Tub." Have them illustrate the story.

2. Ask the children if they can think of something they were supposed to do and didn't, and the consequences were worse than what they were supposed to do. For example, not wearing warm clothes or boots in bad weather and catching a cold was worse than wearing the boots. At this point we are talking about cause and effect relationships, and the age and maturity of the children need to be taken into consideration. You might ask, "Which is worse—taking a bath or having vegetables grow out of your head so no one will know you or play with you?" "Which is worse—dressing warm and wearing boots or catching a cold?" "Which is worse—brushing your teeth or getting a cavity and having to go to the dentist?" Ask the children to come up with questions.

Extensions

1. Draw a picture of the rain coming down and washing the little boy clean.

2. Buy seeds and plant them and grow a vegetable and/or flower garden or take individual clay pots and have the children paint a face on the pot. It will give the effect of plants growing out of his head.

3. Put a picture of a little boy on the bulletin board and have the children create vegetables and flowers and attach them to his head.

4. Most dogs don't like to take baths. If you were to convince your dog to take a bath, what would you say?

ACTIVITY TWO: THE AMAZING BATHTUB

Objectives

–To develop creative thinking
–To develop language skills
–To develop visual expression

Introduction

Give the children the opportunity to create a new and exciting bathtub that any boy or girl would love to take a bath in. Children can bring their favorite bathtub toys to school for show and tell. The children can also create bathtub toys or songs and rhymes about fun in the tub. For example:

Fun in the tub.
Fun in the tub.
It's time to scrub.
Scrub a dub, dub, dub,
Dub, dub, dub.

Materials

any drawing materials and/or paints and brushes
boxes, tubes, and any other scrap materials like aluminum foil or cellophane glue
the Amazing Bathtub worksheet
a large refrigerator box to be used as a bathtub

Procedure

1. Children can decorate shoe boxes as bathtubs or the large refrigerator box, depending on what is available. What kind of bathtub do you think

all boys and girls would like to be in? Could you make a bathtub that was so much fun that all boys and girls would love to take a bath?

2. The boys and girls can brainstorm while you list all of their ideas on the board. Ask the children what things could be put in or on the tub that would really make it fun to take a bath.

3. Depending on their age and ability, have the children draw their tub or make a three-dimensional tub or use the Amazing Bathtub worksheet.

4. Other options for very young children would be to bring in a wash tub and decorate it or to cut a big bathtub out of poster paper, put it on a bulletin board and have all the children add things to decorate it.

5. Have the class or individual students write a recipe for fun in the tub. Example: Take a tub full of water, a small amount of bubble bath, two rubber duckies, a beautiful wash cloth, some bathtub crayons, and Raffi in the background. Mix together, splash a little and wash until one sparkling and squeaky clean child emerges.

Language Development

Create bathtub songs using water sounds. Have the children see how many water sounds such as "gurgle, gurgle, swish, swish" they can think of. You could use a song like "Old MacDonald": "Old MacDonald had a tub, C-L-E-A-N, and in his tub he had a sponge, C-L-E-A-N, with a squish, squish here and a squish squish there, C-L-E-A-N," and so on. You can add water, splish, splash; soap, slip, slip; bubbles, gurgle, gurgle. Children can create movements to go along with the song.

You can also write poems entitled "When I'm Clean," or "When I'm Dirty." Talk about how it feels to be clean—the smells, the way it looks, and so forth. The same can be done for being dirty. You can use clean and dirty puppets to tell the story. Create a class poem or older children can write poems or stories. They can also write about pets, before and after a bath. Ask the children if they can tell any stories about what happened when they fell in a mud puddle, when they tried to wash their big dog, or when the cat fell in the tub.

Extensions

1. Older children can do a survey and find out how many people like to take showers and how many people like to take baths.

2. Children can do their own set of illustrations for the story and then put them in the appropriate sequence.

3. Create designs for shower curtains.

4. Create new bathtub toys.

5. Have veggies for a snack.

Activity Two, Procedure #3

ALL ABOUT ME: ADDITIONAL STORIES

The following stories that can be told to students relate to the concept or theme "All About Me." If you are not totally comfortable telling stories, these stories may be read to the children. We encourage you to become a teller of tales, but do what feels most comfortable for you.

 The Little Engine that Could by Watty Piper, illustrated by George and Doris Hauman. Platt and Mink Publishers, New York, 1989.

This is a story about a happy little train taking a jolly load of toys and food to all the boys and girls on the other side of the mountain. She suddenly STOPS and simply cannot go another inch. No engines will help until The Little Blue Engine comes along. With all of her strength and determination, "I think I can—I think I can—I think I can," she is able to climb to the other side of the mountain so that the children will not be disappointed.

Suggested Activities

There are several activities that can be built on this story to emphasize that we can do almost anything if we believe we can. The children can sit in a circle and each one can say, "I think I can paint a beautiful picture, I think I can do a somersault, I think I can write my name," and so forth. After the circle activity, each child can do the activity that was mentioned. In most instances, the students, particularly if they are very young, will mention something they can already do. This is fine, just encourage them to elaborate on their skills. If they are older, ask them to think of something they would like to do, tell about it in the circle and then draw a picture about it. Put up all the pictures with an engine in the front and call it the I THINK I CAN TRAIN. If possible, give the children a chance to do the activity.

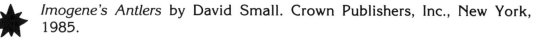 *Imogene's Antlers* by David Small. Crown Publishers, Inc., New York, 1985.

Imogene wakes up one Thursday morning with a pair of antlers growing out of her head. She causes a sensation wherever she goes and finds surprising uses for her antlers. On Friday she wakes up without them but with another surprise.

Suggested Activities

Students can talk about what it would be like to wear a pair of antlers. You can make a hat for the students with antlers and let them wear it for the day or part of the day. What does it feel like to be different? Talk about situations where they might be different. Role play situations where one child is different from all the rest and the others won't play with him or her. How does it feel?

The Carrot Seed by Ruth Kraus. Harper and Row, New York, 1945.

A little boy plants a carrot seed. No one in the family believes that it will come up. He never loses his faith . . . he waters it, weeds it, and FINALLY it comes up!

Suggested Activities

One must have faith and patience. Have the children plant seeds and watch them grow. Have the children write about the planting experience and draw a picture to go with it. Have children create a mural of a vegetable garden or flower garden. Write all the key words related to the planting process on word cards. Have the children sequence them in the appropriate order. Have the children do some creative movement and move as if they were the flower or vegetable growing.

 Biggest House in the World by Leo Lionni. Knopf/Pantheon, New York, 1973.

Father Snail's wisdom teaches Little Snail that some things are better small. He teaches him by telling a story. The story is simple, direct, and filled with imagery.

Suggested Activities

Have the students brainstorm all the small wonderful things that they can think of. Ask them if they think they would be better if they were large. Why or why not? Have the children pretend they are Alice in Wonderland and they drink something that makes them big. Have the children act out what happens in different environments and situations.

 I Wish I Were a Butterfly by James Howe, illustrated by Ed Young. Harcourt Brace Jovanovich, San Diego, 1987.

A poignant story about a cricket who thought he was ugly and wanted to be a butterfly. Along the way he meets a glowworm, a ladybug, and a dragonfly, but it's not until he meets Old One the spider that he finds friendship and realizes his own beauty and specialness. This story would be fun to tell with puppets.

Suggested Activities

Have the students create paper bag or paper plate puppets for each character in the story. Include the children with their puppets in the retelling of the story. The children can also tell what animal they would choose if they could be any animal. They can draw a picture representing the animal they want to be. The children can also draw a picture about themselves and write all the things on the picture that make them special. For example: red hair; I can sing; blue eyes; and so on.

 Timothy Goes to School by Rosemary Wells. Dial Press, New York, 1981.

Timothy faces frustration from Claude, a bully, during his first days of school. Friendship with Violet gives him confidence.

Suggested Activities

For children four years old and up, talk about bullies and what they think about them. Ask them if they can think of any reasons why someone would be a bully. Do some role playing and have them act out the story. Give different children a chance to be the bully. Ask them how it felt.

 Mud Puddle by Robert N. Munsch, illustrated by Sami Suomalainen. Annick Press, Toronto, 1982.

Every time little Jule Ann's mother sends her outside to play she's attacked by a HUGE mud puddle. Each time her mother puts her in a tub of warm, soapy water and washes her until she is very clean. Finally, Jule Ann goes outside armed with two smelly bars of soap. She chases the mud puddle away and it never comes back.

Suggested Activities

Ask the students to tell you about the times they have played out in the rain, running through the mud puddles, and getting all dirty. Ask them, "How did it feel?" "What did your mother say?" "Did you have to take a bath?" Ask them to tell their stories and illustrate them. Ask them to create a dance to chase away the rain and mud.

4
Feelings

THE BOY WHO CRIED WOLF
Adapted from Aesop's Fables

About the Story

This is a story about John the Shepherd who was bored with his job. He thought that tending the sheep was boring and he decided to have some fun. He decided to trick the hunters and pretend that a wolf was threatening his herd. The hunters came to help John and found that he had tricked them—there was no wolf and his sheep were not in danger. John thought this was great fun and tried it a second time with the fishermen. This time, the fishermen were really angry. On the third day, as John was tending his sheep, he heard something that sounded like a wolf. At first, he thought someone was trying to trick him; but then he realized that it was a real wolf who was going to eat his sheep. John ran to the hunters and the fishermen for their help; but they did not believe him because he had lied to them. No one else would believe him either. John was so upset, he didn't know what to do. He ran back to try and convince the wolf not to eat his sheep, but it was too late. The wolf had already eaten his sheep. John had learned his lesson. When he was really in trouble, no one believed him because he had told too many lies.

Key Concepts and Themes and/or Universal Ideas

This story focuses on what happens when we lie and how we lose our credibility and make other people very angry. When we lie, we no longer have the trust of others. The lessons will focus on what happens when we lie to other people and how it makes people angry and disappointed in us. One lesson will deal with exaggeration as a form of lying and how when we exaggerate, people tend not to believe us after a while.

Suggested Companion(s)

a toy wolf
or toy sheep

Preparation

Have you ever told a lie? Has anyone ever told a lie about you? How did it make you feel?

Preparation for Visualization

Tell the Children:

Before we hear the story, we are going to take an imaginary trip. Close your eyes. You are in your room playing with your stuffed animals, dolls, and trucks. You hear a little voice, "Help! Help!" A small fairy is caught in your toy basket and can't get out. It is sparkling and glowing. It is twisting and turning. It is really stuck. You slowly walk over to it. You can't believe your eyes. You have never seen a real fairy before. You are not sure what to do. You are excited but a little afraid. You ask the fairy, "Why should I help you? Who are you?"

And the fairy says, "I'm the tooth fairy who brings gifts to children in exchange for the teeth they have lost. If you let me out I'll give you one of those gifts even though you haven't lost a tooth." You think that might be a fair exchange, so you let the little fairy go.

But the little fairy does not keep its word and flies out the window laughing, "Ha! Ha! I fooled you." You are really angry. The little fairy lied to you. You just don't know if you will ever be able to trust a little fairy again. Now open your eyes and I'm going to tell you a story about "The Boy Who Cried Wolf."

Listen to the Story (Tape 1, Side A)

Follow-up Discussion Questions

1. Did you like the story? Why or why not?
2. Did John do the right thing by tricking the hunters and fishermen?
3. Did you ever tell a lie?
4. How can lies hurt other people?
5. What would you do if you thought someone lied to you or told a lie about you?

ACTIVITY ONE: TRUTH OR CONSEQUENCES

Objectives

—To develop oral communication skills
—To develop critical thinking skills
—To develop an understanding of cause and effect relationships

Introduction

This activity involves a sharing of stories about lies and the child's personal experience with either telling or being told a lie or witnessing the result of a lie. The discussion will focus on how the child felt and some of the consequences of telling lies or trying to fool other people.

Materials

drawing materials
writing materials
Boy-into-Wolf worksheet

Procedure

1. Have the children sit in a circle after the story and tell them they are going to share some stories about when they or someone else told a lie and what happened. You start out with an example and ask the children to volunteer their stories. You might have to guide them along by asking, "Did anyone ever tell you a lie about giving you something and then not give it to you? How did you feel?"

2. The second part of the discussion includes situations the children can respond to. Here are some situations you can use.

   a. Your friend tells you there is a big hole in the seat of your pants. All the boys and girls are laughing. You go into another room and check your pants and find that your friend tricked you. How do you feel? What should you do or what should happen to your friend for tricking you?

   b. Your friends take your lunch box and hide it. When you ask about it, they all say they haven't seen it. When it comes time for lunch, you are very hungry. Your teacher finds it and gives it to you. Your friends have fooled you. How do you feel? What should you do?

   c. Your friend spills her milk. When the teacher asks what happened, your friend blames you for spilling the milk. How do you feel? What do you do?

d. You see someone in your class take another person's pencil. When the teacher asks who took the pencil, no one will tell the truth. You know who did it. How do you feel? What should you do?

e. Your friend tells you that he or she is going to invite you to his or her birthday party. The birthday date comes and you find out you were not invited. How do you feel?

3. Older children can role play some of these situations.

4. Ask the children why they think it hurts other people when they lie.

Language Development

1. Have older children write about "the day I told a lie," "the day someone told me a lie," "the day someone tricked or fooled me," or "the day I tried to trick or fool someone else."

2. Have the class brainstorm how to help someone who tells lies to stop lying.

3. Read or tell the children the story of *Pinocchio* and what happened to him when he lied. Compare him to John in the story. This would work well for both younger and older children.

Extensions

What would have happened to John if everytime he told a lie he began to turn into a wolf? With the first lie he grows a furry tail. With the second lie he grows a long, wet, wolf nose. With the third lie he grows wolf ears. With the fourth lie his

feet turn into paws. With the fifth lie his teeth grow long and sharp. And with the sixth lie, he starts growing hair all over his body. First draw a simple shape of a boy on the blackboard and then have some of the children come up one at a time and add the changes. Have the children use the worksheet to draw their own boy, showing the changes at different stages.

ACTIVITY TWO: EXAGGERATION IS ALSO A LIE

Objectives

- To develop oral communication skills
- To develop creativity
- To develop ability to compare and contrast
- To develop ability to differentiate size relationships

Introduction

This activity will focus on the concept of exaggeration and how exaggeration is a form of lying. The students will exaggerate what happens in the story of "The Three Pigs" and talk about how it changes the story. The children will also discuss what happens in different situations when someone exaggerates.

Materials

drawing materials
writing materials

Procedure

1. Introduce the word *exaggeration* and what it means. Show the children an object. For example, show them an apple and ask them to describe it. Then tell them you are going to exaggerate. Tell them it is the biggest apple in the world and that it is so juicy the juice is just leaking out all over. The apple is so red that it glows like the sun. Ask the boys and girls if you were telling the truth. Ask them what you did and what was not truthful

about what you said. Ask them how they would feel if you told them you were giving them an apple like the one you described but then gave them an ordinary little apple like the one you have in your hand. Ask them if they would be disappointed. Ask them what they would think the next time you described something you were going to give them. For example, you might ask them what they would think if you promised them the best treat they ever had if they did a good job cleaning up the classroom.

2. Tell the children they are going to tell "The Three Pigs" story as a group and change parts of the story by exaggerating. Tell them the story or use the story on the tape as it is. Tell them that they are going to retell the story and exaggerate. For example,

   When the first house was built it was made out of straw that was like spun gold.

   When the wolf blew the house of golden straw down he was like a tornado and the golden straw rained over the land like golden straws.

   When the second pig built his house it was built with sticks that were like skinny logs and when they were blown away by the wolf it was like a hurricane and a blizzard of spears.

   The brick house was like a big, strong stone castle and the wolf blew and blew like a giant monster.

   These are just a few ideas. You can ask the students for their ideas and add to the story or you can use the pigs as an example and then let them do the same thing with another story like "The Three Bears" or the "Loom Pa Pas."

3. After you have done this, ask the children how the exaggerated version of the story made the story different. Ask them if it was believable.

4. For older children, have them draw a picture from the original story and then draw the same picture in its exaggerated version.

Language Development

1. Ask the children if they have ever exaggerated and what happened. Here are some questions to ask:

   Have you ever said that you had a real bad stomach ache so that you wouldn't have to go to school? Was it the truth? What happened? If you did this on many days and your Mom found out, do you think that she might not believe you when you had a real stomach ache?

   Would it be like when John was in real trouble and the hunters and fishermen did not believe him?

Did you ever tell friends that you got a new toy and said it was much bigger and better than it really was? What happened when your friends found out it was just an ordinary toy? Did they think you were lying?

Did someone ever just tap you, or gently bump into you by accident, but you told the teacher they really hit you hard? You were exaggerating. What happened? How would you feel if your friend did this to you and you got punished for something that you really didn't do?

Use some situations that have come up in your classroom.

2. Give children different objects from the room. Have them describe them to the group and exaggerate what they really look like. Have the class tell what parts were changed in the description.

Extensions

Talk about the children's favorite toy. Ask them to draw it and exaggerate. Ask them to make it bigger, fancier, brighter, and more spectacular than it really is. Tell them that it is okay to exaggerate a drawing to make it look more exciting and interesting. This does not hurt anyone.

STORY SUMMARY

I. Introduction to the setting and characters

   A. John is a shepherd.

      1. He takes care of his sheep.

      2. Everyday, they do the same thing. John is bored.

         a. They walk up the hill (ba-a-a).

         b. They eat the green grass.

         c. They play follow-the-leader up one side of the hill and down the other.

         d. And they sleep in the hot sun.

      3. Every evening, they walk down the hill. John eats a boring dinner and goes to bed.

   B. John has a new idea.

      1. He wakes up with a smile on his face.

         a. He takes the sheep up the hill.

         b. They eat the green grass.

         c. They play follow-the-leader up one side of the hill and down the other.

         d. And they sleep in the hot sun.

      2. Now, while his sheep sleep, he plays a trick.

II. John tricks the hunters and the fishermen.

   A. Tricking the hunters

      1. John shouts, "Hunters, hunters, there's a wolf eating my sheep! Help! Help!"

      2. The hunters run up the hill.

         a. "Where's the wolf?" they ask.

         b. "Over there," shouts John. "No . . . over there."

      3. The hunters say, "We don't see any wolf."

         a. John sings, "I tricked you! I tricked you! There is no wolf."

      4. The hunters say angrily, "You'll never trick us again!"

      5. John had fun, fun, fun.

   B. Tricking the fishermen

      1. The next day John wakes up with a smile on his face.

         a. He takes the sheep up the hill.

         b. They eat the green grass.

    c. They play follow-the-leader up one side of the hill and down the other.

    d. And they sleep in the hot sun.

2. While they sleep, he tricks the fishermen.

    a. He yells, "Fishermen, fishermen, there's a wolf eating my sheep."

3. The fishermen run up the hill to help.

    a. They ask, "Where's the wolf?"

    b. "Over there," shouts John. "No, over there."

    c. The fishermen say, "We don't see any wolf!"

4. John sings, "I tricked you! I tricked you! There is no wolf!"

5. The fishermen leave angrily, "You'll never trick us again!"

6. John had fun, fun, fun.

C. John meets the wolf.

1. The next day John wakes up with a smile on his face.

2. He can't figure out whom to trick.

3. He takes the sheep up the hill.

4. While the sheep are asleep, he tries to figure out whom to trick.

    a. He hears, "AHOOOO."

    b. "Who's that?" he says. "It must be someone trying to trick me."

5. He turns around and there is the wolf!

    a. "I'm going to eat your sheep," says the wolf.

    b. "Oh, no you won't. I'll go get my friends," says John.

6. He asks the hunters. They say, "You tricked us once, you'll never trick us again! Go back to your sheep!"

7. He asks the fishermen. They say, "You tricked us once, you'll never trick us again.   Go back to your sheep!"

8. He goes to the townspeople. They say, "Go back to your sheep."

9. John goes back up the hill. His sheep are gone and the wolf is happy and full.

10. "John, you told too many lies. Now when you're telling the truth, no one believes you."

Activity One, Extensions #1

THE FROG PRINCE
A German Folktale Adapted from the Brothers Grimm

The Story

Once there was a princess who was about your age. Her hair was the color of a sunbeam, her eyes the deepest blue of the sky, her laughter sounded like the tinkling of little bells. Everyone who saw her was enchanted by her beauty.

But she did not smile or laugh very often because things were never exactly the way she wanted them. She wanted everything to be PERFECT! If there was the least little spot of dirt on her dress, she would demand a new dress. *[Pantomime a spot on her dress, make your face look unhappy.]* If her mashed potatoes touched her steak, she demanded a new plate with freshly made food. Her silk bed linens were changed each time she laid her perfect little body on them. The King and Queen loved her very much but worried and worried about her. Their perfect little daughter didn't seem to have any fun.

She did have a favorite toy—her perfectly round golden ball! *[Demonstrate playing ball. Throw it up in the air and catch it, joyfully!]* She loved to play with the ball in the sunlight because it sparkled. One day she was out in the rose garden, wearing a white lacy dress, her beautiful blond curls bouncing in the sunlight, her cheeks rosy, playing with her golden ball. She threw it up in the air and SUDDENLY an eagle swooped down from the sky. The Eagle caught the ball in her talons and dropped it into the well.

[Use arms as wings of eagle, pick up the ball in your talons and drop it with a SPLASH! Exaggerate the SPLASH.]

"Oh dear, oh dear . . . my golden ball," cried the perfect little Princess. She ran to the well and peered into the water, but all she saw was her own reflection. She was ready to run back to the castle to get some help when a slimy, ugly frog appeared.

"Oh, Beautiful Princess," he croaked, "I can help you find your ball." *[Use a croaky froggy voice each time Frog talks.]*

"Please help me. I want it back!" she said.

"If I give the ball back to you," said the Frog, his bulging watery eyes looking at her, "I want you to do something for me."

She was desperate. *[Look of desperation on your face]* She wanted her golden toy back, so she smiled sweetly and said,

"What do you want me to do for you? . . . You can have jewelry . . . gold . . . ANYTHING you want, but please find my precious golden ball!"

"Take me back to the castle with you. Let me see the way you live. I want to be at your side, eat from your golden plate and drink from your crystal goblet, and sleep in your little bed."

She laughed her delightful laugh and said, "You are a silly frog. If that is what you want, then I promise I will take you back to the palace. Now go quickly and get my golden ball!"

The frog hopped into the well, swam to the bottom, and came up with the golden ball in his mouth. She reached down and grabbed it from him.

"Thank you, Mr. Frog!"

And off she ran, back to the castle, thinking only of her golden ball and the dirty spots on her dress.

"Wait for me," croaked the Frog. But she was already gone. She had forgotten her promise to the Frog.

She played with her ball the rest of the afternoon. That evening when she was sitting in the Royal Dining Room with her parents, the King and Queen, there came a knock at the door. *Knock, Knock, Knock. [Say it or make the sound.]*

"I'll get it!" she cried as she slipped out of her chair and ran to the door. She opened the door *[pretend to open door],* but no one was there.

"How strange," said the King. "Maybe it was the wind."

The knock came again. *Knock, Knock, Knock.* This time the voice of the Frog said,

> "Beautiful Princess
> Don't you see
> You made a promise to me.
> Your ball is back
> As good as new.
> Now I've come
> To be with you!"

This time the Princess opened the door and looked down, and there was the ugly green frog. She slammed the door quickly. *[Pretend to open door and look down. Look terrified and disgusted.]*

"Who was that, my dear?" asked the King. "You look like you've seen a ghost." *[If you wish, you can use a low voice for King or a gesture such as stroking your beard each time he talks.]*

"No, father, not a ghost, just an ugly old frog!" she replied.

"Is that true what he said? Did you make a promise to him?" asked the King.

"Yes, father *[said fast and passionately].* Yesterday at the well, my golden ball fell into the water. I cried so loud that a frog appeared to help me. I promised him that if he could get my ball that he could live with me in the castle. But I never thought he could live out of water!"

"My dear sweet daughter," said the King. "I have taught you the importance of keeping promises. If you gave him your word, you must keep your promise to the frog."

"I WILL NOT!" *[Having a tantrum.]* "That odious little creature will NOT live with me in the castle . . . eat from my plate, drink from my goblet. He's ugly . . . slimy and, and he smells like the pond!"

"Let the frog inside," demanded the King.

The frog hopped over to the King's chair, bowed to him *[bow],* then hopped onto the table and plopped himself beside the Princess's golden plate and began to eat.

"Oh, he's disgusting *[look of disgust],*" cried the Princess. "I will not eat at the table with a slimy frog. Have my food brought to my Royal chambers."

She turned on her heels and ran out of the room. She did not realize that the frog had attached himself to the lacy hem of her dress. She slammed her bedroom door, threw herself on her bed and sobbed.

"I won't have that frog in the palace, I won't!"

The little frog hopped up on her pillow and started to cry. *[Pantomime tears with fingers from eyes to cheeks.]* The Princess looked at him and her heart softened and she said,

"Please don't cry."

"I was a Prince, once," croaked the Frog, "but I broke a promise and was turned into a frog. If I can keep someone from breaking a promise, then I can be the Prince again. Please, Princess, let me stay with you!"

"How do I know you're telling the truth?" she asked. "You could just be a very clever frog. . . . But your tears look real . . . Oh, all right, you can stay."

And right before her eyes he was transformed into a young adorable Prince! *[Use wide hand movements to show transformation.]* He was wiping away his tears and smiling at the same time.

"Let's play with my golden ball," she said. She was so happy to have someone to play with. *[Pretend to play ball with a child in the audience. Throw the ball back and forth.]*

They made so much noise in her Royal chambers that the King and Queen came running. They were astonished to see the Princess playing with a young boy, just her age. They were delighted when they heard the whole story.

The Prince and Princess ran down to the river. He taught the Princess how to splash and play in the water and in the mud. After all, he had been a frog and frogs know all about these things. *[Look playful and pantomime splashing and swimming. Children can join in with you.]*

And the King and Queen were so pleased for now they had a happy little daughter. And as far as I know, everyone in the palace lived happily ever after.

Key Concepts and Themes and/or Universal Ideas

The main idea for this story is that when we make a promise it should be kept and that when we do not keep our promises, feelings can be hurt, and people can become angry and disappointed. Children need to know that when they don't keep their promises, they not only make another person feel bad but they will not be trusted to keep their word in the future.

Suggested Companion(s)

a frog

Preparation

Has someone ever promised you something and then not kept their word? Have you ever made a promise to do something and not kept your promise?

Preparation for Visualization

Tell the Children:

Before we hear the story, we are going to take an imaginary trip. Close your eyes and imagine we are going to a country that is very far away. It is very foggy but the sun is starting to come through the fog and you are a slimy, green frog sitting near a well watching a little princess. We can hear the little girl laughing. The pretty little princess with long beautiful hair and sparkling eyes dances in the forest near her castle and is playing with her favorite ball. The grass is full of dew and everything is sparkling and smells very fresh. The little girl is having a wonderful time. We are enjoying the wet grass and we really enjoy seeing someone who is so pretty, lighthearted, and happy. As the princess plays with her ball it suddenly bounces near us. We wish we could play with the princess but frogs are not that good at playing ball. All of a sudden the ball bounces past us and falls into the well. The little princess starts to cry. We want to help the princess. What can a frog do? Now open your eyes and I'm going to tell you a story about what happened to the frog and the princess.

Listen to the Story

Follow-up Discussion Questions

1. Did you like the story?
2. Did you think the princess was going to keep her promise?

3. If you had to kiss the frog, would you have kept your word?

4. Has anyone ever broken a promise that they made to you? How did you feel?

5. How would you feel if one of your stuffed animals turned into a special friend for you to play with?

ACTIVITY ONE: KEEPING PROMISES

Objectives

- To develop language skills
- To develop vocabulary
- To develop fine motor skills
- To develop responsibility

Introduction

This activity focuses on keeping promises in the classroom, between friends, and at home. The activity will give the children a chance to practice keeping promises and meeting particular goals or objectives and will teach responsibility.

Materials

the Promise worksheet
the Frog worksheet
paper plates
colored construction paper
glue or paste
crayons or markers
string
small paper bags

Procedure

1. Cut up the Promise worksheets and put them on the bulletin board on separate pieces of colored paper.

2. Tell the children they are going to practice keeping promises so that if they ever have to help out a frog it will be easy for them to keep their promise and not disappoint their friends, teachers, or family. Some of the promises on the sheets are:

- I promise to clean up the blocks.
- I promise to be kind to my classmates.
- I promise to help at home by setting the table.
- I promise to finish my work on time.

3. Ask the children which promise they want to make and put their name on the promise. Have the children do a drawing of their promise. Do not be concerned if it is not recognizable. Ask them to tell you about the drawing.

4. At the end of each day ask the children if they have done anything to keep their promise. Have them tell what they did. Depending on the age of the children and the appropriate amount of time for their age level, if they do not keep their promise, they turn into a frog, by the end of the day or week.

5. Either give the children the Frog worksheet or let them create their own on a paper plate. The worksheet only provides the outline of the frog head. The children have to fill in the sheet and create their own frog head. After they paste their head on the paper plate, punch holes in the sides, and add string, they will have frog masks. Don't forget to cut out holes for eyes. If the children do not keep their promises, they wear the mask and turn into the frog. When someone else in the class helps them keep their promise, they get to take off their mask.

6. The children can also use the masks in the next activity, for creative dramatics and to act out "frog feelings."

Language Development

1. Have children sit in a circle and talk about the story. If the princess had not kept her promise, what would have happened to the frog? Have the children talk about how the story might have ended.

2. For older students, have them write about how they feel when someone (a parent, friend, or teacher) breaks a promise to them.

3. Brainstorm a list of descriptive words to describe the princess, the frog, the prince, and the place where they lived. For example, for the princess they may say she is spoiled, pretty, mean, and so on. After they have a list for each character and the place, have the children pick one of them and do an illustration or create a paper bag puppet, keeping all the words in mind. Display all the princesses together, the frogs together, the princes together, and the places together and put the words up all around them. If the children make paper bag puppets, they can continue the story of the life of the prince and princess, telling about the fun they had together and how they were so fond of frogs that they continued to have many frog friends.

4. Ask the boys and girls, "If they could turn their frog into the perfect playmate, what would he or she be like?" Have the class do this as a group. Put the words up on a piece of paper, and depending on their skills, have the children write a group or individual story about their ideal playmate.

5. Have the children write a promise about helping at home to take home to their family and have the children come back and tell what they did.

6. Have the children brainstorm other animals that could have played the role of the frog and how the story would have been different. What if the frog was a dinosaur, a turtle, a parrot, a monkey, and so on.

Extensions

1. Have the children use the blocks or other building materials and create a wonderful place to play for the prince and princess.

2. Have the children write a thank you note from the prince to the princess for changing him back into a prince.

ACTIVITY TWO: FROG FEELINGS

Objectives

—To develop language skills
—To develop vocabulary related to feelings
—To develop fine motor skills
—To develop students' creative expression

Introduction

The focus of this activity is on feelings. The students will each try to create a frog showing a different feeling. They will also try to imitate these feelings through creative improvisation while they and the other children try to guess what "frog feelings" are being demonstrated. Bring pictures of real frogs and hang them up around the room for the children to see. They may be helpful when they create their frog pictures.

Materials

light green construction paper
green markers and other colored markers
the paper plate frog masks from Activity One
the Feeling Word Card Worksheet
blocks or other building materials

Procedure

1. Have the children brainstorm different feeling words. Present different situations related to broken promises. Ask them how they feel as a result of the broken promise. Sample situations:

   You were promised ice cream for dessert and your Dad forgot to bring it home.

   Your friend promises to sleep over and then calls and breaks the date just before he or she was supposed to come over to your house.

   Your brother or sister promises to read you a story after dinner and forgets and goes off with a friend.

   Add your own examples that fit your classroom and students.

2. Take your own lists of feeling words or cut up the ones from the worksheet or use both. Have the children each pick a word without looking or distribute the words to the children.

3. Have each child act out his or her word. Have them put on the frog masks. They are to act out the feeling on the card and the other children are to guess their word.

4. The children are to draw their own frogs showing the feeling on their card and the feeling they acted out.

Language Development

1. Create a frog alphabet book or a fairy tale alphabet book. Emphasize feelings.

2. If the children are old enough to write, have them write a story about the feelings that they illustrated and something that has happened in their life.

3. Have the children sit in a circle and make up stories about silly frogs, angry frogs, and so on. Emphasize the feelings but change the characters to dinosaurs or other creatures.

4. Create frog and princess paper bag puppets. Use paper bags decorated with junk collage items such as yarn, construction paper, buttons, or feathers. Have the children recreate the conversations between the frog and the princess and make up some of their own.

Extensions

1. Have the children create a place for the frog to live. Instead of a dog house, have them create a frog house, using blocks or other building materials that are available in the classroom. Have the children listen to frog songs while they are working or after they have completed the activity.

   - *Five Little Frogs* from Raffi's "Singable Songs" or
   - *Who Put a Frog?* from Jim Post's "Children's Collection I"

2. Get a frog to be the class pet.

3. Create little frog bodies for each day of the month when you do this activity and pin them on your calendar. Put a picture of the prince under one of the heads. Each day remove one frog head. When the students come to the date that covers the prince, they can celebrate the day the frog turned into a prince. Have frog cupcakes and do frog, prince, and princess dances. Make up songs. Decorate the room like a castle.

The Calendar

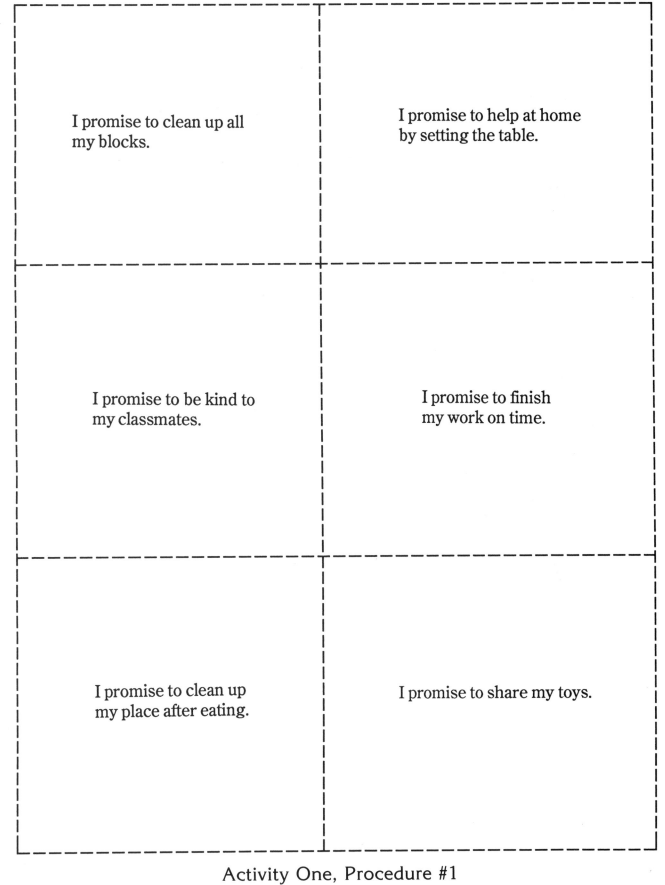

I promise to clean up all
my blocks.

I promise to help at home
by setting the table.

I promise to be kind to
my classmates.

I promise to finish
my work on time.

I promise to clean up
my place after eating.

I promise to share my toys.

Activity One, Procedure #1

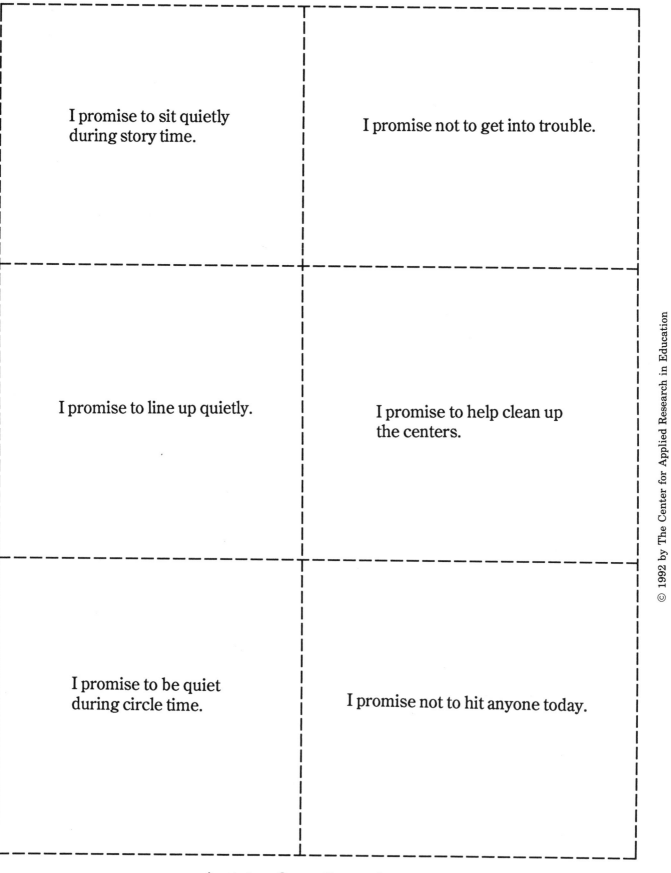

I promise to sit quietly during story time.	I promise not to get into trouble.
I promise to line up quietly.	I promise to help clean up the centers.
I promise to be quiet during circle time.	I promise not to hit anyone today.

Activity One, Procedure #1

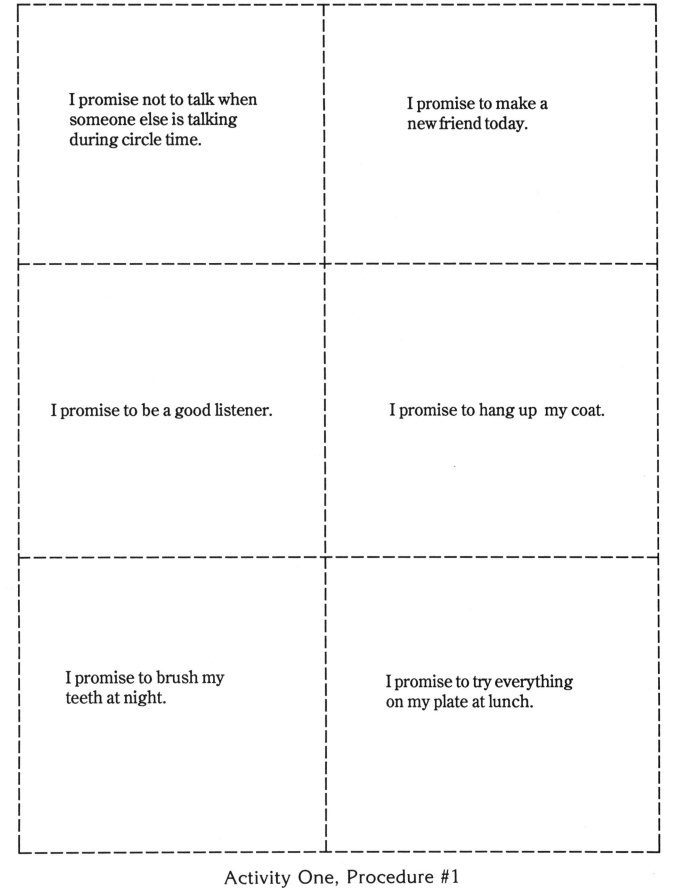

I promise not to talk when someone else is talking during circle time.

I promise to make a new friend today.

I promise to be a good listener.

I promise to hang up my coat.

I promise to brush my teeth at night.

I promise to try everything on my plate at lunch.

Activity One, Procedure #1

Activity One, Procedure #5

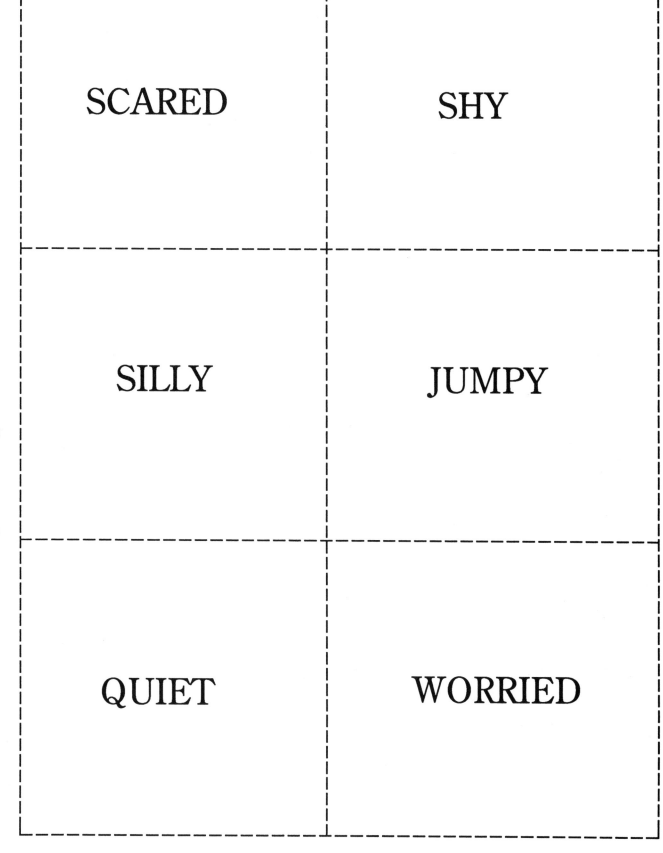

SCARED

SHY

SILLY

JUMPY

QUIET

WORRIED

Activity Two, Procedure #2

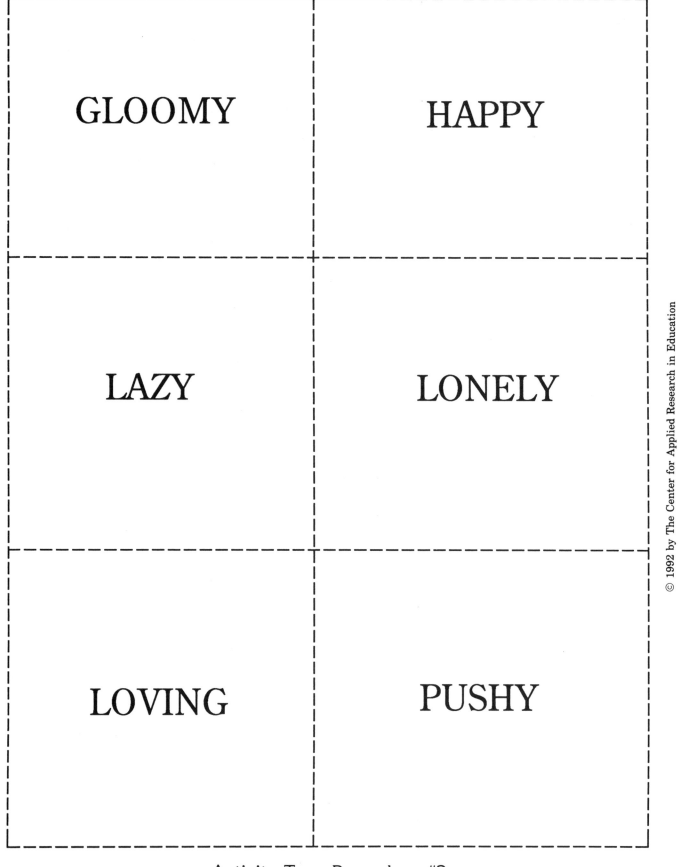

GLOOMY	HAPPY
LAZY	LONELY
LOVING	PUSHY

Activity Two, Procedure #2

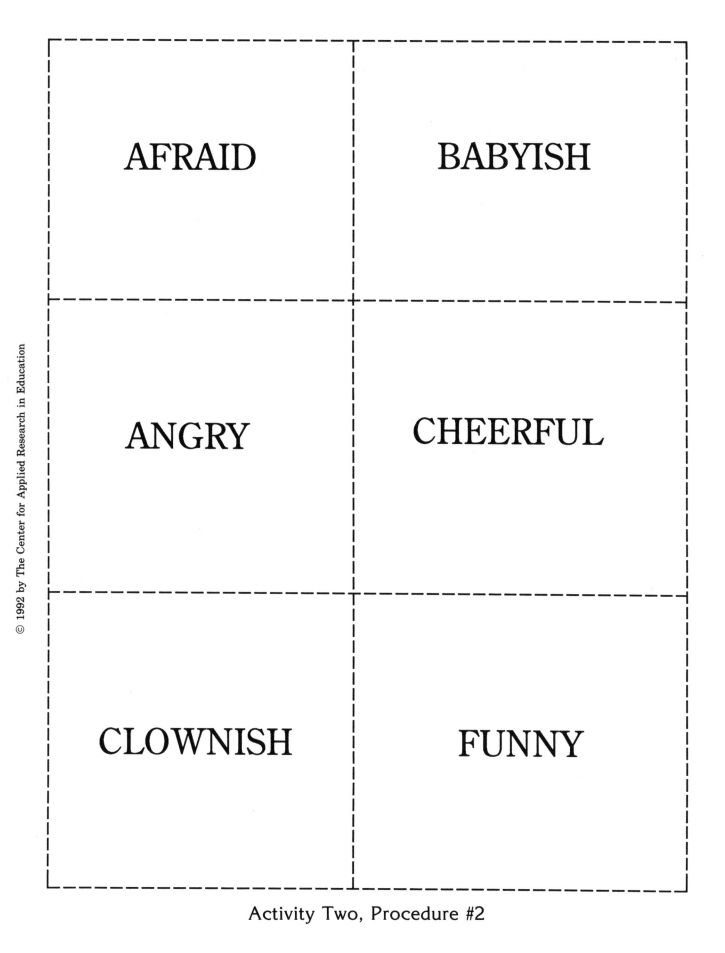

AFRAID

BABYISH

ANGRY

CHEERFUL

CLOWNISH

FUNNY

Activity Two, Procedure #2

FEELINGS: ADDITIONAL STORIES

The following stories to be told or read to students relate to the concept or theme of feelings.

 Hansel and Gretel, adapted from a German folktale collection by Jacob and Wilhelm, the Brothers Grimm.

Hansel and his sister Gretel find themselves alone in the forest. The first time Hansel cleverly leaves a path of pebbles, which leads them back home. The second time he leaves a path of bread crumbs but they are eaten by the birds. The lost children are attracted to a house built of cake and sugar candy and find themselves in the power of a wicked witch. Gretel saves the day when she pushes the witch into the heated oven and frees Hansel.

Children are concerned, scared, and then ultimately relieved during the telling of this well-loved fairy tale.

Suggested Activities

There are several activities related to this story. Making gingerbread cookies is a favorite activity that reinforces the fantasy.

The teacher can bring pebbles to school or children can go out and collect pebbles. All the children can close their eyes while one child makes a path with the pebbles. The rest of the class will open their eyes while the whole class or two of the children follow the pebbles and find either the child or a surprise that was left at the end of the trail.

A related idea is to leave a trail of bread crumbs after lunch and make a trail outside. Come back the next day and see if it is really true—that the birds came to eat them. Have the children write or tell about what they thought happened to the crumbs.

Children can also tell how they felt when Hansel and Gretel (1) were lost in the woods alone, (2) found the witch's house, (3) found out she was a witch, and (4) were finally free and reunited with their father. Have the children tell their own stories about when they thought they were lost and couldn't find their parents.

 It Could Always Be Worse by Margot Zemach. Scholastic, Inc., New York, 1976.

There was once a man who was miserable! In his tiny little hut lived his children, his animals, his wife, and his mother-in-law—such misery! so noisy! so crowded! So he went to the Rabbi for advice. His advice leads to ludicrous pandemonium when he brings his chickens, his goats, and his cow into the house! Then the Rabbi tells him to take them out again; and when he does, his children, his house animals (pets), his wife, and his mother-in-law are the only ones who are left in the hut, leaving plenty of room to breathe. He realizes that he is truly a lucky man.

Suggested Activities

The activities will encourage children to talk about problems that make them miserable and that they think are unsolvable, until they realize it could be worse. Examples will be given and students will respond with personal stories. For example, "Do you like it when you have to share your toys? Think of it this way, isn't it fun to have someone to play with?" or "Do you like it when you have to share your room? Isn't it nice to have someone to share the room when it is dark and lonely at night?" "Did you ever think you only got a little bit of dessert and then thought about what it would be like if there was no dessert?" The teacher can have the children dramatize the story by drawing a circle on the floor and getting the children to play the different roles to get the feeling of what was happening in the story. Then ask, "Did the size of the house change?" "No." "Then what happened?"

 Nana Upstairs and Nana Downstairs, written and illustrated by Tomie De Paola. Putnam and Sons, New York, 1973.

Tommy had a grandmother and a great-grandmother. He loved them both very much. This book is about Tommy's special visits with his two Nanas. The book shows the love and caring between the two Nanas. When the 94-year-old woman upstairs dies, Tommy learns about death.

Suggested Activities

Talk about grandparents and have children bring in photographs or drawings of their grandmothers and grandfathers. Talk about their age, where they live, if the children ever stay over at their homes, and things they do together. Talk about grandparents who have died and the children's feelings. Talk about how the children can keep their grandparents alive in their memories by telling stories and drawing pictures about them.

Other Stories

 Angry Arthur by Haiwyn Oram. Puffin Books, New York, 1982.

Where the Wild Things Are by Maurice Sendak. Harper and Row, New York, 1984.

Ira Sleeps Over by Bernard Weber. Houghton Mifflin, Boston, 1973.

 Timothy Goes to School by Rosemary Wells. Dial Press, New York, 1981.

 Caps for Sale by Esphyr Slobodkina. Scholastic Book Services, New York, 1940.

 The Animal by Lorna Balian. Abington Press, Nashville, 1980.

The Big Fat Enormous Lie by Marjorie Weinman Sharmat, E.P. Dutton, New York, 1978.

5
Family

> ## GRANDPA'S ENORMOUS TURNIP
> ### Adapted from an Old Russian Folktale

About the Story

This story is about an old man who plants a turnip seed. Grandpa watches the turnip grow and grow until it becomes a giant turnip. When Grandpa decides it is time to pull the turnip from the ground, he finds that it is so huge, he cannot pull it from the ground. He tries and tries but has no luck. Grandpa calls Grandma for help and she pulls Grandpa as he tries to pull up the turnip, but it does not come up. Grandma calls for help from Cousin Mel but the same thing happens and the story continues. Old Cow Bess, Piggy Wiggy Tess, Little Dog Fess, Skinny Cat Jess and Squirrely Burly Shirl, the squirrel, all join in the effort. Squirrely Burly Shirl is the last one to come and is added to the chain of characters trying to pull up the turnip and it finally comes up. The story ends with everyone feeling very good and Grandma Bell making turnip soup, turnip stew, turnip bread, turnip salad, and turnip ice cream for everyone to eat.

Key Concepts and Themes and/or Universal Idea

The main idea of this simple story is that while some jobs are too big for one person, with the help and collaboration of family and friends we sometimes can get a very difficult task completed. You will want to talk with the children about how they help around the house and how the whole family works together to get a job done, such as cleaning up after dinner. You will also want to talk about all the things one can make from a vegetable garden.

Suggested Companion(s)

a turnip

Preparation

Ask the students if there is anything that they do around the house with other family members to get a big job done, like cleaning up after dinner or planting a garden. If it is spring, you may want to use this activity to generate some excitement for planting a vegetable or flower garden in or around your school.

Preparation for Visualization

Tell the Children:

> Before we hear the story, we are going to take an imaginary trip. Close your eyes. Your family was all together and it was your brother's (father's, mother's, sister's, insert which persons seems most appropriate) birthday and the whole family has to help get ready. Everyone was helping by decorating, cooking, and getting ready for the party. Mom asked you to go out into the garden and get some flowers for the table. You went out and found some GIANT daisies and they smelled soooo good. You tried and tried to pull some out but they were so big you could not do it, so you called your brother who pulled you as you pulled on the flower, but nothing happened. Your brother called the dog and the dog pulled your brother and he pulled you and the flower wouldn't come out. The dog called the cat and the cat called the rat and they all pulled and pulled and the daisies came up. They were almost as big as a tree and they smelled just like perfume. You brought them into the house with the help of your brother, the dog, the cat, and the rat. Your Mom was so pleased, she said "What giant flowers, they are almost as big as a tree." She cut back some of their stems and put them in a huge pot with water and everyone thought they were the prettiest part of the decorations for the party. Now open your eyes and I'm going to tell you a story about Grandpa's Enormous Turnip.

Listen to the Story (Tape 1, Side A)

Follow-up Discussion Questions

1. What happened in Grandpa's garden?
2. Can you imagine how big that turnip was?
3. How was Grandpa's story like the story about the flowers?
4. Have you ever helped around the house to get a job done?
5. Has anyone ever helped you when your room was a big mess and had to be cleaned up?
6. What do you do to help around the house or garden?

ACTIVITY ONE: THE GREAT RAINBOW TURNIP

Objectives

- To develop the ability to cooperate
- To develop oral communication skills
- To develop students' ability to write their name
- To develop fine motor skills
- To develop color identification skills
- To develop creative thinking

Introduction

This is a simple activity which allows the children to work together to reach a common goal. They will all contribute to the decoration of a giant turnip using the colors of the rainbow and printing their name on their own part of the turnip. The children will then talk about how they might get the rainbow turnip into the sky. Let them use their imaginations and think about ways a rainbow turnip could fly up to the sky. Wouldn't it be wonderful if we could have food flying around in the sky and whenever we get hungry we could just grab a bite? This idea is similar to the book *Cloudy With a Chance of Meatballs,* by Judi Barrett.

Materials

a large pre-cut giant turnip made out of poster paper or kraft paper (make two if your class is large)

tempera paint and brushes or crayons or oil crayons

Vegetable worksheet

Procedure

1. Before sharing the story, draw a huge turnip on a piece of kraft paper or poster paper (about six feet long).
2. Show it to the children after they hear the story.
3. Tell them that you are like Grandpa and can't get the whole job done without help, and you want to make a rainbow turnip with all the colors of the rainbow.
4. Display each color of the rainbow and go over the colors with the students, red, yellow, orange, green, blue, indigo (a blue-green), and violet. Put up colored paper or paint different swatches of paper and put them up. Put the color name under each color.

5. Go over the colors with the children, giving them only the colors of the rainbow. Ask the students to match the paint colors or crayon colors to the color swatches.

6. Tell the children they are each going to have a chance to paint a color on the turnip to make it into a rainbow turnip. Give each child a chance to add color to the turnip. Give them a black crayon to put their name at their place if they can write their name. If they can't, print it together.

7. Once the rainbow turnip is completed, put blue paper on the bulletin board or on the wall that will represent the sky.

8. Ask the boys and girls to think of ways a rainbow turnip could get into the sky. (Could it fly, would it grow, could someone throw it out of an airplane?)

9. Hang the turnip in the sky. Ask the students, what else could be put into the sky? (Clouds, rainbow birds, rainbow butterflies, rainbow kites, or rainbow airplanes) Have the children create all the different things to be put into the sky to keep the rainbow turnip company. They can also create other rainbow vegetables so the creatures in the sky have something to eat. If they are very young, do not be concerned if their additional objects bear no resemblance to the actual object. You can cut out the objects they suggest and let them decorate them with rainbow colors. Do what is appropriate for their age level. Emphasize the cooperative spirit of the project.

Language Development

1. Have each child tell a story about helping around the house.
2. Have the children create a group story about the rainbow turnip and the rainbow sky.
3. Have the children tell about how everyone helps each other in the classroom. Give an award for helper of the day for a week.

Extensions

1. Bring in food magazines. Make a list of vegetables with the students. Have the students find vegetable pictures in the magazines and tear them out. Make a class vegetable book. Continue to emphasize the spirit of cooperation.
2. Give the children the Vegetable worksheet. Have them cut out the vegetables. Give the children a piece of blue paper. Give them strips of brown and green paper. Have them paste the brown strip on the bottom and then the green strip on the top of the brown strip. After the children paste the vegetables in their garden, give them the names of their vegetables and have them label their picture. If they cannot write the letters, do it for them. Older children can draw their own vegetables without using the vegetables on the worksheet.
3. As a class, create a recipe for a good salad. Have the students tell you what should be in the salad and how to put it together. Write on chart paper and make a salad for the class.

ACTIVITY TWO: A PLAY

Objectives

- To develop oral communication skills
- To develop sequencing skills

Introduction

The students will put on a simple play about Grandpa's turnip. All the children can take part by playing the roles of villagers who help the other characters when they call for help. Their role is to be the chorus. There are eight characters in the story, but if you want you can add one or two more. There are several activities that go along with the play. You can make it as simple or as elaborate as you want.

Materials

poster paper

tempera paints and brushes

large paper bags

cut paper

drawing materials

scissors

paste

Character Cards worksheet

Procedure

1. Retell the story with the children. Ask them whom they would like to play. You are the narrator. The chorus repeats the part where they pull the turnip, "They pulled and they pulled and they pulled." They also repeat the part where each character is named as they pull the turnip. The individual characters go and get the next character and ask them for help as they join the line of characters who are trying to pull up the turnip. See the outline at the end of this activity. Use the outline to develop a script and the Character Cards to help the children remember who the characters are.

2. Use a large piece of poster paper for scenery and have the children paint sky, grass, trees, bushes, and some vegetables.

3. Use large paper bags for costumes. Cut up the middle of one side of the bag and cut a hole out of the bottom for the child's neck. Cut arm holes on the sides of the bags. The bags become vests that can be decorated according to the role the child plays. They can paint the bags or tear paper and glue it to the bags.

4. Create a large turnip with cardboard or poster paper and have the children paint it white. Attach some green yarn or pipe cleaners or whatever you have for the stem. Put a heavy weight on the turnip so that it is held down. Use whatever is simple and that will work. A big brown box with books in it might do the job.

5. Have the children create invitations to their parents and to other classes to come and see their play.

6. Create a large program for the wall showing the children's names, their photograph (mounted on a turnip), and their part in creating the play. The children who can write their name can put it on the program. The children can make pictures of the different characters and put them on the program. The children can decorate the program making turnip

prints. Cut the turnip in half, dip it into some tempera paint and stamp it onto the giant turnip program.

7. Cut up turnips and make a dip to serve as a snack for the students and/or their audience.

Language Development

1. Have the children sit in a circle and retell the story. Allow the children to keep adding characters to the story. As they add the characters, ask the children to repeat each character from the beginning. Use the character cards to help them remember. When they add new characters have them draw a picture of the character to add to the cards.

2. Give individual students the character cards and have them arrange them in the order they appear in the story.

Extensions

1. Make vegetable soup where everyone helps. Make sure you put in turnips. After they make the soup, read the story *Stone Soup* to the children. Emphasize the cooperative spirit.

2. Bring in different kinds of seeds and have the children create seed pictures.

STORY SUMMARY

I. Introduction of characters and setting

    A. Once, Grandpa planted a tiny turnip seed.

        1. He watered it.

        2. He'd say, "Grow little turnip day by day, grow big and enormous in every way."

    B. Soon it began to grow.

        1. It grew and grew and grew until it was ready to pull up.

        2. He pulled and he pulled and he pulled again, but he could not pull up the turnip.

II. Everyone helps to pull up the turnip.

    A. Grandpa asks Grandma Bell for help.

        1. "Grandma, where are you?   Help me pull up the turnip."

        2. Grandma Bell pulled Grandpa and they pulled and they pulled and they pulled *BUT,* they could *NOT* pull up the turnip.

    B. Grandma Bell went to get Cousin Mel.

        1. "Where's Cousin Mel?" asked Grandpa.

        2. Cousin Mel was milking the cows. "Grandpa, what do you want?"

        3. So Cousin Mel pulled Grandma Bell and Grandma Bell pulled Grandpa and they PULLED.

    C. Cousin Mel went to get his Old Cow Bess.

        1. M-O-O-O. "Come on, Bess, we need your help," said Mel.

        2. So Old Cow Bess pulled Cousin Mel, Cousin Mel pulled Grandma Bell, Grandma Bell pulled Grandpa. So they PULLED.

    D. Old Cow Bess (MOO) went to get Piggy Wiggy Tess (OINK).

        1. "Come on, Piggy, give us a hand," said Grandpa.

        2. So Piggy Wiggy Tess pulled Old Cow Bess, Old Cow Bess pulled Cousin Mel, Cousin Mel pulled Grandma Bell and Grandma Bell pulled Grandpa. So they PULLED.

    E. "Piggy, ya got any friends?" asked Grandpa.

        1. Piggy Wiggy Tess (OINK) went to get Little Dog Fess (BARK).

        2. So Little Dog Fess pulled Piggy Wiggy Tess, Piggy Wiggy Tess pulled Old Cow Bess, Old Cow Bess pulled Cousin Mel, Cousin Mel pulled Grandma Bell, Grandma Bell pulled Grandpa. So they PULLED.

    F. "Little Dog, you think maybe you can get that little cat that lives in the barn?" asked Grandpa.

    1. So Little Dog Fess (BARK) went to get Skinny Cat Jess (MEOW).

    2. So Skinny Cat Jess pulled Little Dog Fess (BARK), Little Dog Fess pulled Piggy Wiggy Tess, Piggy Wiggy Tess pulled Old Cow Bess, Old Cow Bess pulled Cousin Mel, Cousin Mel pulled Grandma Bell, and Grandma Bell pulled Grandpa. So they PULLED.

G. Squirrely Burly Shirl, the farm squirrel, came by and asked, "What's going on here?" "We're trying to pull up the turnip." "Come on Squirrely Burly, give us a hand."

    1. So Squirrely Burly Shirl pulled Skinny Cat Jess, Skinny Cat Jess pulled Piggy Wiggy Tess, Piggy Wiggy Tess pulled Old Cow Bess, Old Cow Bess pulled Cousin Mel, Cousin Mel pulled Grandma Bell, Grandma Bell pulled Grandpa. So they pulled and they pulled and they pulled again this time, and they pulled UP THE TURNIP!!

III. Grandma served the turnip.

A. She took the turnip and made:

    1. Turnip soup, turnip stew, turnip bread and salad, too.

    2. For dessert she made–TURNIP ICE CREAM.

B. Everyone enjoyed the food and now you know what happened to Grandpa's Enormous Turnip!

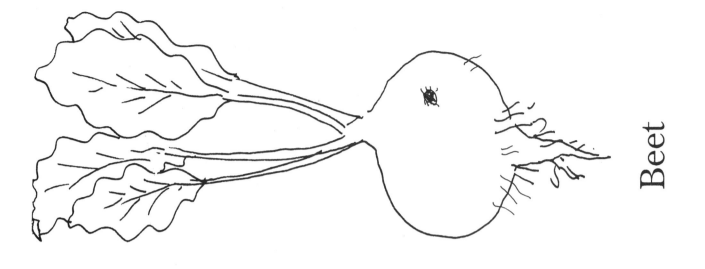

Beet

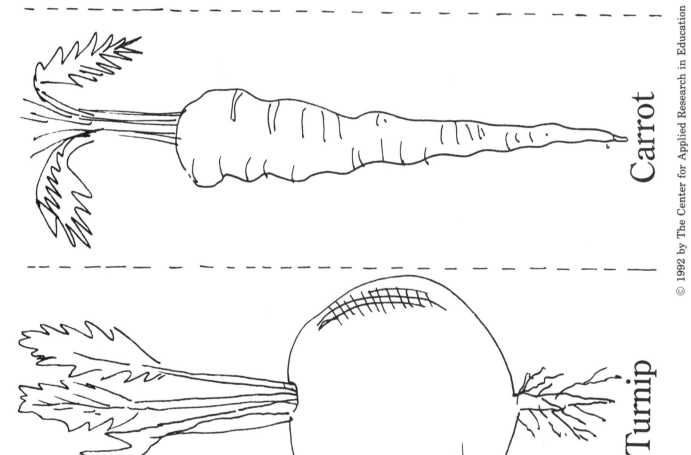

Carrot

Turnip

Activity One, Extensions #2

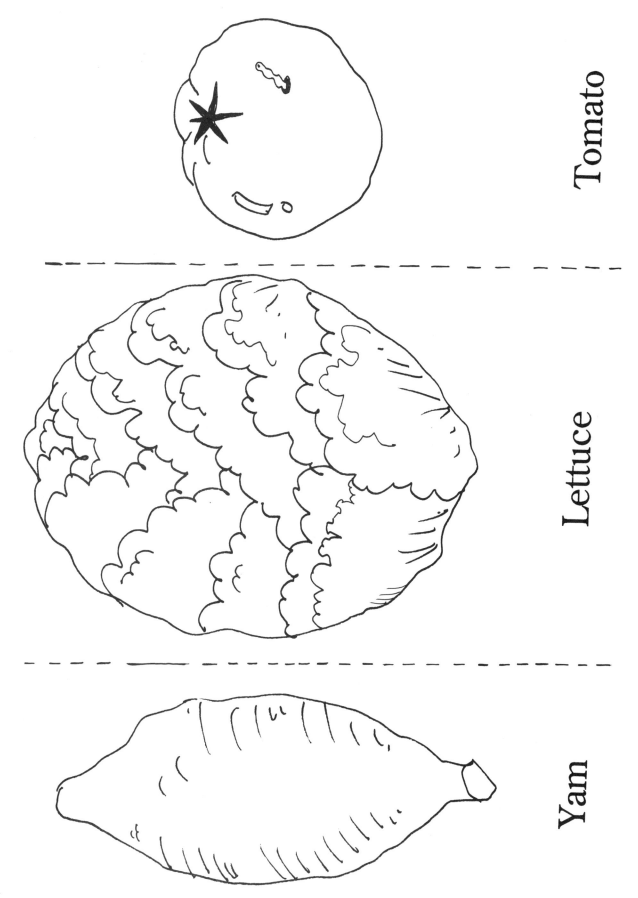

Tomato

Lettuce

Yam

Activity One, Extensions #2

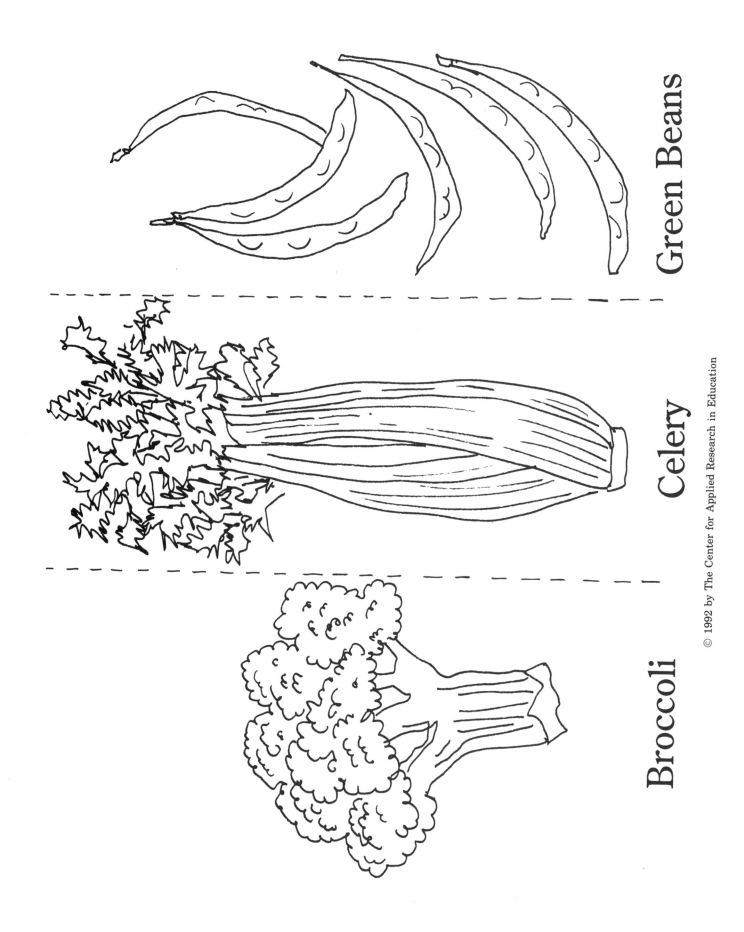

Green Beans

Celery

Broccoli

Activity One, Extensions #2

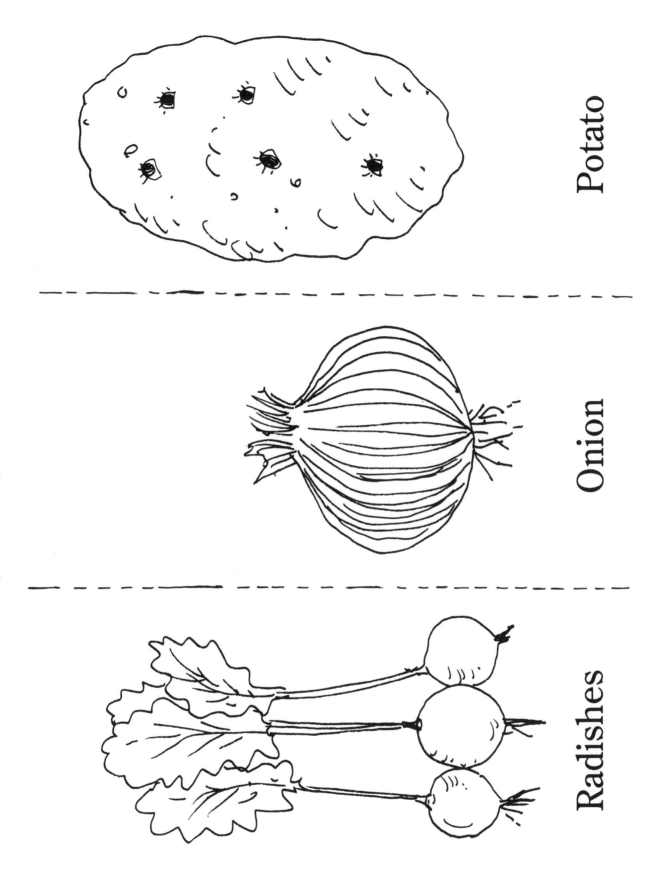

Potato

Onion

Radishes

Activity One, Extensions #2

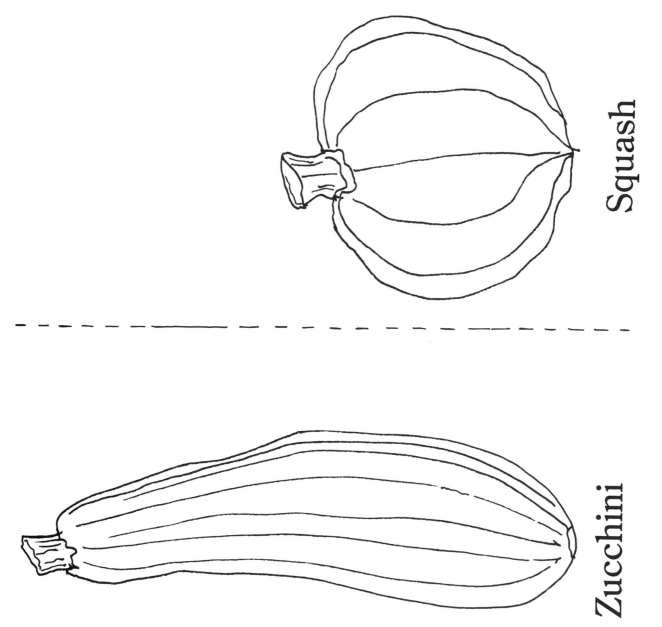

Squash

Zucchini

Activity One, Extensions #2

Grandpa

Grandma Bell

Cousin Mel

Old Cow Bess

Activity Two, Procedure #1

Piggy Wiggly Tess

Little Dog Fess

Skinny Cat Jess

Squirrely Burly Shirl

THE THREE BEARS
Adapted from the Old English Folktale

The Story

Once upon a time there were three bears. They lived in their very own house deep in the forest. There was Papa Bear, a great big bear; Mama Bear, a middle-sized bear; and Baby Bear, a wee little bear. Each of the bears had its own bowl for porridge: a big bowl for Papa Bear, a middle-sized bowl for Mama Bear, and a wee little bowl for Baby Bear. They each had a chair to sit in: a big chair for Papa Bear, a middle-sized chair for Mama Bear, and a wee little rocking chair for Baby Bear. There were three beds to sleep in: a big bed for Papa Bear, a middle-sized bed for Mama Bear, and a wee little bed for Baby Bear.

One day Mama Bear made porridge for breakfast and poured some into the three bowls. Papa Bear tasted the porridge and said, "This porridge is too hot. Let's take a walk in the forest." And so they did.

A little girl named Goldilocks was walking through the forest and saw this snug little house nestled in the trees. She looked in the window, then peeked through the keyhole; but no one was there.

She tried the latch and the door was not locked so she walked right in. She saw the three bowls of porridge on the kitchen table. It smelled so good and Goldilocks was hungry. She walked over to the big bowl of porridge and tasted it, but it was toooo HOT. Then she tasted the porridge in the middle-sized bowl; it was toooo COLD. Then she tasted the porridge in the wee little bowl and it was JUST RIGHT. So she ate it all up.

Now Goldilocks looked in the parlor and saw three chairs. She sat down in Papa Bear's big chair, but it was toooo HARD. Then she sat in Mama Bear's middle-sized chair, but it was toooo SOFT. So she tried Baby Bear's wee little rocking chair and it was JUST RIGHT. ROCKITY, ROCKITY, ROCKITY, BOOM! The bottom fell out and it broke into many pieces.

Goldilocks walked upstairs to the three bears' bedroom. First she laid down on Papa Bear's big bed, but it was toooo HIGH at the head for her. Mama Bear's middle-sized bed was toooo HIGH at the foot for her. But Baby Bear's wee little bed was not toooo HIGH at the head and not toooo HIGH at the foot; it was JUST RIGHT. She covered herself with Baby Bear's wee little quilt and fell fast asleep.

The three bears finished their walk and came home for breakfast. When Papa Bear saw the spoon that Goldilocks left in his porridge, he said in a great big voice, "SOMEBODY HAS BEEN TASTING MY PORRIDGE." Goldilocks had left the spoon in Mama Bear's middle-sized bowl of porridge, too. Mama Bear said in a middle-sized voice, "SOMEBODY HAS BEEN TASTING MY PORRIDGE." Then Baby Bear looked at his wee little bowl and said in his wee little voice, "Somebody has been tasting my porridge and has eaten it all up." Baby Bear began to cry.

The three bears walked into the parlor. Papa Bear saw the cushion was not straight in his big chair and he said in a great big voice, "SOMEBODY HAS BEEN SITTING IN MY CHAIR." Mama saw the cushion was squashed down in her middle-sized chair and she said in her middle-sized voice, "SOMEBODY HAS BEEN SITTING IN MY CHAIR." Then Baby Bear looked at his chair and said in a wee little voice, "Somebody has been sitting in my chair and broke it to pieces." And Baby Bear began to cry.

The three bears went into their bedroom. Papa Bear noticed that his pillow was out of place in his big bed and he said in a great big voice, "SOMEBODY HAS BEEN SLEEPING IN MY BED." Mama Bear noticed that the blanket was wrinkled on her middle-sized bed and she said in her middle-sized voice, "SOMEBODY HAS BEEN SLEEPING IN MY BED." Then Baby Bear looked at his wee little bed and said in his wee little voice, "Somebody has been sleeping in my bed and there she is." Goldilocks woke up, opened her eyes and saw the three bears. As quickly as she could she rolled off the bed, ran to the open window and jumped down. She ran into the forest never to be seen by the three bears ever again.

Key Concepts and Themes and/or Universal Ideas

The Three Bears were a close-knit family who lived in a nice little house. Goldilocks was a little girl who had not learned her manners and who used other people's belongings without asking. The Bears were very upset with Goldilocks and gave her the scare of her life. Talk with the children about asking permission, and about apologizing when they have used someone else's things and broken them. Talk about family breakfasts and sharing.

Suggested Companion(s)

porridge
small rocking chair
stuffed bears

Preparation

Prior to telling the story, talk with the children about what happens if they use something that belongs to a family member without permission. Ask them what their family eats for breakfast and if someone has ever eaten their food when no one was around.

Preparation for Visualization

Tell the Children:

Before we hear the story, we are going to take an imaginary trip. Close your eyes. You are in your warm cuddly bed and it's toasty and warm and you begin to wake up. You wiggle your nose and you smell wonderful hot cereal. You want to sleep a little bit more and you wiggle and snuggle in a little more. You hear your Mom call and you answer, "I'll be there soon." After a while you stretch and stretch and slowly get out of bed. You put on your robe and slippers and go down to breakfast. By the time you get downstairs, breakfast is over and your brother has eaten your cereal. When you ask your brother why he did that, he says he was hungry, he didn't think you were coming down for breakfast, and he didn't think you'd mind. How do you feel? Now open your eyes and I'm going to tell you a story.

Listen to the Story

Follow-up Discussion Questions

1. What do you think about what Goldilocks did?
2. Did she do the right thing? Why or why not?
3. How would you have felt if you were Goldilocks? Papa Bear? Mama Bear?
4. If you were Goldilocks, what would you have done?

ACTIVITY ONE: FAMILIES, FAMILIES, BEARS, AND MORE

Objectives

—To develop oral and written communication skills
—To develop creativity
—To develop sequencing skills

Introduction

This is a simple activity that allows the children to create their own stories using the format from "The Three Bears" for other animal families. Older children will use the story format that is provided on their own. With younger children, you can enlarge the format, make a transparency, or write it on the board or chart paper—whatever works for you.

Materials

Story Format worksheet
writing and drawing materials
18″ by 24″ manila paper

Procedure

1. After the discussion about the story, tell the students that they will make up their own story.
2. Provide the older children (children who can read) with the Story Format worksheet and the choices. You can give each child a piece of large manila paper divided into five sections and tell them to put one part of the story in each section. If needed, help the children fill in the blanks. After they have completed their stories, have them illustrate each section. The children can also fill in the blanks with pictures instead of words. Emphasize small, medium, and large: Small Baby Bear, Medium Mama Bear, and Large Papa Bear.
3. Do a group story with the younger children and individual stories for older children. Have the children stand up and tell the class their stories.
4. Display the written and illustrated stories for the whole class.

Language Development

1. Have the children play the role of Goldlilocks or another visitor and write an apology for what he or she did. After the children have written their notes or after you have created a class note with all of the children, read the children *The Jolly Postman.* The first letter is an apology from Goldilocks.
2. Have children tell the class about their favorite family breakfast and what their families do together at breakfast time. Does everyone help make breakfast? Does their Mom make breakfast like Mama Bear? Are Sunday breakfasts different?
3. Did they ever take something that was not theirs or break someone else's toy? Have them tell the children a story about what happened.
4. Have children practice asking permission to use other people's toys and so on.

Extensions

1. Have the children create a special make-believe breakfast for their stuffed animals using play food.

2. Have the children set the table for the special breakfast. Talk about what they need to set the table.

3. Have the children create special place mats for "The Three Bears" breakfast.

ACTIVITY TWO: BABY BEAR'S NEW CHAIR

Objectives

—To develop creativity
—To develop fine motor skills
—To develop visual communication skills

Introduction

The purpose of this activity is to encourage the children to develop their creativity. In the story Baby Bear's chair was broken. The children are going to design a new chair for Baby Bear using the enclosed worksheet or a large piece of drawing paper.

Materials

drawing materials
Design a Chair worksheet
18″ × 24″ drawing paper
magazines
glue
colored construction paper
scissors
scrap fabric
yarn

Procedure

1. Talk about Baby Bear's chair and what happened to it. Ask the children what a wonderful chair for Baby Bear would look like.

2. Tell the children they will have a chance to create a new chair for Baby Bear. If you use the worksheet, the children can cut colors and shapes from magazines and fill in the chair or they can draw designs on the chair or both.

3. Older children may want to draw their own chair on large paper and fill in the chair with assorted fabrics, yarn or colors and shapes cut from magazines.

4. Create a bulletin board labeled the "BABY BEAR CHAIR STORE." Display the chairs on the bulletin board.

5. If you have some plain wooden rockers available to you that could use a coat of paint, use acrylic paint and give the children a chance to decorate the rockers. One possibility would be to have them paint bears or some other animals all over the chairs.

Language Development

1. Have each child point out his or her chair and tell why Baby Bear would like that chair.

2. Have each child draw a picture of their Dad's or Mom's special chair and tell the class about it.

Extensions

1. Have the children design a new quilt for Baby Bear's bed or for the animal family in Activity One. Each child can create a separate patch.

2. Have the children act out the story using assorted props.

3. Buy some Grammy Bears™ cookies or Teddy Bear Grahams™ which are available in several varieties and do a match activity with the children. Have them sort the cookies by flavor (vanilla/chocolate), create patterns, and count them into sets.

ANIMAL FAMILIES

FISH
CATS
DOGS
BIRDS
GOATS
DUCKS
SNAKES

TEMPERATURE

HOT
COLD

CHAIRS

ROCKING
STUFFED
FANCY

PLACES TO LIVE

OCEAN
BARNYARD
DESERT
TREES
POND
CAVE
MOUNTAIN

BEDS

FLUFFY
HARD
CUDDLY

BREAKFAST FOODS

WORMS
EGGS AND SAUSAGE
CEREAL
BAGELS
FRUIT
SPIDER FLAKES
BUG MUFFINS

VISITOR

CURLY BROWN
SUSIE CUTIE
SALLY BRAIDS
RUSTY CURLS

BABY BED

BEAUTIFUL
COLORFUL
PRETTY
BRIGHT
FLUFFY

WAYS TO MOVE

RUN
WALK
SWIM
FLY
WADDLE
HOP
WIGGLE OR SLITHER

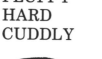

Activity One, Procedure #2

STORY FORMAT FOR "THE THREE BEARS"

Once upon a time, there was a family of three _____.
They lived in their own house in a/an _____. One
morning when they came down for their breakfast of
_____, they found it was too _____, so they took a
_____ in the _____.

While they were gone, a visitor came into their house.
_____ came in and tried out their breakfast of _____
and ate it all up.

She (He) went on to another room and found three
_____ chairs. She (He) tried each one and really liked
Baby _____'s chair, but when she (he) sat in it, it broke.

She (He) went on to the bedroom and found three
_____ beds. She (He) tried each one and Baby _____'s
was just _____. It was _____ and _____. _____
cuddled up in the bed and fell asleep.

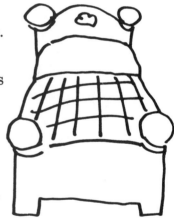

When the three _____ returned, they found that
someone had been there. That someone had eaten Baby
_____'s breakfast all up. That someone had sat in Baby
_____'s chair and broke it. The three _____ went into
the bedroom and found _____ snuggled up in Baby
_____'s bed sound asleep. The three _____ scared
_____ and she (he) _____ out the window and _____
away.

Activity One, Procedure #2

Activity Two, Procedure #2

FAMILY: ADDITIONAL STORIES

The following stories which can be told or read to students relate to the concept or theme of family.

 Anansi the Spider: A Tale from the Ashanti, written and illustrated by Gerald McDermott. Henry Holt and Company, New York, 1986.

Anansi, the West African spider hero, has six sons, and each one has a special talent. They combine their talents to save their father who has been swallowed by a big fish.

Suggested Activities

The children will be encouraged to tell stories about their family members and their special talents starting with themselves. They will be encouraged to tell how they could use their special talents to help each other. For example, if I can draw beautiful pictures I can give them to other members of my family to make them feel good. Children will be encouraged to demonstrate their special talents, like telling a story, singing a song, drawing a picture, showing how they can help around the house. Children will tell stories about things their family does together.

 Frederick by Leo Lionni. Pantheon Books, Random House, New York, 1967.

The little field mouse family gathers food and straw for the winter, while Frederick gathers warmth, colors, and words. When the food runs out, Frederick's words and poems help them through the cold winter days and nights.

Suggested Activities

Frederick looked at the aesthetic or sensory qualities of the objects, while his family focused on the functional or utilitarian aspects of life. Take the children outside and have them look at objects as Frederick did. Use all five senses. Let them look, feel, smell, listen, and taste (when appropriate) the trees, flowers, grass, and so on, outside the school. They can play the game, "I see or hear something red or soft . . ." while the other children guess what it is. After they come in, they can make up poems or paint or draw pictures about what they experienced. Children can also tell about what they can do to make their families feel good. Children will be encouraged to make up songs, dances, and stories to go home and share them with their families.

Love You Forever by Robert Munsch. Firefly Books, Ontario, 1986.

A mother holds her new baby boy and sings, "I'll love you forever, I'll like you for always, as long as I'm living my baby you'll be." Throughout all of the stages of childhood the mother repeats the loving song; and when she grows old, her son holds her and sings it to her.

Suggested Activities

Have the children talk about all the people they love. Have the children create an "I love you" picture with an "I love you" message for their mother or someone else in their family that they love very much. For younger children teach them how to make hearts and have them fill their paper with different colored hearts. Then have them dictate a love message for their mother or whomever the picture is for. This is a good activity for Valentine's Day.

 Mother, Mother I Want Another by Maria Polushkin, illustrated by Diane Dawson, Scholastic Book Services, New York, 1978.

It's bedtime in the Mouse House and Mother Mouse takes Baby Mouse through his usual bedtime rituals. He gets his PJs on, brushes his teeth, gets tucked in bed, and demands, "Mother, Mother, I want another, Mother!" Mother Mouse tries desperately to find another Mother, bringing back Mrs. Duck, Mrs. Mouse, Mrs. Pig, and Mrs. Donkey! Finally Baby Mouse explains that he just wants another kiss. He gets kisses from all the mothers! This is a great idea for Mother's Day.

Suggested Activities

Have the children talk about what it would be like to have many different kinds of mothers. What would it be like to have a kangaroo mother, a giraffe mother, an elephant mother, a snake mother, and so on. Talk about what it would be like if each of these mothers gave them a big, juicy kiss or a big squishy hug.

Have the children draw a picture of their own mother and encourage them to add lots of details. Older children can write about their mothers and the wonderful things she does for them.

Stevie, written and illustrated by John Steptoe. Harper and Row, New York, 1969.

The story is narrated by a young black boy who is relating his frustrations about family life. Stevie stays with another family while his Mom works and causes havoc with the life of the boy and his part-time family. When Stevie and his Mom move away, the other boy realizes that Stevie was a nice boy and he misses him.

Suggested Activities

Ask the children to imagine what it would be like if a child from another family moved in with their family. Talk about how they would feel, what they would share, and what fun they could have. Older children can use this idea as the main theme for a story. Have the children sit in a circle and each say one good thing about this new situation. Then the children could repeat the activity stating one problem that might occur. After this you can ask the children how they could turn the problem into something positive.

Ask Mr. Bear by Marjorie Flack. Macmillan, New York, 1932.

Danny goes to the farm animals for a gift for his mother's birthday. Mrs. Hen offers eggs; Mrs. Goose offers feathers for her pillow; Mrs. Goat offers milk for cheese; Mrs. Sheep offers wool for a warm blanket; and finally Mrs. Cow offers fresh farm milk. But Danny's mother already has all of these things. Danny goes to see Mr. Bear and he whispers into his ear the perfect gift. So Danny goes back home and gives his mother a BEAR HUG for her birthday.

Suggested Activities

Ask the children if they know when their mother's birthday is. Ask them what they usually do for their mother's birthday. Tell them that birthday presents don't necessarily have to cost anything; for example: kisses, birthday songs, dances, stories, their own artwork, or a helping hand. Have the children brainstorm all the things they can think of that would be free. Have them create some of them.

Other Stories

Patchwork Quilt by Valerie Flournoy, illustrated by Jerry Pinkney. Dial, New York, 1985.

My Mother Is the Most Beautiful Woman in the World by Becky Reyher. Lathrop, New York, 1945.

The Jolly Postman or Other People's Letters by Janet and Allan Ahlberg. Little, Brown and Company, 1986.

A Chair for My Mother by Vera B. Williams. Mulberry Books, New York, 1982.

Stone Soup, written and illustrated by Marcia Brown. Aladdin, New York, 1947.

 The Carrot Seed by Ruth Kraus. Scholastic, New York, 1945.

 The Biggest Pumpkin Ever by Steven Kroll. Holiday, New York, 1984.

Eating the Alphabet by Lois Ehlert. Harcourt Brace, New York, 1989.

6
Seasons

THE SNOW PARLOR
By Elizabeth Coatsworth

About the Story

The Snow Parlor is about a curious little boy who was very anxious to know where the snow came from. He asked several animals but none of their answers were satisfactory except for that of the snowbird who gave the little boy the best piece of advice. The snowbird said, "The best way, my child, is to see for yourself. Climb on my back and I will take you there." So the boy did what he was told. They flew and flew until they came to the edge of the world and they found an icy mountain with a hole in the center. Snowflakes were coming out of its crater and blowing in every direction. As the boy approached the mountain, he came upon an enormous number of small bears chopping off ice at the base of the mountain. The snowbird took the boy into the mountain where he saw the big snow bears cutting the ice into snowflakes. After the little boy was satisfied, the bears blew him back home.

Key Concepts and Themes and/or Universal Ideas

The little boy was curious. He wanted to know where snow comes from. Long ago when we didn't know as much about science and we did not have scientific answers to explain the hows and whys of the world around us, people made up stories to explain nature and our environment. The little boy who wanted to know where snow comes from was given some good advice. He was told to find out for himself. When it is possible, one of the best ways to learn is to see for one's self, to experience as much as we can. The little boy saw the bears cutting out the snowflakes and blowing them off the mountain into the winds. The story's key ideas are the importance of curiosity, how myths have been created to explain natural phenomena like snow, and why it is important to encourage children to explore, ask questions, do research, and find out about things for themselves.

Suggested Companion(s)

cut-paper snowflakes
ice cream, icicles, or a pan of fresh snow if available
stuffed polar bears

Preparation

Prior to hearing the story, talk with the children about being curious. Ask if they wonder where snow, rain, and ice come from. Ask if they ever wonder where other things in nature come from. Ask them if they wonder why there are different seasons.

Preparation for Visualization

Tell the Children:

Before we hear the story, we are going to take an imaginary trip. Close your eyes. You are outside on a winter day and it is very cold. The wind is blowing across your face and your nose is getting cold. All of a sudden some white flakes land on your nose. How does it feel? Suddenly the sky is filled with white flakes and they're all over your face and clothes. How does it look, how does it feel? As you take a few steps forward, it feels like walking through a curtain of snow, but you never reach the other side. The snow sparkles and it feels and smells so fresh. It keeps swirling around you. Now open your eyes and I'm going to tell you a story.

Listen to the Story (Tape 1, Side B)

Follow-up Discussion Questions

1. What did you see?
2. What pictures do you see?
3. Do you think the boy expected to see what he did?
4. How many of you thought that bears create snowflakes?
5. How many other ways do you think snow is made?

Have one child play the role of the boy and the other children play the roles of different animals or people. Have the child go up to the other children, one at a time, and ask them "How is snow made?" The children are to make up an answer. Another way to do it is to have the child ask the class and the children can volunteer their ideas by raising their hands so they can be called on. The purpose is to encourage creative thinking and divergent thinking skills. The answers should be as fanciful as possible. Don't make judgments.

ACTIVITY ONE: WHITE SNOW, SNOW WHITE

Objectives

- —To develop creative thinking and divergent thinking skills
- —To develop sensory awareness
- —To develop fine motor skills
- —To develop sequencing skills
- —To increase knowledge about seasons and related concepts
- —To improve oral communication skills

Introduction

This activity explores the color white and gives students an opportunity to create white worlds, cut out their own snowflakes, and create white collages using a variety of textures. Students will explore the idea of what it would be like to live in northern Canada or in an all-white world. The students will also become aware of the many different shades of white and the many different kinds of white papers and materials.

Students will learn to cut out snowflakes and will understand that there are no two snowflakes that are alike, just like there are no two people who are alike.

Materials

white construction paper

scissors

glue

white tempera paint

brushes

large white or light blue mural paper

white things: cotton balls, paper towels, kleenex, doilies, paper napkins, wrapping paper (any kind of white paper or light weight material)

magnifying glass

Foot worksheet

Procedure

1. After the discussion about the story ask the students to name all the white things they can think of. Make a long list on large paper and post it on a bulletin board. Ask the students to think about white winter things. Ask the children to bring white "things" to school. Ask the children what if all of the objects in the world were white? What would it look like? Read the children the "White Poem" from *Hailstones and Halibut Bones* to give them more ideas.

   Hailstones and Halibut Bones by Mary O'Neill, illustrated by John Wallner. New York: Doubleday, 1989.

2. Provide all of the white materials and ask the students to make some white things for their white world. Have them use the ideas from their list or other ideas. Put up the white or light blue mural paper and have the students glue up their objects. Students can create white houses, white animals, white flowers, white moons, white suns, or white cars. Younger children can just glue up white materials.

3. After the students create their white world, ask them if they would like to make snowflakes and add them to their world. Find pictures of snowflakes and give the children a magnifying glass to look more closely at the snowflakes and see how they are different. If you do this when there is snow on the ground, go outside with the magnifying glass or bring in some snow. Have the children look and see how different each snowflake is. If you are really desperate, have no pictures, and live in a warm climate, scrape some shavings from an ice cube to create a simulated  snowflake or iceflake and have the children look through the magnifying glass at the structure. Give older children 9″ × 9″ and 6″ × 6″ squares of white paper and make snowflakes.

4. After each child makes two or three snowflakes, have them pretend they are the bears and blow them around the room or use an electric fan. If the children are too young, give them pre-cut snowflakes. After this, have the children add their snowflakes to the mural. The children can also create a snowman out of the snowflakes for the mural.

Language Development

1. After the children have made their snowflakes and, before they glue them to the mural they can also act out the *Snow Parlor* story.

2. What if one day snow came down in different colors? What would happen if you had a purple snowstorm? a yellow snowstorm? a chocolate snowstorm? and so forth. Draw pictures and tell what would happen in your snowstorm.

3. Have the children create a group or individual story about "How the whole world became white or black or green or red. What would it be like if the whole world was white?" Use the original student lists of "white things" and the "What if the whole world were white?" ideas from the first part of the lesson. Ask the students if they can find all the w's in the question. The students can also add to the "What is white?" poem. You can do this for any color.

4. Have the students create a list of "w" words. Have them write them along with a list of "white" words and add them to their white world.

5. Have the students brainstorm a group of snow words. For example, snow cone, snowshoes, snow mobiles, snowshoes, snow sled, snow bunny, snowblower, and so forth. Write them for the children and begin to make a snow book.

Extensions

1. Adapt the white world idea and create a black world. Talk about opposites. Compare and contrast with the white world. How are they alike or different? Point out the only real difference is color.

2. Use the Foot worksheet and have the children create shoes on the foot for different seasons; i.e., summer sandals, winter boots, galoshes for spring rain, fall hiking boots, ice skates, and so on.

3. Create a snow sculpture using Ivory flakes and water. Add to the sculpture with styrofoam shapes, toothpicks, and so on.

4. Have a white day. Ask the children to wear all white clothes and eat all white foods that day like marshmallows, mashed potatoes, milk, vanilla ice cream, whipped cream, coconut, turnips, white chicken breasts, and so forth. Decorate the room with white paper and sheets. Have fun!

ACTIVITY TWO: WHY THINGS HAPPEN

Objectives

—To develop oral and written communication skills
—To develop divergent thinking skills
—To be able to compare a fantasy, myth, and fact
—To encourage questioning and curiosity

Introduction

The purpose of the activity is to encourage students to ask questions, to begin to explore the concept of myths, and to begin to understand some basic science concepts. The little boy in the story was curious and wanted to know where snow came from. This activity encourages the students to wonder why things happen and to ask some questions and begin to explore. The activity is more appropriate for children who are about four and a half and up. The students will have an opportunity to tell and write their own stories and to create group stories. The outcome might be a book of class myths and a book of science concepts. Encourage the children to ask questions about what they are curious about. Create a class list and keep adding to it. Tackle the different questions at appropriate times.

Materials

ingredients for ice cream
ice cream maker
a globe
ice and a fan
18″ × 24″ manila paper
drawing materials or paint markers

Procedure

1. Talk about being curious. Ask if they wonder about where snow, rain, and ice come from. Ask the children what they wonder about. Have a weather person come in and talk to the children. Encourage the children

to ask questions of the weather person. Prepare some of the questions before the weather person comes to the class.

2. Ask the children what all the good things about snow are. What are all the bad things? What are some of the things we do in the winter when there is snow? How do we have to prepare for snow? For example, we can play in the snow, we can ski on the snow, and snow makes everything clean and pretty. But, we have to prepare our cars for snow, we have to shovel a path so people won't fall, and we have to put salt and sand on the streets so they are not dangerous.

3. Encourage the students to ask questions about other things that they wonder about. You can relate the questions to weather or anything they want. To get them started, ask the children, "Do you wonder about where the sun goes at night?" Show them a globe and a round ball and demonstrate how the earth moves around the sun. Show them where the sun is in the winter and where it is in the summer. Talk about the different seasons and why there is no snow in the summer. Other questions might be, "Why is the grass green?" or "Why do trees lose their leaves?"

Language Development

1. The children can tell stories about what they like about the snow. They can also write these stories, create snow pictures using mixed media, and create a class or individual snow book.

2. Students can talk about animals that like the cold and snow such as bears, seals, and penguins. Students can talk about how the animals live in cold climates.

Extensions

1. You can have the children create other stories to explain natural phenomena and create a class book. You can also present them with scientific information and have them make a class science book.

2. Ask students if they wonder where ice cream comes from. Make ice cream with the class.

3. Have the children create a dance. Divide them into four groups. Find appropriate music. Have one group do a summer dance, and the others do a winter dance, a spring dance, and a fall dance. Talk about what they could do for each dance. They could be falling leaves in the fall, a blizzard in the winter, or flowers growing in the spring. Ask them how they would move their arms, their feet, and how fast or slow they would move.

4. Have the students create a dance. As a group talk about how one would move as a snowflake in a blizzard; as a snowflake in a light cold wind; as a piece of sleet in an ice storm. Encourage the students to experiment

with different speeds and levels of moving their bodies. To embellish this activity use hand-held scarves, tinsel wands, white crepe paper streamers, and light wands. Cotton balls can represent snow. Musical selections to accompany creative movement for this activity are:

The Four Seasons	Antonio Vivaldi
"Snowflakes Are Falling"	Claude Debussy
"Autumn to Spring"	George Winston
"Concert for the Earth"	Paul Winter

5. Divide students into three groups and create movement improvisations for winter, spring, summer, and fall. Choose appropriate music and props to accompany their creations.

STORY SUMMARY

I. Introduction to characters and setting
A. Once there was a boy who loved to ski.
1. He skied every day.
2. He wondered where the snow comes from.
3. He skied into the forest to find out.
B. He asked the forest animals.
1. He saw Mr. Fox.

Boy asked: "Hi, Mr. Fox, could you tell me where the snow comes from?"

Fox answered: "I don't know where the snow comes from and I don't really care where the snow comes from. I'm busy finding food in this winter forest, now be gone with you."

"Goodbye, Mr. Fox," said the boy.
2. He continued to ski and saw Mrs. Squirrel scampering up a tree.

"Oh, Mrs. Squirrel."

"Oh dear, oh dear, it's one of those children. They always ask so many questions."

"No, Mrs. Squirrel, I only have one question. I want to know where the snow comes from."

"I don't know where snow comes from. All I know is if you don't bother it, it won't bother you. Now I've got to go organize my nuts."
3. A huge snow storm came up.
a. One of the flakes was larger than the rest. It was a bird.
b. "Are you a Snow Bird?" he asked.
c. "Oh yes, I am a Snow Bird."
d. "Oh goodie, you can tell me where the snow comes from."
e. "I can do better than that. I can take you where snow comes from. Climb on my back and we'll go."

II. Going where snow comes from
A. They flew almost to the end of the world.
1. They flew over houses, schools, the forest.
2. In front was a huge icy mountain, with a big hole in the center. "Is that where snow comes from?" said the boy.
3. There were little tiny bears at the base of the mountain, chopping off big chunks of ice (chop, chop, chop).

a. They put the clumps of ice on their backs.

b. They marched up the mountain (march, march, march).

c. They counted 1-2-3 and threw the ice down into the hole in the mountain.

B. The Snow Bird took him into the mountain.

1. It is beautiful but cold in there. At a big marble table big snow bears with scissors are taking the ice and cutting out snowflakes (cut, cut, cut).

2. "Snow Bird, I didn't know snow bears made the snowflakes. How do the flakes get out of the hole in the mountain?" "Just watch and listen," said Snow Bird.

3. The biggest of the bears stood up and shouted, "STOP." All the bears put down their scissors and sang:

> "One for the money
> Two for the snow
> Three to get ready
> Now BLOW, BEARS, BLOW!"

a. And the snowflakes went up, UP, UP, UP and out the big hole in the mountain and then down, down, down over the houses, the schools, and the forests.

C. The boy stays and helps.

1. He got to chop (chop, chop, chop), march (march, march, march), cut (cut, cut, cut) and blow (one for the money) until he was ready to go home.

2. "Snow Bird, I'm tired and cold and hungry. Can I go home now?"

3. Snow Bird whispered in the ear of the biggest bear.

a. He cut out the biggest snowflake he had ever seen (cut, cut, cut), put it down on the table, and shouted, "STOP."

b. All the bears put down their scissors and sang, "One for the money."

c. He blew, UP, UP, UP and out of the hole in the mountain and down, down, down right in front of his home.

III. Home for Dinner

A. His mom called him in for dinner, "DINNER!"

B. Over dinner, he told his mom all about where snow comes from.

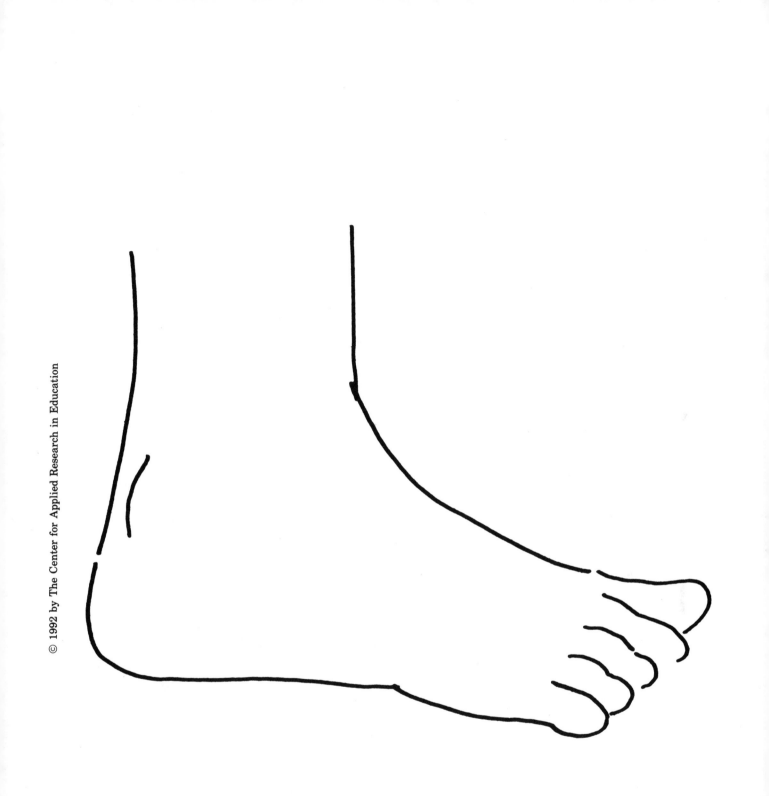

Activity One, Extenstions #2

THE TWELVE MONTH BROTHERS
Adapted from a Slavic folktale

The Story

[Note: Teach the season song before telling.]

There was once a young girl whose name was Katrina. She lived with her stepmother and stepsister in a tiny house on the edge of a forest. They did not like her because she was happy, sweet and very, very beautiful. So they did everything in their power to make her MISERABLE. She worked around the house from sun-up to sun-down. They were very cross with her and gave her many orders and complaints. *[Said with mean voice. Both Stepmother and Stepsister have cross, mean voices!]*

"The soup is too salty! The cows need milking! The house needs sweeping . . . the windows are dirty!"

She did all that they asked of her. She was polite, hard working, and pleasant. She sang happy little songs to herself as she worked and grew more beautiful every day.

"What are we going to do about her?" *[said with mean voice, with conviction]* asked the Stepmother one day. "If a young man comes calling he'll never look at you, my dearest daughter, if Katrina is around. We must get rid of her!"

Winter was especially cold that year. The icy wind whistled through the chimney. No matter how much wood Katrina piled on the fire, the house was still cold.

One day the house got full of smoke and the Stepmother threw Katrina out in the cold and said,

"You stupid fool! You can't even build a fire without filling the house with smoke!"

118

"Please, let me back inside, it's so cold out here, I don't even have my coat on. . . . I'll fix the fire. . . . I'm sorry, Stepmother . . . but let me in . . . please," begged Katrina.

"If you wish to get back into the house, you miserable worm, you must find violets so that I can be reminded of spring!" called back Stepmother.

"And make sure they are fresh!" added Stepsister.

Katrina was chilled to the bone, she only had on her thin cotton dress and old wooden shoes. *[Have audience shiver with you.]* She sadly turned away from the house and slowly walked into the forest. Perhaps the trees would give her some warmth. She was surprised to see a light in the distance and hear voices.

She came to a clearing in the forest and was astonished to see twelve men sitting in a circle around a blazing fire.

"Don't be afraid," said a man with a low friendly voice *[find a deep voice for January]*. "Warm yourself by the fire."

Katrina moved closer to the fire and thanked the old man.

"We are the Twelve Month Brothers. I am January," he said. "Perhaps we can help you."

Katrina looked around the circle and indeed the twelve brothers ranged from very old to very young. January had a long white beard and hair.

January spoke again, "What are you doing out on such a cold winter's day?"

"I came to pick violets for my Stepmother. And I cannot go back home until I have found them."

"Violets?" said January. "Don't you know the violets grow in the springtime, not in the winter?"

"I know," Katrina said, looking very sad. "But I must find them."

"We can help you," said January. "I will pass my wand to March and the seasons will change."

[Sing seasons song to the tune of "Three Blind Mice."]

> Twelve long months,
> Twelve long months.
> Watch the seasons change,
> Watch the seasons change.
> Old winter's snow melts into spring.
> And spring gives way to our summer fling.
> When summer ends, it's time for fall.
> Then back to winter, now that is all.
> The twelve long months.
> The twelve long months.

January passed his wand to February who passed it to March. *[Gesture the wand going from brother to brother.]* The snow melted, the sun warmed the green grass, the birds began to sing, and the sweet violets began to grow.

"Pick them quickly, little one. Then go and be safe," said kindly old January.

Katrina picked as many as her dress pockets could hold, quickly thanked the Twelve Month Brothers and headed home. *[Gesture picking flowers and filling up her pockets.]*

Her Stepmother and Stepsister were very surprised to see her return so quickly with pockets full of sweet smelling violets.

"Where did you find them?" her Stepmother asked crossly.

"Under the trees in the forest," answered Katrina.

They did not share them with Katrina, but the fragrance filled the house and she could enjoy their sweetness.

The next morning, Stepsister called Katrina into her bedroom and said,

"Fetch me some strawberries! They will improve my delicate complexion."

"Make sure they are sweet and juicy," added Stepmother.

Katrina knew the strawberries grew in the Summer.

At least she had time to put on her coat and scarf. She headed back to the clearing in the forest to seek the help of the brothers again.

"Come, little one, warm yourself by the fire," said January. "Why have you returned?"

She walked up to the fire.

"Now my Stepsister wants juicy, red strawberries for her complexion," answered Katrina.

January quickly passed his wand again to February to March to April to May and finally to June.

[When the song is repeated, children join in.]

>Twelve long months,
>Twelve long months.
>Watch the seasons change,
>Watch the seasons change.
>Old winter's snow melts into spring.
>And spring gives way to our summer fling.
>When summer ends, it's time for fall.
>Then back to winter, now that is all.
>The twelve long months,
>The twelve long months.

Katrina watched as winter melted into spring, and spring into summer. Small white flowers covered the ground and turned into berries which ripened into plump, red, juicy strawberries.

Katrina bent down and picked them quickly. Once again she thanked the Twelve Month Brothers and ran home through the forest. Stepmother and Stepsister were thrilled with the strawberries and ate them quickly without sharing them with Katrina.

On the third day, Stepmother wanted some apples. So Katrina once again hurried to her friends, the Twelve Month Brothers. It seemed that January was expecting her.

"And what do they want now?" he asked.

"Apples, Brother January."

"Warm yourself by the fire, and I'll pass the wand to September and October."

[Repeat song.]

> Twelve long months,
> Twelve long months.
> Watch the seasons change,
> Watch the seasons change.
> Old winter's snow melts into spring.
> And spring gives way to our summer fling.
> When summer ends, it's time for fall.
> Then back to winter, now that is all.
> The twelve long months,
> The twelve long months.

This time the wand went to January, February, March, April, May, June, July, August, September, and finally October. In front of Katrina was a huge tree, filled with apples.

"You may only pick two apples . . . hurry and be safe."

Katrina picked two large, juicy, red apples, put them in her pockets and hurried home.

"Only two?"

"Well, Stepmother, that was all they allowed me to pick," said Katrina.

"Who is they?" asked Stepmother.

"The Twelve Month Brothers," answered Katrina. "They live in the forest."

Katrina's Stepsister quickly put on her warm coat, hat, gloves, boots, and scarf *[use gestures to show her dressing]*.

"No one will stop me! I'll pick as many apples as I wish."

She went out into the cold winter's night to find the Twelve

Month Brothers. She walked up to the fire, ignoring the twelve brothers, warmed herself and asked,

"So which one of you is October?"

"Who are you?" asked January.

"None of your business, old man, just show me October, so I can pick as many apples as I wish," said Stepsister.

January lifted up the wand and in one swift movement of the wand, a fierce winter storm brewed. *[Use big gestures to show wand and storm brewing.]* Thick snow came out of the heavens and the winds began to blow. Stepsister stumbled into the forest and lost her way.

Stepmother sat at the window waiting for her daughter to return. She worried about her freezing to death in this cold winter's storm. Finally, she dressed warmly and followed her daughter out into the stormy night. They NEVER returned, both of them were lost in the cold winter's night.

Each night Katrina kept a candle in the window, in case they could find their way back, *but they never did.*

Each time the seasons would change, Katrina thought about her good friends, the Twelve Month Brothers, and she would be happy.

Key Concepts and Themes and/or Universal Ideas

The emphasis in this story is on the change of seasons and how each season brings us something different. The seasons will not be the same for children in different parts of the country, but it is important for young children to know about the seasons and how the earth changes throughout the year. The activities emphasize what the Earth brings us at different times of the year and will provide children with the opportunity to share ideas and feelings about what happens during each season and about the related celebrations.

Suggestion Companion(s)

a spring flower, a strawberry, and an apple (or pictures)

a wand

Preparation

Have you ever wondered what it would be like to live in a place where there is only one season all year round and there were no changes? For example, what if it was winter all year and there was always snow on the ground? Even in the jungle there are changes, such as the rainy season, during the year. Some places are like that. Do you live in one of those places or do you live in a place that has seasons?

Preparation for Visualization

Tell the Children:

Before we hear the story, we are going to take an imaginary trip. Close your eyes and imagine you are sitting in your yard and it is too cold to stay outside. You are shivering and turning blue, you are cold and you don't want to go inside. All of a sudden a little frosty fairy lands on your knee and says, "I ccccannnn hhhharrdddlllyyy sssstannnddd ssssttttillll. YYYooouu aarree sssshhhiivveeerrinng." You tell the frosty fairy that you are cold, but you like it outside and wish it was warmer so that you could stay out and play. The frosty fairy flies around your head and says, "I have something for you that will help you get your wish," and she gives you a long wand that is made up of four colors: white, green, bright yellow, and orange. You ask what you have to do. The fairy says that all you have to do is wave the wand and wish for the season you want it to be. Then wait and see what happens; but you have to say something nice about that season or else it will not happen. If you cannot say something about the season that is wonderful or if you do not tell about things that really happen in that season, it will stay winter. The seasons like to hear nice things about themselves, so wave the wand and talk to the season and see what happens. Now open your eyes. What season did you wish for? I'm going to tell you a story about the wonderful things that happen in each season and how the Twelve Month Brothers helped a lovely little girl in trouble.

Listen to the Story

Follow-up Discussion Questions

1. Did you like the story?
2. Would you like to have a wand like the one in the story?
3. What would you do with the wand?
4. Do we live in a place that has four different seasons? What is our weather like all year?

ACTIVITY ONE: THE GIFTS OF THE SEASONS

Objectives

—To develop the ability to compare and contrast
—To develop fine motor skills
—To develop the use of descriptive vocabulary
—To develop creative expression

Introduction

The students will be involved in several activities that will help them to develop an understanding of the characteristics of each season and what makes them unique and special. The children will create torn paper murals and stories about the seasons. The activities in this unit can relate to other science activities.

Materials

colored construction paper

glue or paste

large mural paper

Seasons worksheet

12″ × 18″ construction paper

markers or crayons

scissors

Procedure

1. Make multiple copies of the worksheet and cut it up into the individual pictures. You may want to laminate them before you cut them up. Give the children a set of pictures and a set of season title cards. Have the children work alone or in pairs. You may use this as an activity for the whole class or in small groups. Have the children match the pictures to the appropriate season. Relate the discussion back to the story as you talk about how the Earth changes for each season. If you don't want to cut up the sheets, the children can circle the pictures to match each season with a different colored marker for each season.

2. After the children have done the worksheet and you have continued the discussion about what happens in different seasons, brainstorm nouns and adjectives that describe each season. Put these words on individual cards (cards that are large enough to be seen from a distance) and save them to be put on the students' murals. Put winter words on white paper, spring words on green, summer words on bright yellow, and autumn words on orange.

3. Divide the children into four groups for mural making. If you have colored kraft paper, give each group a different color to match the word cards for each season. If the children are very young, have them tear paper to create the objects and characteristics that make up each season for their mural. You may create a simple outline for some of the objects to get them started. For older children have them create a torn paper mural

for each season. Discuss the organization of their mural with them before they get started and coach them as they go along, reminding them of the words on the colored paper. Put the words on their mural.

Language Development

1. Have the children create a picture about whatever season you are experiencing at this time. If they can write, have them write about this season. Have them focus on what grows during this season, how the animals behave and the characteristics of the season at this time. If the children cannot write, have them dictate a sentence about their picture to you. Create a class book. As the year continues, create a class book for each season.
2. Have the children create stories about each season or have the children act out the part of the story that relates to their mural, using the mural as a backdrop. The children can make hats for the months of the season that they want to be. Make a simple cone or crown shape for a hat and have the children draw or paste on decorations that relate to their month.

Extensions

1. Have older children create clothes for each season and create a fashion magazine.
2. Have the children go through magazines and tear out pictures related to the seasons and have them create a collage for all seasons.

ACTIVITY TWO: THE MAGIC WAND

Objectives

—To develop students' imagination
—To develop students' creativity
—To develop students' gross motor skills
—To develop students' oral communication skills

Introduction

The students will sit in a circle and pretend they have the magic wand as they share ideas about the seasons and act out activities related to each season. The students will create dances or do creative movement activities related to each season.

Materials

a wand
tapes of appropriate music
tape recorder

Procedure

1. Have the children sit in a circle. The children will pass the wand from one child to another. One child will stand in the center of the circle, select another child and say the name of one of the seasons. The child who receives the wand will have to say something about the season. It may have to do with the Earth, the weather, things they like to do during the season, whatever they want. They may also act out an activity related to the season and have the other children guess what  it is. Younger children may need help with ideas. When finished, the child states the name of another season and passes the wand to another child.

2. Play some music for the children and ask them what season it reminds them of. Divide the children into four groups. Have them all stand. When you point the wand in their direction and call out the name of a season, tell them they are to move to the music. You may want to guide their movements. For example:

   It is spring and the wind is blowing you all around or you are trying to fly your kite and you're running through the field and it's pulling and twirling.

   You are a little plant trying to grow out of the ground. You are reaching and stretching and growing.

   It is winter and you are rolling in the snow and sliding down the hill. You are running and playing in the snow.

You are a snowman and the sun is out and you begin to melt.

It is summer and you are swimming and splashing. The sun feels great on your face.

You dance through the fields picking daisies.

You are a beautiful butterfly flying over the garden trying to decide what flower you want to sit on.

It is fall and you are a pumpkin growing in the pumpkin patch.

You are the leaves gently falling from the trees. You are floating in all directions.

You are the same leaves being raked into one big heap all nestled close together.

Language Development

1. Talk about winter and winter activities and compare winter to the other seasons. For older children, have one child act as the *Season Changer*. Ask another child to start a story about "A Winter Snow Storm." When the Season Changer points his wand at the next student and calls out a different season, the new student continues the story but changes the season. The class has to listen carefully to see if the story events and setting match the season.

2. The children can create a group story about a tree or a seed and what happens to it throughout the year during each season. The tree is bare in winter, begins to grow leaves in the spring, is full in the summer and loses its leaves in the fall. They can talk about how the tree feels. Have the children role play two trees as they go through the changes. What would they say to each other? Have the children compare their tree to the tree in the story of "The Little Pine Tree." Do the same thing with the caterpillar and butterflies, flowers, animals that hibernate, and so on.

Extensions

1. Have the children create illustrations related to the changing tree, hibernating animals, or the changing caterpillar.

2. Create a special dramatic play center for the seasons. Put appropriate seasonal clothing in the center. Have the children bring in natural and man-made objects relating to a particular season. Have them tell about the objects for show and tell. Have the children dress up and act out seasonal activities.

3. Have the children create a picture of one season and put something in it

that doesn't fit, such as a snowman in a picture of summer with everyone at the swimming pool. Help the children with their individual ideas. Hang the pictures up and have the children look at each picture and try to find the part that does not fit.

4. Music suggestions:

"Concert for the Earth"	Paul Winter Consort
Symphony No. 6	Ludwig van Beethoven
"Saving the Wildlife"	Mannheim Steamroller
"The Dreams of Children"	Shadowfax
"Beyond Boundaries"	Earthbeat
"Holidays and Special Times"	Greg and Steve
"Burning Rhythms of Haiti"	Konbit
"The Moldau"	Bedrich Smetana

Winter	Spring	Summer	Fall
Starts in December	Starts in March	Starts in June	Starts in September

Activity One, Procedure #1

SEASONS: ADDITIONAL STORIES

 Sylvester and the Magic Pebble by William Steig. Simon and Schuster, Inc., New York, 1969.

Sylvester is a donkey who lives with his loving parents on Acorn Road in the town of Oatsdale. He collects rocks and pebbles. One fall day he finds a magic pebble. Unfortunately he makes a foolish wish and disappears. His parents spend all winter looking for him. Then one spring day he suddenly reappears and the family is together again.

Suggested Activities

Have the children talk initially about how their parents would feel if they disappeared for a year and how they would feel if they were Sylvester. The children can then role play to see if they can keep Sylvester entertained during each season. The children can create different leaves, snowflakes and flowers for each season and put them around Sylvester. They can tell him stories and try to make him happy. They can dance and sing for him. How did Sylvester feel during each of the seasons? The children can write letters to Sylvester's parents telling them how they could find him and giving them a map.

 Frog and Toad All Year, written and illustrated by Arnold Lobel. Harper, New York, 1976.

The stories in this book are about the adventures of frog and toad related to the seasons. The story ideas include sledding, falling leaves, and melting ice cream.

Suggested Activities

Ask the children to tell about different things they like to do with their friends in the summer, spring, winter, and fall. For example, whom do they like to go swimming with in the summer? Whom do they go get an ice cream with in the summer? Whom do they make snowmen with in the winter? And so forth. Have the children tell about their own adventures and do a group story creating a new adventure for frog and toad related to whatever season you are experiencing at the time. You can turn the new frog and toad story into a play or puppet show.

 Mousekin's Golden House by Edna Miller. Prentice Hall Books, Simon and Schuster, New York, 1964.

In the fall forest, the little Mousekin finds the perfect place to spend the winter.

Suggested Activities

Have the children close their eyes and imagine what it would be like living in a giant pumpkin. Talk about where they would sleep, eat and play. Talk about what it would be like living in another large fruit or vegetable. Have the children draw a house made out of one of these fruits or vegetables.

Other Stories

Waiting for Spring Stories by Robert Bethany. Harper and Row, New York, 1984.

The Snowman, written and illustrated by Raymond Briggs. Random House, New York, 1978. (A beautiful videotape is also available.)

The Snowy Day, written and illustrated by Ezra Jack Keats. Puffin, New York, 1962.

The Winter Wren, written and illustrated by Brock Cole. Sunburst/Farrar, Straus, New York, 1984.

7
Holidays

THE SHOEMAKER AND THE ELVES
A Version of the Folktale from the Brothers Grimm

About the Story [Recorded as a rap]

This story is a tale about clever elves who put some shoes on the shoemaker's shelves. The shoemaker and his wife were good people. In their time of need the elves came at night and made their shoes. They were so fine that people were willing to pay a great deal of money for them and the shoemaker and his wife became wealthy. One night they stayed up to see who was helping them out by creating beautiful shoes while they were asleep. They observed the elves and saw that they had no clothes and decided to do something to thank them. So, they made the elves some very fine clothes for Christmas. Once they received the clothes the elves were very pleased at the way the shoemaker and his wife showed their appreciation. The elves decided that the shoemaker and his wife no longer needed their help and left.

Key Concepts and Themes and/or Universal Ideas

The story illustrates how one good turn deserves another. The shoemaker needed some help and the elves provided the help he needed without asking for anything, expecting thanks, or letting anyone know what they had done. The shoemaker, being a good person, was very grateful. When he discovered what the elves were doing, he wanted to thank them in some way. He chose Christmas time to give them something to show his appreciation. The shoemaker's wife noticed that they did not have any clothes and that they might be cold, so they made new suits of clothes and shoes and left them for the elves. By now the shoemaker had become rich and could get along without the elves, so the elves happily took their gifts and went dancing on to help someone else.

133

The holidays are a time when we can give thanks and share what we have with people who have helped us or people who are less fortunate.

Suggested Companion(s)

a toy elf or a pair of shoes or both

Preparation

Ask the boys and girls what they do at holiday time for other people. Ask them who is kind to them. Who is kind to them at the school?

Preparation for Visualization

Tell the Children:

Before we hear the story, we are going to take an imaginary trip. Close your eyes and imagine you have been trying to keep your room clean, but no matter what you do you never get all your toys put away before it is time to go to bed and your Mom and/or Dad are not very pleased with you. See yourself trying to pick up your toys and put your books away. Everything is such a mess; your Mom says, "Time to get in bed, no story unless your room is cleaned up." You just sit down in the middle of your bed and are really sad because you still didn't get everything put away. You just don't know how to get it done in time. One night the same thing happens as usual, but the next morning there is a big surprise. Everything is neatly put away and your Mom is just as surprised as you are. She says if your room is like this tonight, we can read a story. Well, you are so excited and you try not to be too messy. Your Mom reads you a story after your dinner and you go up to your room to play. Before you know it, the room is a mess. Your Mom calls, "Time to go to bed," and you don't have everything finished in time. This happens for several days. When you wake up, your room is all clean. Your Mom reads you a story after dinner and everything is fine. But, who is cleaning your room at night? One night you decide to stay up and see what happens. You crawl under the covers and your eyes peep out and you wait and watch. Along comes some cute little elves who put everything in its place. You watch them carefully so that you can see how they do it. As they work you hear them say, "What fun it would be to have some of these toys for our birthday." You go fast to sleep. The next night you clean up your whole room before going to sleep. The elves have shown you how. You decide to pick out two of your favorite toys and leave them with a thank-you note for the elves. You also wish them happy birthday. You decide to stay up again and peek out from the covers and see what happens. The elves come and see the neat room and the present and dance happily away to some other child's house to help out. Now open your eyes and we are going to hear a story about some other helpful elves.

Listen to the Story (Tape 1, Side B)

Follow-up Discussion Questions

1. Tell me about the story.
2. Did you like the rap?
3. Have you ever heard a rap before?
4. Would you like to make up a rap for a fairy tale?
5. Why do you think the elves were so kind to the shoemaker and his wife?
6. How was the story like the one about the little child who had trouble cleaning his room?
7. Who are some of the people who give you help during the year? (parents, grandparents, sisters, brothers, teachers, librarian, school nurse, the principal, neighbors, friends, and so on)
8. What kinds of gifts and help can you give them at holiday time to thank them?
9. How do you help other people during the year?

ACTIVITY ONE: A GIFT OF THANKS

Objectives

- To develop oral and written communication skills
- To develop fine motor skills
- To develop ability to compare and contrast
- To develop sensitivity towards others

Introduction

Discuss what we do at holiday time for other people. Discuss gifts for friends and family, food for the poor, toys for the poor, or warm clothing for people who have none. Maybe your class can start collecting now for the poor and donate something even when it is not a holiday. This activity is going to focus on gifts of time and help for other people.

Materials

drawing materials

writing materials

odds and ends depending on what you decide to do

Thank-You Note worksheet

vegetables and waterbase ink or tempera paint mixed with a little liquid starch

Procedure

1. Have the children talk about all the people who are kind to them at home and around the school. Talk about the things they do. Make a list on the board.

2. Talk about these people and how the children can help them or give them something they would like such as a special picture, poem, story, song, or a gift of help.

3. Have the children choose one of these people and create something special or create a card telling them what they will do for them. With young children you will have to help with the writing. The children may make decorations for the principal's office or the nurse's office, or they may offer to come one day a week and help put the chairs around the tables in the library at the end of the day.

Language Development

1. Have the children use the Thank-You Note worksheet and write or draw a thank-you note from the shoemaker to the elves or the elves to the shoemaker. They can also use the note for someone they know. Have them add decorations to the card. Help them brainstorm ideas for the card and write them on the board to be copied if they are too young to write. If they are too young to print, help them fill in the card and have them do the decorations or have them just draw a card.

2. Have the children create a thank-you rap for the elves or the shoemaker.

Extensions

1. Use vegetables or other stamps and create a border design for the stationery. Stamp the vegetables in tempera paint or ink and use them as a stamp around the border. Have the children practice before they

do it on the stationery. The children can use the same technique to create wrapping paper.

2. Have older children brainstorm gifts that can be given that do not cost money. For example, a gift of love, kindness, or help, a hug, and so on.

3. Have them design an elf stamp for the envelope.

ACTIVITY TWO: ELF FASHIONS

Objectives

—To develop body awareness
—To develop imagination
—To develop visual expression
—To develop fine motor skills

Introduction

This activity is intended to stretch the children's imagination and ability to be playful. The children are going to create clothing for the elves. You can do one of two things. You can have the children lay down and outline and cut out each other's bodies or they can draw elves on large paper.

Materials

large poster paper or 12″ × 18″ manila paper
magic markers
colored construction paper
scissors
glue or paste
assorted papers (wrapping paper, wallpaper)
buttons, yarn, etc.
large and small brown paper bags

Procedure

1. Talk with the children about what they think elves look like. As they tell you, write some of the characteristics on the board or chart paper. You might want to share different descriptions from different fairy tales or stories. Ask them if they were the shoemaker and his wife, what kinds of clothes would they make for the elves.

2. Have them lay down and draw around each other's bodies and cut them out or have them draw an elf on their own.

3. Have them use a combination of markers, paper, yarn, buttons, etc., for the elves. Talk about elf shirts, pants, hats, and so forth.

4. Display the elves with their new clothes. Have an elf fashion show. Invite other classes to come. If you are working with older children, have them make invitations to the elf fashion show.

Language Development

1. For older children, work with the music teacher and create a rap for another fairy tale.

2. Have the children create a list of gifts that elves might like to have. Do it on the board or chart paper as a class.

3. Teach the rap to the children after they have listened to the tape. Make elf costumes and have two children become the shoemaker and his wife and put on the rap for another class. Have the children use large paper bags for elf vests and make elf hats out of smaller paper bags. Use the materials from the list to decorate the costumes.

Extensions

1. Have the children draw around their own feet and then create elf shoes. Have them use the same materials that they used for the elf fashions.

Children can also create shoes for other creatures such as elephant shoes, chicken shoes, lion shoes, and so on.

2. In approaching such a project, the students should translate the tale into a poem form so that the meter or rhythm can be set. Use a metronome while creating the piece so that the students can regulate the tempo or speed of the words.

3. The movement used to enhance the rap should be very rhythmical. The students should use their "shoes" to create the rhythm of the rap. Tap shoes could be worn or cleats could be applied to regular shoes. Percussion instruments could accompany the sounds.

STORY SUMMARY

This is a tale about clever elves
who put some shoes on the shoemaker's shelves.

It all began when a shoemaker said,
"I have the blues, I'm going to bed."

Boo baba boo and ratta tat tat
Tell me what happened after that.

Just before he turned out the light
He took some leather and cut it just right.

He got into bed and was snoring away,
When two elves appeared, but not to play.

Boo baba boo and ratta tat tat
Tell me what happened after that.

They hammered and nailed, they stitched and sewed,
They did not stop 'til the rooster crowed.

The shoes were a masterpiece in every way.
They took the shoemaker's breath away.

Boo baba boo and ratta tat tat
Tell me what happened after that.

The shoes were neat, oh so nice,
The shoemaker sold them for double the price.

All that money took away his blues,
He bought fine leather for two pair of shoes.

The elves came back the following night,
And finished the shoes by the bright moonlight.

The shoemaker sold them the following day.
Folks came a' running and a' willing to pay.

Boo baba boo and ratta tat tat
Tell me what happened after that.

The shoemaker cut, the elves sewed the stitches.
In time the shoemaker increased his riches.

One night, near Christmas his wifey said,
Tonight we stay up, we're not going to bed.

Boo baba boo and ratta tat tat
Tell me what happened after that.

They stayed up very late that night.
They peeked through the curtain, Oh my what a sight.

Boo baba boo and ratta tat tee
Tell me real quick what did they see?

Two elves as naked as the day they were born.
Working on the shoes to be ready by morn.

They've made us rich, and happy too.
We're thankful, said wifey, what shall we do?

Boo baba boo and ratta tat tat
Tell me what happened after that.

Let's make them clothes for a Christmas gift,
It will keep them warm, and give them a lift.

They sewed shirts and pants, to fit just right.
And left them for the elves on Christmas night.

Boo baba boo and ratta tat tat
Tell me what happened after that.

When the elves came out under darkened skies,
They were in for a very big surprise.

Instead of leather they found clothes you see,
They tried them on and danced with glee.

Boo babba boo and ratta tat tat
Tell me what happened after that.

The happy elves never came again,
And the shoemaker did just fine.

THE END

Dear

Thank you for

Yours truly,

Activity One, Language Development #1

WILLIWU, THE LONELY LITTLE WITCHGIRL
By Ruthilde Kronberg

About the Story

There are two ways in which *Williwu* can be told. Both ways the audience is informed beforehand that there is a refrain that Williwu hears throughout the story. The storyteller chants or sings it, and then teaches it. The audience is requested to chant or sing the refrain when it's time, as follows:

> It's up to you, Williwu,
> This is something you must do,
> If you don't do it very soon,
> You won't make it to the moon.

The tale is greatly enhanced by having the audience be Williwu's prompter. A second way that works well with children is to encourage them to join in whenever there are repetitions, which occur frequently throughout the story.

The Story

Long, long ago, next to the Cahokia Mounds *[or insert name of local area]* stood a little house in which lived seven little witchgirls. Six of them were perfect toughies. They fought all day and went around doing as much mischief as they possibly could. But the seventh one, whose name was WILLIWU, was different.

No matter how hard she tried, Williwu could not manage to be bad. That caused a lot of trouble between her and

143

her witchgirl cousins. They had been taught by all the old witches that being good was the same as being stupid. And who wants to be stupid? Not those little witchgirls! So they despised Williwu. They played tricks on her, they called her horrible names, they tripped her while she walked, laughed at her—and who do you suppose was forced to do all the dirty work around the house?

WILLIWU!

Poor Williwu—with no one to talk to—she was a lonely little witchgirl.

One bright Halloween Day, the witchgirls told Williwu to get their flying brooms out of the closet and dust them off for their trip to the moon. This was a big event, in fact the most important and most wonderful thing they did all year. On the night of October thirty-first, without fail, at midnight, all the little witches and the big witches mounted their flying brooms and were off to the moon for a big party. (Some day I shall tell you about that party, but right now I want to tell you what happened that morning to Williwu.)

No sooner did she open the closet door than hundreds of little house mice scampered out, and Williwu saw they had eaten all the branches of the brooms. They had left only tiny little stubs! And that wasn't all they did! The broom*sticks* were full of little toothmarks where the mice had tried to bite into the wood too! These brooms could take no witch anywhere! These brooms could not even fly as high as the housetop—and they would surely NEVER make the moon!

Williwu called her cousins over and when they saw what had happened, they began to wail and scream and screech most horribly!

Only Williwu stayed calm. "Why don't we go to the witchbroom maker," said Williwu, "and buy seven new brooms?" For once, the cousins did not make fun of her idea. They dashed off to the witchbroom maker's house, yelling:

"Witchbroom maker, Witchbroom maker,

QUICK! QUICK!

Sell us each a broom, so we can fly to the moon."

But the witchbroom maker said, "I'm sorry, I have only six brooms left. One of you will have to stay home tonight."

"Let it be Williwu," screamed the six witchgirls wickedly, and before the witchbroom maker could stop them, they pushed him aside, stormed into his shop, grabbed the six brooms and flew away.

"Come back, you little brats!" cried the witchbroom maker furiously. "You didn't even pay! I never saw naughtier witchgirls than you!" And then shaking his fist at them far up in the sky by now, he said, "If ever I get my hands on you, I'll give YOU knuckleheads instead of brooms."

"Oh!" he stormed to himself as he went back inside and shut the door. "I HATE TO BE TREATED LIKE THAT!"

All of a sudden he noticed that not all the witchgirls had left. One was still standing inside his house, off in a corner, and her eyes were filled with tears.

"What are you doing here?" snarled the broommaker. "Are you waiting for a knucklehead?"

"No, I get plenty of those from my cousins," cried the girl. "I am Williwu, and I stayed here because I hate to go home. My witch cousins will laugh at me all afternoon for not having a broom to fly to the moon."

"That's the nastiest bunch of witchgirls I ever saw!" said the witchbroom maker. "You seem to be much nicer."

"That's my problem," wailed Williwu. "I simply cannot manage to be bad. Sometimes I wonder if I really am a witchgirl. I never do anything the way I'm supposed to. But this is the worst thing that has ever happened to me, because any witch or witchgirl who doesn't make it to the moon on Halloween night will be the laughingstock of all the other witches forever and ever."

"I know how you feel," said the witchbroom maker. "To be laughed at hurts more than being scolded. I know because kids used to make fun of me, too. As you can see, my legs are a little crooked, so I can't run like other people."

When Williwu looked down at them, drying off her tears, she saw that his legs were more than a *little* crooked. They were *very* crooked. But she was too polite to say anything, and the witchbroom maker went on. "Let me see, maybe I can help you so those hooligans can't make fun of you for not getting to the moon. You'll have to be real quick, though. Run to the willow tree and ask him to give you an armful of branches. I think I have just enough time to make a very fine broom, so you can fly to the moon."

The witchbroom maker expected Williwu to be delighted at the very idea, but Williwu was not used to kindness. She was also frightened. She said,

"Oh, gee, I don't even know the willow tree. Please—would you come along with me?"

"I can't," said the kind old witchbroom maker. "You know I can't run. We'd never make it in time."

And then he said, slowly and clearly . . . *[to audience]* . . . "Can you guess what he said?" *[Don't wait for words. Lead audience to say with you:]*

"It's up to *you,* Williwu,
This is something you must do,
If you don't do it very soon,
You won't make it to the moon."

"All right, I'll try," said Williwu with a sigh. She took a deep breath and ran all the way to the willow tree. When she got there, she said, all out of breath and in a rush, "Willow tree, dear willow tree, I am Williwu, the little witchgirl. Would you please give me some branches so I can take them to the witchbroom maker? He promised to make a broom so I can fly to the moon."

In a weak little voice, the willow tree replied, "I wish I could, but look at me! Ever since the well stopped sending me water, my branches stopped growing. My roots are so dry, I think I'm about to die.

"Would you run to the well and ask him to send me some water? If I got some water, I could give you some branches to take to the witchbroom maker. I am sure he could make you a fine broom so you could fly to the moon."

"Oh, dear," said Williwu, "I don't know how to talk to the well. I wish someone could come along with me."

"I can't move, as you can see," said the sad old willow tree. And then Williwu heard those words again.

She wasn't sure whether the willow tree said them, or whether they came to her from the air, but all the same, *she heard them.* *[Ask audience.]* What did she hear?

"It's up to *you,* Williwu,
This is something *you* must do,
If you don't do it very soon,
You won't make it to the moon."

"All right, I'll try," said Williwu with a sigh. She took a deep breath and ran all the way to the well. When she got there, she said, "Dear well, I am Williwu, the little witchgirl. Would you kindly send some water to the willow tree, so he can give me some branches to take to the witchbroom maker? He promised to make a fine broom to fly me to the moon."

"Ahhh," moaned the well. "I wished I could. But look and see, a hurricane rolled a stone on top of me. I can't send water to anybody, and I am about to burst! Could you please help me?

"If you would roll the stone off me,
I could send water to the willow tree,

So it could give you branches to
take to the witchbroom maker.
I am sure he could make you a fine broom
so you could fly to the moon."

"Oh, that should be easy!" cried Williwu. And she began to push
the stone. She pushed, and she pushed, and she pushed—as hard as
she could.

But the stone was far too big to be moved by one little witchgirl.
When Williwu realized that all her efforts were in vain *[or, for
younger audiences, that "she just couldn't do it"],* she threw herself
on the ground and sobbed,

"Witches spells and witches brew,
I wish I could get rid of you!"

Then she tried all the spells she knew, but nothing worked.
Finally she began to cry. Her tears fell all over the stone, which
moved him to say, "Little witchgirl, listen to me. You don't need a
spell to push me off the wall. What you need is a friend."

"A FRIEND?

"What is a FRIEND?" asked Williwu, bewildered.

"Don't you know what a friend is?" asked the stone, amazed.

"No," replied Williwu, shaking her head sadly.

"A friend is someone who helps you when you need help,"
explained the stone.

"Listen—go to the white house on top of the hill. It belongs to a
little girl whose name is Valerie. She is very nice. Ask her to help
you to roll me off the well."

Williwu took a few steps back and said, in a trembling voice, "Is
there nobody else who could go in my stead? I've never spoken to
any real girls."

"No," said the stone. "As you can see, there is no one else here
but you."

And then she heard those words again.

"It's up to *you,* Williwu,
This is something you must do,
If you don't do it very soon,
You won't make it to the moon."

"All right, I'll try," said Williwu with a sigh. She took a deep
breath and ran all the way to Valerie's house.

When she got there she knocked on the door, and Valerie
appeared. "I am Williwu," said the little witchgirl, very fast.

"Please, will you help me roll the stone off the well, so he can send some water to the willow tree, so it can give me branches to take to the witchbroom maker, who promised to make me a broom so I can fly to the moon."

"Sure," said Valerie. "Can I bring my brother Daniel and all our friends along? We were just getting ready for a Halloween party."

"That would be great," said Williwu. "Would they be willing to help us to push the stone away?"

"Of course," said Valerie. "Friends are always willing to help."

Then she called out to her friends inside the house.

"Come on, everybody! We're off on an adventure!"

They all rushed out of the house and followed the little witchgirl down the hill. It was a good thing they did come along because it took ALL of them to push the stone off the well.

The well gurgled with relief—and immediately sent huge waterwaves to the willow tree. The willow tree soaked up every drop and gave the children some of its best branches. When they brought them to the witchbroom maker, the kind old man allowed them to stay and watch while he made the finest broom ever . . . long enough so Williwu could invite all the children to come with her to the moon! And the broommaker too!

And off they flew! Now what could be better than a Halloween party on the moon? Williwu, Valerie, Daniel, the witchbroom maker, and the children played wonderful new games and danced all kinds of strange new dances until they could dance no more! And never did they meet any of Williwu's cousins because they were partying on the dark side of the moon.

Not before the morning star rose did they leave. But on the way home Williwu seemed sad, and when Valerie asked her what was troubling her, she began to cry and said, "I wish I wouldn't have to return to my cousins."

"You won't have to return to your cousins," cried Valerie. "Please come with us. We would love to have you."

Nothing nicer could have happened to the little witchgirl! She moved into Valerie's and Daniel's house right away, and it wasn't too long before she became a regular little girl, just like Valerie. And she was never laughed at again or scolded for being good and trying to help.

Key Concepts and Themes and/or Universal Ideas

There are several points you will want to stress. One is the difference between the good little witch and the bad little witches. In this story bad and good has to do with being kind to each other. Other concepts you will want to discuss have to do with making choices, learning to do something for oneself, and making new friends.

Suggested Companion(s)

a picture of a witch or a broom

Preparation

Ask the boys and girls if they think all witches are mean or if there are some nice witches. Most children will be familiar with good witches and bad witches from *The Wizard of Oz.* Ask them what kinds of things the mean witches do. Ask them what kinds of things the nice witches do.

Preparation for Visualization

Tell the Children:

Before we hear the story, close your eyes and imagine it is Halloween night. Imagine that you can see into the land of the witches. They are very busy getting ready for a big evening. Look carefully. Can you see them? There are big ones and little ones, fat ones and skinny ones, ugly ones and pretty ones, green ones and purple ones. I bet you didn't think there were so many different kinds. They are rushing around and making so much noise. Don't you wish you could hear what they were saying? Get a little closer; but be careful, don't let them see you. You don't know what they might do if they thought you heard their secrets. Are you closer now? Can you hear a little better? You hear them laughing and cackling and teasing one little witch. They are telling her she is not mean enough. They are poking her and tickling her and messing up her beautiful black cape and hat. Big tears are rolling down her face, she doesn't know what to do. You feel so sorry for her. She is afraid she is going to be left out of all the Halloween activities. The other witches keep laughing and teasing her and she runs off into the forest sobbing. Now open your eyes and get ready to listen to a story about a good little witchgirl and maybe you would like to be her friend.

Listen to the Story

Follow-up Discussion Questions

1. Did you like the story?
2. Did you like the ending?
3. Would you have liked to be Williwu's friend?
4. Would you have helped her?

5. Did she make a good choice by going to find the things needed to make the broom and getting help?

6. Are you ever mean to friends, brothers, sisters, or cousins?

7. What do you do?

8. What are some of the nice things you do?

9. Williwu learned that sometimes you can't do everything yourself and you need a friend's help. How do your friends help you? Do you help your friends?

ACTIVITY ONE: PORTRAITS OF THE MEAN AND KIND

Objectives

- To develop the ability to compare and contrast
- To develop fine motor skills
- To develop visual expression
- To develop vocabulary skills

Introduction

This activity will provide the children with an opportunity to explore the characteristics of the mean and the good little witchgirls. The children will tell you how a mean witch would look and how Williwu might look. They will then create either a mean witch portrait or a portrait of Williwu using simple cut paper and markers.

Materials

12″ × 18″ purple and light blue construction paper

cut-up pieces of construction paper

markers

glue or paste

scissors

writing materials

Procedure

1. Brainstorm with the children. Ask them what a mean witch would look like and write all of their words on chart paper or the board. Do the same for Williwu.

2. Tell them they are going to make a portrait of one of the two. If they have

time they can do both. Remind them about where the eyes, nose, ears, mouth, and hair would be. Have them look at each other or themselves in the mirror.

3. Use green paper for the mean witches and light blue for Williwu. Give the children some precut construction paper shapes to use for the face and hair. They may want to add a hat or whatever else they think would be appropriate. For children who can cut, they may want to cut additional shapes that might be more appropriate.

4. Give them markers for details when they think they have put on all the necessary cut paper shapes. Do not give them the markers too soon. Encourage them to elaborate as much as possible. Remind them to keep in mind the character they are creating. The two kinds of witches should look different. Encourage them to use their own ideas and make choices.

5. Display all of the witches and write a group description of the characteristics and behavior of the mean witches and another one for Williwu. Have the children tell you what to write and display it with the portraits.

Language Development

1. For older children, have them write a letter to Williwu telling her they would like to be her friend and all the things they could do together if they were friends.

2. Have the children sit in a circle and tell a story about Williwu's adventures with her new friends.

3. Have the children tell about when someone was mean to them and what they did.

Extensions

1. Have the children draw or use other materials of their choice and create a fantastic new broom for Williwu. Remember it has to be a broom for three. You may want them to create a broom of the future for her.

2. If it is Halloween time, have the children dress up as good or bad witches and have a party on the moon. Create moon games and activities. Snacks may be moon juice and moon crackers.

ACTIVITY TWO: MAKING CHOICES

Objectives

—To develop problem-solving skills
—To develop oral communication skills
—To develop role-playing skills

Introduction

This activity will provide the children with different kinds of problem situations and they will have to decide which behavior might be the best choice and why.

Materials

Problem-Solving Cards worksheets

Procedure

1. Have the children sit in a circle. Tell them they are going to play a game about solving problems. If the children are in first or second grade, they may want to role play the problems. Cut up the problems from the Problem worksheets and put them in a box or bag.

2. The child will pick a problem without looking. You will read it to them and the class and then they will try to solve it. If they are having trouble, ask the class for help. If they say, "Tell the teacher," tell them they need to solve the problem themselves or with a friend.

3. Older children can write about a problem they have had with a friend or relative.

Language Development

1. Create a class alphabet book about friendship.

2. Write a class letter to the mean witchgirls telling them not to be so mean and giving all the reasons why they should be kind to Williwu.

3. Put different Halloween characters up for the children to see. Ask them, "If you could have any one of these for a friend, who would it be and what would you do together?" For example, Peter Pumpkin, Catherine Cat, George Ghost, Wilma Witch, and so on.

Extensions

Give each child a piece of paper and have them write a huge W on the paper and tell them to turn it into two witches playing together.

Your best friend becomes friends with someone else and you get left out of some of their activities.

What do you do?

It's time to get partners for an activity. Everyone gets one but you.

What do you do?

You give your friend a birthday present that you want because you don't have it.

What do you do?

Another child comes along and pushes you.

What do you do?

Your friend told a mean lie about you.

What do you do?

You would like to be line leader and your teacher hasn't picked you for this job for a long time.

What do you do?

Activity Two, Procedure #1

Your cousins or your brother or sister's friends come over to your house to play. They won't let you play. They say you are too young.

What do you do?

What happens when your friend gets into trouble for something you did?

What do you do?

You are in line for recess and the same boys and girls always push into the line ahead of you.

What do you do?

You are sitting and reading quietly and someone keeps bothering you.

What do you do?

Someone in the class lost his pet. It ran away.

What do you do?

Your friends are working a puzzle and they are upset because it is difficult and they are having a hard time.

What would you do to help them?

Activity Two, Procedure #1

HOLIDAYS: ADDITIONAL STORIES

 Humbug Witch by Lorna Balian. Abingdon, Nashville, 1965.

A funny little story about an unusual witch. All of her is little except her BIG NOSE. There is a surprise ending when we find out that this is really not a witch at all but a young girl!

Suggested Activities

Get out the costume bag and let the children dress up as different creatures and animals. Use paper bag or paper plate masks and make the ugliest witch you can think of.

 Potato Pancakes All Around: Hanukkah Tale by Marilyn Hirsh. Hebrew Publishing Co., New York, 1978.

When Samuel the peddler reaches the village, it is the first day of Hanukkah. He's welcomed warmly by Mama, Papa, Grandma Yetta, Grandma Sophie, and the children. It becomes a festive holiday evening with everyone cooperating in making Samuel's potato pancakes. Samuel shows them how to make the potato pancakes from a crust of bread. The result is delicious pancakes for everyone.

Suggested Activities

If it is possible the class should make potato pancakes and the children should be encouraged to tell about their holiday food and share a story about a holiday meal. Favorite holiday dances and songs can also be introduced but the emphasis should be on the stories including elements about special relatives who visit and favorite activities. Drawings, paintings, and stories can be created by all age children. For older children a class book titled *Favorite Holiday Meals* which includes written stories, illustrations, and recipes can be started. This story can be thought of as another version of *Stone Soup*. Have the children dictate their favorite recipes and create a recipe book.

 The Puppy Who Wanted a Boy by June Thayer. William Morrow and Co., New York, 1958.

Petey the puppy wanted a boy for Christmas. When his mother fails to find him a boy, he goes out into the world to find one. He doesn't find one boy for Christmas, he finds an orphanage with 50 boys.

Suggested Activities

Ask the children, "If you were to be a holiday gift for an animal, what kind of animal would choose you as their owner and why? What would you do to make a wonderful home for them? How would you change your house? What special foods would you find for them?"

Other Stories

The Polar Express, written and illustrated by Chris Van Allsburg. Houghton, Mifflin, Co., Boston, 1985.

Molly's Pilgrim, by Barbara Cohen and illustrated by Michael J. Deraney. Lothrop, New York, 1983.

8

Animals and Pets

THE NERVOUS LITTLE HARE
Adapted from an Old Folktale from India

About the Story

They say that long, long ago in the land of India, before Buddha was born, he would come down to earth in the form of a lion to help his fellow animals. The story of "The Nervous Little Hare" tells how the lion helped a little hare who worried about everything. She was always afraid that something dreadful would happen to her.

"What if the earth would fall in?" Little Hare would ask Mother Hare.

"My foolish Little Hare, the earth will not fall in . . . do not worry." At night Mother Hare would hold her in her arms and sing,

> You are safe, my Little Hare.
> Peacefully sleep without a care.

But Little Hare worried and worried anyway. The story tells how the little hare was frightened by a piece of fruit falling from a tree and how she mistakenly thought the earth was falling. The frightened little hare ran through the forest telling each animal as she ran that the earth was falling. The little hare ran. She ran, ran, ran, ran, ran. She ran until she ran right into BIG HARE. As the BIG HARE, the LITTLE DEER, the MONKEY, the LEOPARD, the TIGER, and the ELEPHANT came across her path, she told them,

157

> I knew it, I knew it
> I knew it would come true.
> The Earth is falling, Earth is falling,
> What shall I do?

Each animal followed her singing the same chant. Until the animals ran into the LION who took them back to the tree and showed them what really happened.

Key Concepts and Themes and/or Universal Ideas

The main idea of the story is that sometimes we may worry too much and things that frighten us may not be what they seem. It also implies that we need to check out our suspicions very carefully and ask lots of questions so that we can find out what the real problem might be. Children need to begin to find out that the more information they have, the less there is to be frightened of, although there are certain situations that require caution and care such as saying no to strangers and crossing the street carefully. A child needs to know that most animals are friendly but that there are appropriate ways for approaching strange animals if they do not want to get hurt.

Another topic for consideration is that animals are frequently frightened by loud noises. When an animal is frightened by a loud noise, many times it will run off and hide. Children need to be careful not to frighten their own pets and other animals.

Suggested Companion(s)

a big juicy piece of fruit

Preparation

Ask the children what frightens them, what worries them, and if loud noises frighten them. Ask them if a loud noise ever frightened them and then they found out it was something different from what they originally thought.

Preparation for Visualization

Tell the Children:

Before we hear the story we are going to go on an imaginary trip. Close your eyes and imagine it is time to go to sleep. The room is dark and quiet. You are warm and snug in your bed. Your favorite stuffed animal is next to you and is soft and cuddly. It is summer and there is a light breeze. Everything smells fresh and cool. As you begin to fall asleep you hear a creaking noise. CREAK! CREAK! It doesn't stop. You begin to get frightened. You don't know what it is. You stick your head under the covers but you can still hear it. You decide to call your Mom and just as you sit up and get ready to call, you look out into the room and you see two green eyes and you realize it is your pet cat and he is rubbing up against the closet door which is causing the creaking. You feel so much better and you invite the kitty up onto the bed. Now open your eyes and I'm going to tell you a story.

Listen to the Story (Tape 1, Side B)

Follow-up Discussion Questions

1. Did you like the story?
2. Did you think the Little Hare was silly?
3. Why do you think he was so frightened?
4. Why do you think the animals followed the Little Hare?
5. Would you have followed the Little Hare? Why or why not?
6. Have you ever been frightened like the Little Hare?

ACTIVITY ONE: RUN, HARE, RUN

Objectives

—To develop sequencing skills
—To develop oral communication skills
—To develop fine motor skills
—To develop gross motor skills

Introduction

This activity is similar to the circle game, "Duck, Duck, Goose." The students will sit in a circle after hearing the story for the first time. The teacher will tell the story again and the children will participate.

Materials

large poster paper for a bulletin board	paint
colored construction paper	brushes
glue or paste	scissors

Procedure

1. After the discussion, create a large tree trunk for your bulletin board. Put it on the floor. Have the children cut or tear green paper for leaves and paste them to the tree. Have the children cut or tear red paper for apples and add them to the tree. Keep a few apples for the floor.

2. After creating the tree, have the students sit in a circle and ask them to tell you who the hare ran to first. Continue asking the students what animals were involved in the sequence of their appearance in the story.

3. This will take some coaching, but once the children do it a few times they should get the pattern. Ask one student to be the hare and explain to the students that you are going to tell the story again. When you say, "Run, Hare, Run," the child should run on the outside of the circle while the whole class chants:

> Run, Hare, Run
> Run, Hare, Run
> Run, Hare, Run, Hare
> Run, Run, Run.

The child runs around once and then stops behind another child. The child who is seated says, "Where are you going, Little Hare?" The Little Hare says, (the other children can help),

> I knew it. I knew it.
> I knew it would come true.
> The Earth is falling, the Earth is falling.
> What shall I do?

The child asks, "Can I come along?" The Little Hare says, "Yes, Bigger Hare!"

The children run around the circle together as the group chants the same chant, except they change the word "Hare" for "Bigger Hare." They stop behind another child and that child becomes the Little Deer. The activity proceeds in the same manner.

The game continues including the Monkey, the Leopard, the Tiger, and the Elephant until they come to the Lion who ROARS, "Why are you all running?" The whole class chants again changing the animal name to Lion. The Lion tells the other animals,

> You must have heard something else.
> Look around you, the Earth is quiet.
> Why are you animals having a RIOT.

The Lion asks each animal, "Who told you the earth was falling in?" Each child tells or points to the animal (child) until they come to the Little Hare. The Lion tells him to show him the place. The Hare is frightened, but the Lion convinces him to go.

The Lion takes the other children to the tree and shows them the fruit. And the whole class says, "See the earth is not falling."

4. Ask the children if they can tell you the order of the animals' appearance in the story. Have all the children who played animals stand up and get in line in the order of their appearance in the story.

Language Development

1. The children can continue the game and add other animals to the story.

2. Ask the children to brainstorm different ways the Hare could have moved as he went from animal to animal. The children can change the chant by exchanging the word run with another kind of movement such as hop, skip, slide, and so on.

3. Read or tell the class the story about Henny Penny (the sky is falling). Have them compare and contrast the two stories.

Extensions

1. The students can create the animals in the story and put them up around the tree. They can cut them out or draw them and then cut them out. Allow them to create their own animals even if they are unrecognizable. Another option is to have them use large paper, large brushes, and paint.

2. Have the children talk about all the different fruits that might grow on the tree. Have them create the fruits and add them to the tree.

ACTIVITY TWO: SCARY THINGS

Objectives

   —To develop oral communication skills
   —To develop expressive language skills

Introduction

The purpose of this activity is to have the students share stories about things that have frightened them.

Materials

none needed

Procedure

1. Talk to the students about things that are frightening. Ask them to tell you about things that frighten them. Ask the children to tell the class a story about something that frightened them, but turned out to be OK like a noise or dream.

2. Encourage the children to tell their stories. Keep asking them to add details.

   - Were they alone?
   - Was it real or something they imagined?
   - Was it at night or during the day?
   - Who helped them?
   - Are they still afraid of it?

3. Encourage the children to listen to each other's stories. Ask them if they are afraid of some of the same things.

4. Have each child draw a picture about their story or about what they are afraid of. Have them label the pictures or write sentences about the pictures. Older children can write their own stories.

Language Development

1. Ask the children to think of all the scary sounds they know and to make up even more. Have each child make a scary sound. Write it on the board. If the children are old enough, have them tell you how they think the sound should be spelled. Ask them to act out the sound and have the rest of the class guess who or what animal is making the sound. Ask the children to draw what the sound would look like.

2. The children can create a scary creature and write about it.

Extensions

1. Have the children create a list of things that they should be careful about. For example, they should not talk to strangers or get in their cars. They should look carefully before crossing the street and hold an adult's hand. And so forth.

2. Talk about the Lion and how he explained what was really happening to all the animals. Ask the children to tell you who are some of the people

they could go to if they were afraid of something and what that person might tell them. For example, parents, grandparents, teachers, the police officer, older brothers and sisters, and so on.

3. Ask the children if they have pets. Ask them what kinds of things scare their pets. Ask them if it is kind to try and scare pets. Is it kind to make loud noises around their pets? Should their pets really be afraid of the mailman? Is the pet being smart when it barks when there is a stranger at the door?

4. Using a large white sheet and a lamp, have the children do a shadow play. Have them be animals and creatures. Have them act out the story.

STORY SUMMARY

I. Setting the scene, introduction of characters

    A. The story takes place in India.

        1. Before he was born Buddha would come down to Earth in the form of a LION.

        2. This is one of those stories.

    B. Introduction of Little Hare and her mother

        1. She was always nervous, worried about EVERYTHING.

        2. She asked her mother, "What if the Earth would fall in?"

        3. Mother sang each night:

> "You are safe, my little hare.
> Peacefully sleep, without a care."

II. The Earth is falling in.

    A. There was a loud noise in the forest.

        1. Little Hare was asleep in the forest by a river.

        2. A piece of fruit from a nearby tree fell into the river with a loud noise.

        3. Little Hare cried:

> "I knew it, I knew it
> I knew it would come true.
> The Earth is falling, Earth is falling
> What shall I do?"

        4. So Little Hare ran, ran, ran, ran, ran.

    B. She ran into Big Hare.

        1. Sang verse, "I knew it," etc.

        2. "Can I come along?" asked Big Hare.

        3. "Yes, but hurry," answered Little Hare.

        4. They ran, ran, ran, ran, ran.

    C. They ran into Deer.

        1. Sang verse "We knew it!"

        2. The deer joined them.

        3. They ran, ran, ran, ran, ran.

    D. They ran into Monkey, then Leopard, then Tiger, then Elephant.

        1. Each time the verse is repeated.

        2. One by one they joined the others.

        3. "They ran, ran, ran, ran, ran" is repeated at the end of each segment.

E. They finally run into LION.

    1. Verse repeated.

    2. Lion ROARS! and says "Look around you, the earth is quiet! Why are you animals having a RIOT?"

    3. Elephant, who told you the Earth is falling in?

> It was Tiger.
> Tiger, who told you?
> It was Leopard.
> Leopard, who told you?
> It was monkey.
> Monkey?
> It was Little Deer.
> Little Deer?
> It was Big Hare.
> Big Hare?
> It was Little Hare.
> Little Hare?
> "I heard it with my own ears."

F. Little Hare took LION back to the place by the river.

    1. Lion told Little Hare to watch and listen.

    2. Little Hare watched a piece of fruit break loose and make a loud NOISE.

    3. "That's it!"

III. The Earth is not falling.

A. Lion and Little Hare go back to the other animals.

    1. "The Earth is not falling," Little Hare told them.

    2. They all agreed LION was very wise and they were foolish.

B. Little Hare never worried about the Earth falling in again.

THE BREMENTOWN MUSICIANS
A German Folktale Adapted from the Brothers Grimm

The Story

Note:

1. Teach song (see below).
2. Divide audience into the four animal sounds: Hee-haw, bark, meow, cock-a-doodle-doo.

Once there was a farmer who had a VERY old donkey. The donkey had worked hard for the farmer for many, many years. Now he was too old to do the heavy farmwork. One day the farmer said,

"You eat too much, and you're too old to work. You are no longer useful to me. Leave at once!"

The sad old donkey left the farm and headed toward the city.

And he sang: *[Sung to the tune of "Twinkle, Twinkle." Sing twice so audience can join in.]*

> I am very old, you see.
> No one gives a hoot for me.
> I have no home or place to go.
> What will I do? I do not know.

As he walked along, an idea popped into his head. *[Use a special voice for Donkey. You can add some hee-haws.]*

"I know what I can do. . . . I can go into Brementown and become a great musician!"

So he walked along, and walked along ALONE.

As he walked toward the city he noticed a dog asleep on the side of the road. As the donkey passed by, the old dog woke up and started whimpering.

"What's wrong, old friend?" asked Donkey. "Why are you sleeping by the road?"

"I'm old! My master cannot take me hunting anymore, so he sent me away! A-rrrrr." *[Sound whimpering.]*

And he sang *[Have audience join in]* :

> I am very old, you see.
> No one gives a hoot for me.
> I have no home or place to go.
> What will I do? I do not know.

"Why don't you come along with me?" suggested Donkey. "I'm going to Brementown to be a great musician. You can join me!"

"I'd like that!" said the dog, feeling better already.

So they went along and they went along, TOGETHER.

They had not gone very far when they met up with an old Tabby Cat. She was so thin that her ribs showed through her orange and white fur.

"What are you doing out here in the middle of the road?" asked Donkey.

"I cannot chase mice anymore. *[Cat-like with meows.]* My master was going to throw me in the river!" said the Cat.

And she sang *[have audience join in]:*

> I am very old, you see.
> No one gives a hoot for me.
> I have no home or place to go.
> What will I do? I do not know.

"Why don't you come along with us? We're on our way to Brementown to be great musicians. You have a beautiful voice, come and sing with us," said Donkey.

"Thank you!" said Cat. "I will come with you. I always wanted to make a little night music."

So, they walked along and walked along, TOGETHER!

It was almost dark when they came upon an old Rooster, pecking at the grass along the road.

"What are you doing away from your farm?" asked Donkey. "Are you lost?"

"I'm just an old Rooster. *[Crow like a rooster.]* Sometimes I oversleep and then no one at the farm wakes up on time. The farmer's wife tried to put me in the soup!"

And he sang:

> I am very old, you see.
> No one gives a hoot for me.
> I have no home or place to go.
> What will I do? I do not know.

"Come along with us," said Donkey. "We're going to Brementown to be great musicians. You can sing with Cat."

"I'd love to!" said Rooster. "Singing suits me just fine."

So Rooster joined his new friends.

[By this time children are joining in with this sentence.] So they walked along, and walked along, TOGETHER.

By this time it was getting very dark and they were in the forest. They decided to sleep in the forest, and to continue their journey in the morning. The night air was cold and the winds began to blow. Donkey found a warm place under a large tree. Cat and Dog slept next to him snuggling as close as they could. Rooster flew to the top of the tree, to be the lookout for danger.

"Oh look!" said Rooster. "I can see a light. It must be a house."

"Let's go to the house," suggested Dog. "Maybe we can find a warmer place to sleep, and some food to eat."

Together they headed toward the house, Rooster leading the way. When they got there, they heard voices inside. Donkey looked in the window, Dog climbed on Donkey, Cat climbed up on Dog, and Rooster flew up onto Cat's head. They all peered into the window. *[Pretend to look in a window.]*

They saw four robbers sitting around a big table, eating delicious hot food. They were all laughing and talking about robbing people and warming themselves by the fire.

"How can we get some of that food and a warm place to sleep?" asked Cat.

They talked it over and decided on a plan. They got back into position: First Donkey, then Dog, then Cat, then Rooster, so they could all see inside the house.

Donkey counted *[make this part important]:*

"One, two, three—NOW!"

They all sang as loud as they could. Donkey brayed *[hee-haw]*, Dog barked *[woof-woof]*, Cat meowed *[meow!!]*, and Rooster crowed *[cock-a-doodle-doo!]* *[Direct the children with their sounds!]* They broke through the window and tumbled into the room with a CRASH!

The frightened robbers ran out of the house as fast as they could and disappeared into the forest.

They left their money, their food, and their warm blazing fire.

"The house is ours!" shouted all four animals.

They warmed themselves by the fire, ate the delicious food and looked for a place to sleep.

"I'll sleep by the warm fire," purred Cat.

"I'll sleep under the table," said Dog.

"I'll sleep in the barn," said Donkey. "I like sleeping on the hay."

"I'll sleep on the roof," said Rooster. "I'll watch out for the robbers."

They settled into their places and fell asleep.

Meantime, the robbers were so cold in the forest that they decided that they left the house too hastily. *[Shiver.]* Now, the house looked quiet and peaceful and safe.

"I'll go back inside, and check things out," said one of the robbers.

He crept back into the house. All was dark and quiet. He found a candle in the kitchen, so he went to the fire to light it. Cat who was sleeping by the fire, woke up, opened her eyes, and the robber yelled. *[Cats meow.]*

"Great balls of fire!" Cat hissed and scratched. The robber fell onto the table and the dog bit him. *[Dogs bark.]*

"YOWL!" screamed the robber, dancing around, holding his sore foot. He hobbled out of the house and Donkey kicked the robber with his two hind legs. *[Donkeys hee-haw.]* At the same time Rooster yelled, "Cock-a-doodle-doo!"

[Roosters cock-a-doodle-doo.]

The robber ran into the forest as fast as he could, shouting,

"Run for your life! There are monsters in that house! When I go near the fire there were two great balls of fire, then something threw me against the table and cut me with a knife. I ran to the door and another monster kicked me and yelled, 'Tell you what I'll do! Tell you what I'll do!' I didn't stay around to find out what he was going to do to me."

"Let's get out of here," said another robber. They disappeared into the forest.

The next morning when the animals woke up, they looked around and saw that the robbers were GONE.

They decided to stay in the house, where it was safe and warm. They never got to Brementown, but they sang together every evening, celebrating their friendship and their happiness. And if you should go into the forest, listen carefully, for you just might hear them singing. *[Lead the animals in music—each animal using the appropriate sound.]*

Key Concepts and Themes and/or Universal Ideas

The donkey brays, the dog barks, the cat sings serenades, and the rooster cock-a-doodle-doos. The animals found each other after their owners rejected them because they were too old to do their usual jobs well. They all had talent and decided to become musicians. Then after their success with the robbers, they had renewed self-confidence and went on to live a full life as musicians. The story reminds us that although people become older and can't do their jobs as well as they could when they were younger, they may have other talents and can still lead useful lives. The focus should be on the valuable contributions that senior citizens can contribute to our lives and community. You may want to explain that senior citizens are like grandparents.

Suggested Companion(s)

musical instruments

photographs of senior citizens who are musicians or doing other things

Preparation

Prior to hearing the story, ask the children what their grandparents do and if any of them are retired from their jobs. Find out if they know what *retired* means. Explain the term with some examples. Ask them about some of the fun things they do with their grandparents or an older adult who is their friend or relative. Ask them if any of their grandparents can sing or play a musical instrument.

Preparation for Visualization

Tell the Children:

Before we hear the story, we are going to visit an imaginary place. Close your eyes. Pretend you are a very old person and you are a baker in a bakery. You have always baked the best breads, cakes, and cookies. Imagine how they smelled. Can you smell them? Everyone came from far and near for your bakery goods. Listen to all the people as they talk about how good your bakery goods are: "OOh, those chocolate chip cookies are so good. OOh that bread makes my sandwiches just perfect." Now your boss tells you that because you spill the flour sometimes and because you are not working quite as fast as you used to, you are getting too old to do your job. You feel very sad. You cannot imagine what you will do. You love being a baker. What will you do? Now open your eyes and I'm going to tell you a story.

Listen to the Story

Follow-up Discussion Questions

1. What did the masters do to the animals?
2. Why did the masters want to get rid of the animals?
3. What did you think about what they did?
4. What did the animals do to the robbers?
5. Did the animals act like they were old?
6. How did the animals feel after they scared away the robbers? Why?

ACTIVITY ONE: MY TALENTED GRANDPARENTS

Objectives

—To develop an appreciation and respect for the talents and knowledge of older adults
—To develop oral and written communication skills

Introduction

The activities in this lesson introduce the students to the many talents of older adults and help them appreciate the skills and talents of their grandparents. The students will look at pictures and talk about the talents of these individuals and how they can enjoy sharing in these talents. Senior adults should be invited into the classroom to share their talents in the arts and crafts, storytelling, cooking, etc. The children should not only be an audience but have opportunities to share in activities with these individuals.

After telling some stories about their grandparents and visiting with older adults, the students will create their own book about their grandparents. Younger students can tell their stories and then you can create a class book about "Our Grandparents Can . . ."

Materials

pictures of older adults involved in productive activities
drawing and writing materials
12″ × 18″ drawing paper

Procedure

1. Brainstorm with the class. Ask them about the special things that older people can do. This list can include just about anything. Ask the children to tell stories about their grandparents and the special things they can do. Encourage the children to bring in pictures of their grandparents.

2. Have the children create invitations to their grandparents to come to the class to share their jobs and hobbies.

3. The children can draw a picture of their grandparents on one page and something to show their talents on a second page. If the children are older, six and seven years old, they may want to add more pages about their grandparents doing special things. The children should be able to present their book to their grandparents on a special grandparents day.

Language Development

1. Read books or tell stories to children that center around older adults and their talents. (See additional stories.) Talk about how important it is to respect older adults and learn from them.

2. Have children talk about the animals in the book and how animals can help us. Create a class alphabet book on animals and their special

talents. Examples: A is for anteaters. They eat ants. B is for bees. They make honey. Have the children draw the animals as if they were old. How could you make the animals look older?

Extensions

1. Have the children make puppets of the Brementown musicians and recreate the story.
2. Have the children act out the story themselves. Emphasize how an old donkey would move or an old dog. Compare and contrast the movements of very young people to very old people.
3. Take children to a retirement center or adult day care center to visit with the senior citizens and share in storytelling activities together.

ACTIVITY TWO: RECYCLED MUSICAL INSTRUMENTS

Objectives

—To develop fine motor skills
—To develop language skills
—To develop listening skills
—To be able to compose and repeat a rhythm

Introduction

The activity is to encourage children to think about how to recycle containers and to think about toys and other objects that can be recycled. You want to develop students' creative thinking by encouraging them to see that objects can be used for more than one purpose. Similarly, people can do more than one job and just because they are old, that does not mean that they can no longer contribute to society.

Materials

containers (milk cartons, oatmeal boxes, coffee cans, cardboard boxes, potato chip cans)
rice, beans, corn, sand, pebbles, macaroni, buttons
sandpaper, wooden blocks, spools, spoons, wooden sticks, long rubber bands
construction paper, paste, crayons, markers, masking tape
photographs or drawings of musical instruments from around the world

Procedure

1. If possible have someone come in with simple African instruments and/or instruments from other countries and demonstrate them for the children. Encourage them to talk about how they are made and the materials they are made from. If you cannot do this, show them pictures and talk about the pictures.

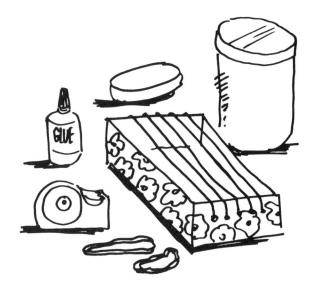

2. Show the children an oatmeal container or coffee can and ask them how many different ways they can use these containers to create a musical instrument. Put some other objects in front of them so they can experiment. Encourage them to be creative.

3. Bring out several other containers and the rest of the materials and encourage the children to experiment. Tell them to explore the sounds made by rubbing objects together, filling them with beans or other objects, shaking them, tapping them against each other, and so on.

4. Follow the students' lead and help them to create an instrument based on their experimentation. They may come up with an object filled with smaller objects to create a maraca or shaker, a drum, or a string instrument using a cardboard box and rubber bands.

5. Lead the students in clapping out different rhythms. Play these patterns on their instruments.

6. Now retell the story and assign each child the role of one of the musicians. Whenever one of the musicians speaks or is referred to, the children should shake, beat or strum their instrument.

Language Development

1. The students are to become the Brementown musicians and create their own songs.

2. The students are to create a group story (older children can create individual stories) explaining how they created their instruments. En-

courage the children to describe the sequence of steps that were necessary to create the instrument.

Extensions

1. Have the children take their instruments to a nursing home and play for the senior citizens.

2. Have the children make masks and play the role of each of the Bremen-town musicians.

3. Have a veterinarian come into your class and talk about how to care for animals as they grow older.

4. Some excellent instrument recipe books include:

   Homemade Musical Instruments (Drake Publishers, New York)

   Musical Instruments Recipe Book (McGraw-Hill, Webster Division, New York)

   Simple Folk Instruments to Make and Play (Simon and Schuster, New York)

ANIMALS AND PETS: ADDITIONAL STORIES

 Squeaky Door, an oral Puerto Rican folktale from *An Incredible Journey,* a cassette by Laura Simms.

This is a humorous sequence story taking place at Grandma's farm house. Valerie, the granddaughter, is afraid of the squeaky door so Grandma puts the cat in her bed. Valerie ends up with cat, dog, pig, and the horse in her bed which finally goes BOOM! and collapses. The story is full of funny repetitions and animal sounds.

Suggested Activities

The activities will encourage the students to share stories about their fears at night and what they want to take to bed with them that will help them feel safe. They will be asked to draw a picture about their favorite animal or the animal they would like to take to bed. Children will be encouraged to use words such as cuddly, warm, friendly, and safe, to describe their animals. A class story can be created called "Friendly Feelings in the Dark." Have the older children draw a picture of themselves in bed with all the animals they would like to take to bed with them. Remind them they can be on top of the bed, over the bed, or in the bed.

 "The Turtle Who Wants to Fly South," from *The Keepers of the Earth* by Michael J. Caduto and Joseph Bruchac. Fulcrum, Inc., Golden, Colorado, 1988.

This Dakota (Sioux) Indian tale about Turtle and the birds takes place in the fall forest. When Turtle finds out about delicious food in the south, he wants to fly south with the birds. Turtle holds on to a branch with his mouth and the birds hold either end with their claws and Turtle flies south. Turtle opens his mouth to speak and falls to the earth. He crawls into the nearby pond and sleeps all winter long. Isn't that the way it's supposed to be? Turtles hibernate in the ponds while birds fly south.

Suggested Activities

The activities will focus on the different abilities of animals and people. The students will talk about how each skill or ability is special and how we are not all the same. What if we were all the same, what would the world be like? "The world" for young children is their own immediate environment while the world is large for older children. A discussion of hibernation and what animals do in different seasons will be encouraged. Students will role play the different animals and tell stories about their favorite animals and what they do in different seasons. What would happen if all animals or people could fly? What would it be like to hibernate? Students can write a class story about what would it be like to fly or to hibernate. Use the local zoo as a resource. For younger children, name animals and what is special about them; i.e., giraffe, long neck; elephant, long trunk; owls, they can see in the night. Older children can draw pictures exaggerating the special qualities of each animal.

 The Extraordinary Cat: An Asian tale, told by Pleasant de Spain, Pleasant Journeys II, illustrations by Kirk Lyttle. The Writing Works, Inc., Mercer Island, Washington, 1979.

A Mandarin (King) wishes to find a grand name for his extraordinary cat. He searches for the most powerful name and decides to call him SKY. The name of the cat changes from SKY to CLOUD to WIND to WALL to MOUSE, but ultimately ends up CAT, the name he most deserves.

Suggested Activities

The children can start by telling stories about how they named their pets or what they would name a pet if they had one. The children can draw their pets or their imaginary pets and write all the names they can think of for their pet all around the drawing. The children can think of their animal's special traits and think of related names. For example, POKEY for a slow turtle; RAINBOW for a beautiful fish; BUDDY for a super friendly dog.

 Nothing at All by Wanda Gag. Coward McCann, Inc., New York, 1941.

This unusual story is about an invisible dog named NOTHING AT ALL. He longs to look like other dogs and be visible, so boys and girls will adopt him as a pet. He wants to find his brothers. His friend the Jackdaw has a book of magic and is able to transform him from nothingness to somethingness. Now the adorable round-eared puppy can be seen and he is happily reunited with his brothers.

Suggested Activities

Ask the students what it would be like if magic happened and you became invisible. Explain that being invisible is when no one can see you, but you are really there. Have them put on a magic cape. When the cape is on, no one can see them. What would you do? Ask the children to pretend they are invisible. What would they do? Set up scenes such as being able to be invisible in a toy store, at the zoo, on a farm, and other places that would be of interest to them. Another topic for discussion could be, Do you ever feel like you are invisible? When your older brothers and sisters have friends over, do they act like you're not there? How does it feel? If you were the littlest in your family, how would you get attention?

Other Stories

 Little Peep by Jack Kent. Prentice-Hall, Inc., Englewood Cliffs, New Jersey, 1981.

 Millions of Cats by Wanda Gag. Coward McCann, New York, 1928.

 Who's in Rabbit's House? A Masai tale, retold by Verna Aardema, illustrated by Leo and Diane Dillon. Dial Press, New York, 1969.

For a Particular Mouse by Joseph Low. Printers, Inc., Hartford, Connecticut, 1980.

 There's a Nightmare in My Closet by Mercer Mayer. Dial, New York, 1969.

Linnea in Monet's Garden by Christina Bjork and Lena Anderson. Raben & Sjogren Books, Stockholm, 1987.

 Where the Wild Things Are, written and illustrated by Maurice Sendak. Harper and Row, New York, 1963.

The Song and Dance Man, written by Karen Ackerman and illustrated by Stephen Gammell. Alfred A. Knopf, New York, 1988.

Flossie and the Fox by Patricia McKissack. Dial Books, New York, 1986.

9

Monsters, Witches, Giants

> ### THE LOOM PA PAS
> ### By Annette Harrison

About the Story

This is a story about a little girl who does not obey her mother and goes into the forest and meets the LOOM PA PAS. The LOOM PA PAS are not especially evil but they force the little girl to sing and dance until she almost drops from exhaustion. She does escape them and runs safely home from the forest and promises that she will never disobey her mother again.

Key Concepts and Themes and/or Universal Ideas

This is a fanciful story and the basic theme is that when we do not obey our parents or elders we can get into trouble. It also points out that all monsters, witches, or giants are not completely evil. Stress the fun and the fantasy part of the story. Emphasize that using our imagination can be great fun.

Suggested Companion(s)

a stuffed creature or monster or a vase of flowers

Preparation

Ask the boys and girls if their parents ever asked them not to do something or not to go somewhere and they did not obey their parents and did it anyway. Ask them what happened. Did they get hurt or did something bad happen?

Preparation for Visualization

Tell the Children:

Before we hear the story, we are going to take an imaginary trip. Close your eyes and imagine you are tiptoeing into the forest. Tip toe, tip toe, crinkle, crunch, munch, crackle, crackle. All of a sudden you see two eyes looking at you. And then there are more. There are blue eyes and green eyes and purple eyes, big eyes, little eyes, round eyes, square eyes, yellow eyes. They are looking at you. Some wink. The eyes begin dancing around you and get closer and closer. You start to run and run until you are out of breath and just out of the forest. As you look back you see the eyes disappearing in the forest. You wonder whose eyes were looking at you. Were they mean? What did they want? Were they monsters? You escaped just in time and got away, but will you ever know? Now open your eyes and we are going to hear a story about another trip through the forest.

Listen to the Story (Tape 2, Side A)

Follow-up Discussion Questions

1. Did you ever disobey your parents?
2. Do you think the little girl did the right thing?
3. What would you have done?
4. What did you think of the LOOM PA PAS?
5. Did they scare you?
6. What do you think they looked like?
7. What kind of dance would you have danced for the LOOM PA PAS?
8. What songs would you sing for the LOOM PA PAS?

ACTIVITY ONE: LOOM PA PA PORTRAITS

Objectives

—To develop students' creative thinking
—To develop students' imagination
—To develop students' language skills
—To develop visual expression

Introduction

This is an opportunity for students to use their imaginations and create portraits of the LOOM PA PAS. The activity is a collage experience which allows students to express their ideas through a visual representation of the creatures in the story.

Materials

   scrap materials such as: cotton balls, scrap fabric, yarn, aluminum foil, buttons, scrap paper, and so forth

   paper plates

   glue or paste

   LOOM PA PA Flower worksheets

   OOM PA PA music or any other music that would be appropriate

Procedure

1. Tell the students to close their eyes and to imagine what the LOOM PA PAS look like. Are they mean and ugly? Are they fuzzy and cute? Are they nasty and funny looking?

2. Give each student a paper plate. Ask them to create a monster or a LOOM PA PA head.

3. Encourage them to use the whole space. Remind them to include eyes, nose, mouth, ears, hair, and whatever else they want.

4. Ask the students to make up a name for their LOOM PA PA like Laurie LOOM PA PA.

5. Display the LOOM PA PAS and retell the story with the children's help. Teach the children some of the parts and have them join in the story. Their paper plate LOOM PA PAS can also be used for masks as they tell the stories.

6. You can also use the LOOM PA PA plates for a puppet show.

Language Development

1. With older children, have them retell the story from the LOOM PA PAS' point of view. You can do this as a group story or as individual stories.

2. Have the students use another set of paper plates and scrap materials and create LOOM MA MAS for the LOOM PA PAS. They can also use small paper plates and create BABY LOOM PA PAS and tell a story

about the Three LOOM PA PAS using the story format from the "The Three Bears."

3. Have the children create a LOOM PA PA language or LOOM PA PA sounds. What kind of sounds would the LOOM PA PAS make if they were scared, happy, mean, hungry, joyful, etc.? Allow the children to be creative. Create a LOOM PA PA symphony. Use the body, found objects, or instruments to make sound effects.

Extensions

1. Have the children use the Flower worksheets and create LOOM PA PA flowers by creating faces in the center of the flowers.

2. Have the children tell you about places their mothers or fathers tell them they cannot go alone. What are the rules? Ask them what are the school rules. Where are they not allowed to go without an adult?

ACTIVITY TWO: THE LOOM PA PAS DANCE AND SING

Objectives

—To develop students' oral language skills
—To develop students' gross motor skills
—To develop students' creative thinking skills

Introduction

The students will be encouraged to create their own movements and dances to different kinds of music. Some of the children will sing the chorus while some of the students move creatively. The students will also create a song for the little girl to sing to the LOOM PA PAS or use the one on the tape.

Materials

OOM PA PA music or any other music that would be appropriate

Procedure

1. Ask the students how they think LOOM PA PAS move. Put on some music. Ask them to move around the room like the LOOM PA PAS. Then ask them to think about how a frightened LOOM PA PA would move, a silly LOOM PA PA, a funny LOOM PA PA, and so on. Ask them to move

high, low, fast, slow. Ask them to move under the trees, over the flowers, and around and around the forest.

2. Give the children some movement words and ask them to create a dance.

Movement Words:

galoomp omp
pit pat
high
low
fast
slow
quick
hop
jump
run
wiggle
jiggle
slither
slide

3. After the children have created their dance, ask them to add verses to the OOM PA PA song to entertain the LOOM PA PAS.

> Flowers smell so very sweet.
> That they give me dancing feet.
> OOM PA PA, OOM PA PA, OOM PA PA PA.

Younger children can sing songs they already know or you can change the words to another song. For example, to the tune of "All Around the Mulberry Bush":

> This is the way the LOOM PAS dance,
> the LOOM PAS dance,
> the LOOM PAS dance.
> This is the way the LOOM PAS dance.
> All the live long day.
> This is the way the LOOM PAS jump, skip, clap, run, and so on.

Language Development

1. For older children, see how many words they can make up from the word LOOM PA PA. The words can be real or make-believe as long as they can

give the word a meaning. For example, lap, pop, or a loom broom used by LOOM PA PAS.

2. Write a class letter to the LOOM PA PAS from the little girl's mother about how the LOOM PA PAS should not scare little girls in the forest and how they should be more friendly.

3. Have the children tell other LOOM PA PA stories. One day the LOOM PA PAS were very hungry and. . . .

Extensions

1. Have the children create clay LOOM PA PA monsters.

2. Have the children paint the forest where the LOOM PA PAS live. Put the paper plate LOOM PA PAS in the forest.

3. Have older children create directions and a map for getting in and out of the forest safely.

4. LOOM PA PA, OOM PA PA Music

"Danse Macabre"	Camille Saint-Saëns
"Night on Bald Mountain"	Modest Mussorgsky
"Dances from Galanta"	Zoltan Kodaly
"The Banshee"	Henry Cowell

STORY SUMMARY

I.   Setting the scene, introduction of characters

   A. Near the edge of the forest lived a mother and daughter.

      1. Mother warned daughter about LOOM PA PAS in the forest.

      2. Daughter was very curious, especially about the forest and the LOOM PA PAS.

         a. verse: Is there a LOOM PA PA, mother dear?

            Oh yes, there's a LOOM PA PA, a LOOM PA PA, I fear.

            Where is the LOOM PA PA, mother dear?

            In the forest, the forest, not far from here.

            Don't go in the forest, daughter dear,

            For the LOOM PA PA, the LOOM PA PA,

            the LOOM PA PA is near.

            I won't go in the forest, mother dear.

            I hear your message LOUD and CLEAR.

      3. One day her mother leaves the house and the young girl is curious.

         a. She draws pictures of LOOM PA PAS.

         b. She puts on her jacket and goes out to pick flowers.

         c. She ends up in the forest picking flowers and sings:

            Flowers grow so very sweet

            That they give me dancing feet

            Oom pa pa, oom pa pa, oom-pa-pa-pa.

II. In the forest

   A. She looks up and there are the LOOM PA PAS.

      1. Six huge, roly-poly, poppy-eyed LOOM PA PAS, shouting "LOOM PA PAS love oom pa pas!"

      2. They sing, "Sing for us that oom pa song,

            Sing and we will dance along,

            Oom pa pa, oom pa pa, oom-pa-pa-pa!"

   B. She sang and she sang and she sang. They danced until they could dance no more. They fell to the ground and started to SNORE!

   C. She runs away and they chase her.

      1. Pit pat, pit pat, pat, pat, pat,

         pit pat, pit pat, pat, pat, pat.

2. The LOOM PA PAS woke up and followed her.

    Galoom, galoomp, galoomp, oomp, oomp

    (Repeat pit pats, galoomps, two more times.)

3. The LOOM PA PAS shouted "sing."

4. She sang:

    "Flowers grow so very sweet

    That they give me dancing feet

    Oom pa pa, oom pa pa, oom-pa-pa-pa!"

5. She sang and she sang and she sang. They danced until they could dance no more. They fell to the ground and started to SNORE!

III. She runs away (repeat pit pat, pit pat, pat, pat, pat).

   A. She sees her mother and runs into her arms.

   1. From now on she'll listen to her mother.

   2. She never went into the forest, AGAIN!

Activity One, Extensions #1

THE GIANT CATERPILLAR
Adapted from an Old African Folktale

The Story

Long long ago, on the western coast of Africa, there lived a HUGE GIANT CATERPILLAR. He was as big as an elephant. His red mouth matched his red tail. He had two white horns that came out of his head, and his body was covered with hair. *[Use big gestures to sketch how big and to show the two horns coming out of his head.]*

One day three young brothers were walking towards the bush and there was the Giant Caterpillar asleep on the path. He blocked the entire path. *[Use hand gesture to show his height.]* What could they do? They decided that the little brother would go up to the caterpillar and ask him to move. He was shaking with fright as his two older brothers pushed him up to the monster. He bowed to the caterpillar and said *[pretend to be youngest brother, look small and scared]:*

"G-Good d-day, dear Caterpillar. We need to get by. Would you mind moving over, PLEASE?" The Caterpillar opened up his big red mouth and said *[gesture with hands, heel of hands together]:*

"MOVE ON!" *[Use scary monster voice each time Caterpillar talks.]* And he moved out of the way and let the youngest brother skip on by. Then he moved back and fell back to sleep again.

Now it was the middle brother's turn to ask the Caterpillar to move. His knees knocked together as he walked up to the Caterpillar and bowed to him and said *[pretend to be middle brother and look scared]:*

"Good day, dear Caterpillar, do you mind moving over again, PLEASE? I need to get by."

Once again the Giant Caterpillar opened up his big red mouth and said *[same mouth gesture as before]:*

"MOVE ON!"

And he moved out of the way of the second brother. But then the trouble began. The Caterpillar moved back and the oldest brother walked up to him. He was not very polite. He had his hands on his hips and he shouted *[pretend to be oldest brother, very cocky]:*

"GET OUT OF MY WAY, YOU UGLY CATERPILLAR!"

Nothing moved on the Caterpillar, not even a hair on his body.

"CAN'T YOU HEAR ME, GET OUT OF MY WAY!" the oldest brother screamed.

This time something moved on his body . . . he opened up his big red mouth and swallowed him whole! GULP! *[Actually make a gulp sound!]*

The two other brothers were watching from behind a tree and they trembled with fear. They ran back to the village and they cried *[said with great emotion]:*

"Help, help! Big brother has been swallowed by a Giant Caterpillar. He's as big as an elephant, his red mouth matches his red tail. He has two white horns that come out of his head and his body is covered with hair!" *[Use same gestures again. You might want to let children fill in his words. For example, he was as big as an ____.]*

Their father came running and he said,

"I will go and talk to the Chieftain. He will know what to do."

The Chieftain listened carefully. He called the men together and told them to gather their weapons and to meet him at the market place.

From the market place, the men began to follow the path into the bush. *[Keep a walking rhythm with your hands alternating on your knees. Ask children to join you, keeping the rhythm together.]* They looked to their right, they looked to their left, and then they looked straight ahead, and in front of them was the HUGE GIANT caterpillar, asleep on the path.

The Great Chieftain took one look at this hairy monster and yelled *[use deep Chieftain voice]:*

> See that Caterpillar over there?
> He's as big as an ELEPHANT and covered with HAIR!
> His mouth is as red as the setting sun.
> Throw down your weapons, men, and run! run! run!

They ran past the mother of the three boys. She stopped the Chieftain and said,

"STOP! *[Look very upset.]* Where's my son? Have you found him? Why are you running?"

And the Chieftain replied,

"If you had seen the Caterpillar, you would be running, too! Run for your life, mother of the boys, run!"

An old woman was standing there beside the mother of the boys and she said in an old, frail voice *[use an old crackly voice]*,

"Do not worry. The women will go back to their tents, gather their cooking utensils, and will save your oldest son."

So the women hurried back into their homes, grabbed their many cooking utensils, the wooden forks and spoons, the pots made of calabashes and clay, and the sticks they used to beat the grain. They met in the market place and walked together into the bush. *[Use same rhythm again—with hands on knees.]*

They looked to their right, they looked to their left, and when they looked straight ahead, THERE HE WAS! The Giant Caterpillar asleep on the road.

The bravest of the women took the stick that she used to beat the grain and she walked up to the monster, one . . . two . . . three. . . . Her shadow fell over him and she lifted up her stick and WHACK! *[Pretend to be the woman, gesture lifting stick and whacking the caterpillar.]* She hit him on his back and out came the oldest brother and he was alive and well! They all cheered and celebrated! *[Lead the audience in a happy cheer.]* "What do we do about the caterpillar?" asked one of the women.

"Let him be," said the mother of the three sons. "He will only bother those who bother him."

So the women went back to the village and told their story to the villagers.

Many, many years passed and the GIANT CATERPILLAR grew old and died. So the women in the village cut him up to eat him. Something really strange happened . . . teeny, tiny little caterpillars came out, tens of them, hundreds of them, thousands of them, and they went EVERYWHERE! *[Use fingers to pantomime caterpillars going everywhere.]* Into the bush, into their tents . . . all over the world. That's why to this day there are teeny, tiny little caterpillars where we live. Now you know where they came from!

Key Concepts and Themes and/or Universal Ideas

This is a story that illustrates that politeness counts and that monsters are not always evil. It is also an example of how different cultures have produced myths and legends to explain natural phenomena. In this instance the story explains the origin of caterpillars. The two ideas that you may want to stress through the following activities are (1) the importance of manners, and (2) the use of stories to explain ways of viewing the world and natural phenomena.

Suggested Companion(s)

a toy caterpillar or a picture of a caterpillar

Preparation

Have you ever used bad manners and then someone was mean to you? Are all monsters mean? Did you ever wonder where caterpillars come from?

Preparation for Visualization

Tell the Children:

Before we hear the story, we are going to take an imaginary trip. Close your eyes and imagine you are walking to school. It is a bright, sunny day and you are looking around and enjoying the nice, cool breeze and the sparkling sunshine. As you walk along you are not always looking where you are going because you are enjoying the wonderful weather, and the little squirrels as they play tag and the chirping birds. All of a sudden you trip over something and you almost fall over. This great big giant-sized furry bug looks up at you and says, "Please be careful, little one." You look at it and try and kick it aside, but it won't move and it gets angry. "Is that the way to treat a living creature?" You say, "But you are just a big, old bug." The bug says, "I may be a big, old bug, but I have feelings." You try again, but this time the bug snaps at you. You begin to think. Maybe there is another way to get by. You look at the bug and say, "Please, Mr. Bug, may I get by?" and the bug smiles and slowly moves out of your way as he says, "My, how nice you can be." You continue on to school thinking about your meeting with the giant bug and begin to wonder where that huge bug came from. Now open your eyes and we are going to hear a story about another giant creature.

Listen to the Story

Follow-up Discussion Questions

1. What did you think of the giant caterpillar?
2. Was he really mean or did he just try and teach the little boy a lesson for being so rude?

3. Can you imagine what that caterpillar really looked like?

4. Do you think the woman did the right thing by beating the caterpillar?

5. Could you think of another way to have gotten the boy back?

6. Did you ever wonder where caterpillars come from?

7. Did you ever wonder where other creatures come from? Which ones?

ACTIVITY ONE: NICE CATERPILLAR OR MEAN MONSTER

Objectives

—To develop fine motor skills
—To develop sensory awareness
—To develop vocabulary skills

Introduction

This activity will focus on the characteristics of "The Giant Caterpillar." Each child will have an opportunity to create part of the caterpillar and decide whether he is a mean monster or just a big caterpillar who likes good manners. The emphasis is on a sensory approach to expand on their visual imagery and to develop their descriptive language through the creation of a giant imaginary caterpillar.

Materials

18″ × 24″ manila paper
markers
scrap materials
colored yarn
wall paper books
colored paper
5″ × 7″ paper or paper of a comparable size (a different color for each sense)
glue or paste
Five Senses worksheet
scissors

Procedure

1. After the discussion about the story, ask the children to close their eyes and think about the caterpillar. Ask them to think about how he looks,

how he smells, what he feels like as they run their hands over his hairy body, and what his voice sounds like as he speaks to the young boys.

2. Ask the boys and girls to open their eyes and tell you what they saw. Put the eye from the worksheet on a bulletin board and ask the children to tell you what they saw. Write the words on pieces of paper of the same color and put them up under or around the eye. Some words might be large, big, huge, furry, red, green, long tail, fat, long pointed horn, bumpy, and so on.

3. Ask the boys and girls to tell you what sounds the caterpillar might have made. Put the ear on the bulletin board and and write the words on different sheets of a different colored paper and put them around the ear. Some words might be quiet, low, grunt, groan, or moan.

4. Ask the children to tell you what the caterpillar might have smelled like. Write the words on some other pieces of colored paper. Put them up around the nose. Some of the words might be smelly, stinky, icky, or poo.

5. If they could feel the caterpillar, ask the boys and girls what it would feel like. Write the words on some other pieces of colored paper. Put them up around the hand. Some of the words might be furry, fuzzy, bumpy, slimy, or lumpy.

6. Ask the boys and girls if their Mom cooked up some caterpillar stew for dinner, what would it taste like. Put the words up around the lips. Imagine what those words would be.

7. Give each child a piece of 18″ × 24″ manila paper; or if you have colored paper or wallpaper that is about that size, then it would be even better. If the children are old enough, have them round off the edges with a scissors. If they are not, cut off the edges yourself.

8. Review all the words with the children. Tell them that each child is going to make one part of the giant caterpillar and to keep some of those words in mind as they create their body part. Show them how all the parts will fit together to make the caterpillar so that they will understand how their part fits

in. Allow them to use any materials of their choice. Encourage them to be creative and make their part as exciting and colorful as possible.

9. Select two or three children to work on the tail and two or three to work on the head. Review what the tail and head might look like.

10. For older children, give them strips of paper and have them copy the words that they think describe the caterpillar and stick them to the bottom of their section for legs.

11. Hang the caterpillar around the room or out in the hall. Have the children make mini-caterpillars of their own on small pieces of paper and hang them up around the room. Have the children name their caterpillars and describe them. Help them with the words.

Language Development

1. For older children, have them use the words and write about another caterpillar who came to live at their school.

2. Have the children brainstorm all the monsters from stories they can think of. Have them combine them and create a new giant monster. Have them give the monster a name and tell a story about him or her.

3. Read the children *Where the Wild Things Are* and talk about the wild things. Ask the children if they were monsters. Ask them how they were different and how they were similar to the caterpillar. Ask them what would happen if Max met the caterpillar.

Extensions

1. Ask the children to create a friendly monster. Use the sensory cards and brainstorm ideas about how a friendly monster would look, feel, smell, taste, and sound. Write the words on cards and have the children create a friendly monster who could become the class mascot.

2. Have the children create monster songs, puppets, dances. Use monsters as a theme for a week. Be sure to include monster snacks and games.

ACTIVITY TWO: POLITENESS COUNTS

Objectives

–To develop vocabulary related to manners
–To develop imagination through role playing
–To develop oral communication skills

Introduction

This activity focuses on the role that good manners play in the story. The boys who spoke nicely to the caterpillar got to pass and the caterpillar was very nice. The boy who was rude got eaten. In this activity the children will role play the use of good manners and the appropriate language and behavior to use when asking for something.

Materials

drawing materials
writing materials

Procedure

1. Ask the children why the first two boys could pass the caterpillar and the third boy could not and got eaten. Ask them who had good manners and who did not.

2. Ask them how they behave when they ask someone to do something for them. Ask them what words are important for good manners. Ask them what words they need to use when asking for something and what words they need to use when they get it. The words are "please," "thank you," "may I," "may I have permission," and so on.

3. Remind them of times during the day when it is appropriate to use good manners in the classroom.

4. Bring some objects to the middle of the room. Have one child role play using the materials such as building blocks or drawing a picture. Tell another child to role play wanting to use the same materials. Have them role play the appropriate behavior by asking permission. Set up several situations and have them practice. Give all the children a chance to role play.

Language Development

1. *For older children:* Have the children make signs that promote good manners such as, "Say please when you ask for something," "Say thank you when you receive something," "Don't speak when the teacher is speaking," "Don't interrupt someone when he or she is speaking." If you have made the giant caterpillar from Activity One, put sticks or yarn on the signs and attach them to the caterpillar or have a good manners march to other classrooms. Have them decorate the signs with caterpillars or anything else they want.

2. Read the book *Perfect Pigs: An Introduction to Manners* to the children.

Ask the children if they have good manners or pig manners. Older children can create a similar book called *Perfect Caterpillars, Polite Caterpillars, Caring Caterpillars* and illustrate it.

Extensions

Keep a good manners chart. Put appropriate classroom behavior on one side of the chart and the children's names across the top. Give the children a caterpillar sticker everytime you see them using the appropriate behavior. At the end of a predetermined amount of time the children can receive "The Polite Caterpillar" award.

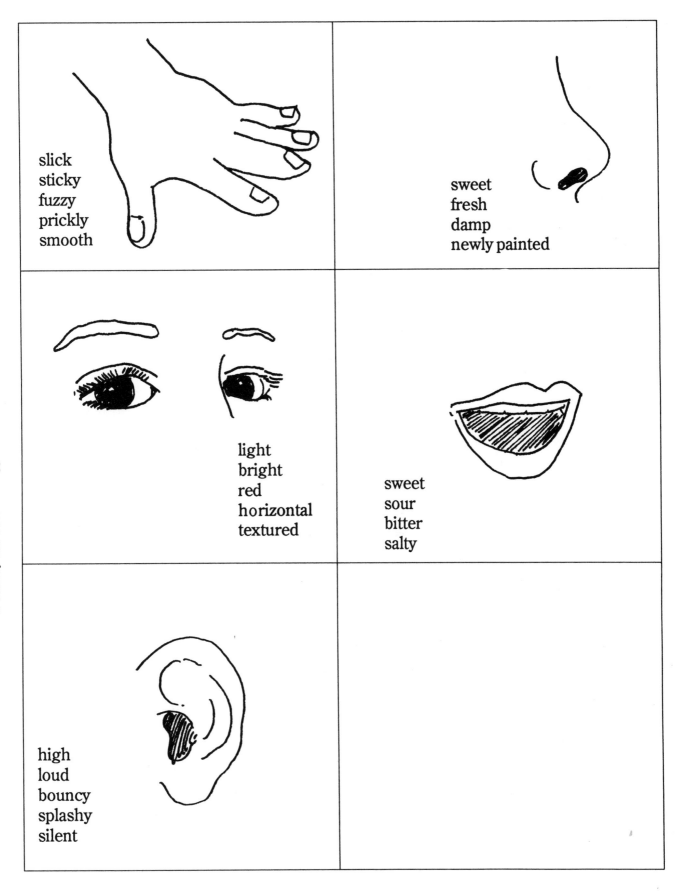

slick
sticky
fuzzy
prickly
smooth

sweet
fresh
damp
newly painted

light
bright
red
horizontal
textured

sweet
sour
bitter
salty

high
loud
bouncy
splashy
silent

Activity One, Extensions #1

MONSTERS, WITCHES, GIANTS: ADDITIONAL STORIES

The Little Boy's Secret by David L. Harrison, illustrated by Phillippe Fix. McGraw-Hill, Canada, 1972.

A young boy leaves school early because he has a secret to tell his mom. He takes the short cut home and meets three giants who want to know his secret, each one bigger, uglier, and meaner than the last. Funny things happen as they each find out the secret. The terrified giants run away and the boy is free to go home and finally tell his mom his secret. She doesn't yell and run away, she puts him to bed and feeds him a good supper, because he has the MEASLES!

Suggested Activities

Did you ever have a secret? Can you think of a secret that would scare away monsters and giants? Why would someone be frightened of the measles? The children will be encouraged to role play the characters in the story. The children will be asked to portray big, mean, ugly giants who are frightened when you tell them your secret. The children will be asked to tell stories about secrets they have had or might have had that would frighten other people. The children can illustrate the big, mean, ugly giants and how they might look with measles. Most children will not have had measles or chicken pox because of the vaccines, but some children may have had them. They will want to tell their story or tell a story of when they were sick and no one wanted to come near them because it was catching, like a cold or the flu.

Hobyahs, adapted from *The Hobyahs* by Simon Stern which was adapted from Joseph Jacobs' collection of English fairy tales. Prentice-Hall, Inc., Englewood Cliffs, New Jersey, 1970.

This is an English folktale about a family who lives in a Turnip house and are bothered by little scary monsters called Hobyahs. When the old man, old woman, and the little girl go to sleep and all is quiet, the Hobyahs come to visit. Turpie, their little dog, comes to the rescue, saves the little girl from the Hobyahs and eats up every single Hobyah. So no one needs to worry about little nocturnal scary monsters, ever again.

Suggested Activities

Talk about monsters that come at night and sleep all day. Are there some animals that are nocturnal like bats and owls? Are they scary? Students can draw their own version of a Hobyah and make up their own story about a

Hobyah. For very young children, a free-form torn piece of construction paper can be given to each child to decorate and turn into a monster. The children can name their monsters and create monster sounds, movements, and songs. Then the boys and girls can create sounds and movements to scare the monsters away.

 Where the Wild Things Are by Maurice Sendak. Harper and Row, New York, 1962.

This is the story of Max who wore his wolf suit and was sent to bed without his supper after misbehaving. He had been creating "mischief of one kind and another." His mother called him "Wild Thing!" and Max said, "I'll eat you up!" At this point he was sent to bed without his supper only to dream a strange and marvelous dream about going to the land of the wild things and living with them until he became lonely and began to smell wonderful things to eat and woke up to find his warm dinner waiting for him in his room.

This story gives young children permission to be angry and act upon their feelings in an acceptable manner through their fantasies. It also illustrates that we can misbehave and have angry feelings, but we will still be loved and accepted by our family. Children need to accept responsibility for their own behavior. They also need to learn that it is all right to be upset or angry with adults and that they will still be loved and accepted. They need to know there are acceptable ways to act upon their feelings and that one of them is through dreams and fantasies when we do not actually act on our feelings.

Suggested Activities

The children will brainstorm different words that will describe the wild things. Ask them what words you would use to describe their terrible claws, terrible eyes? terrible teeth? For very young children, you begin by supplying the words and see if they agree or disagree. For example, "Were they ugly, creepy, scaly, lumpy, or hairy?" Ask them if the wild things in the story remind them of other monsters they have seen. What did they look like? Give children large paper and brushes and paint and/or drawing materials. Ask the children to create the scariest monster they can think of. Remind them to use the whole space.

Other Stories

Perfect Pigs: An Introduction to Manners by Marc Brown and Stephen Krensky. Wm. Colins Sons and Co. Ltd., United Kingdom, 1983.

 The Boy Who Ate More Than the Giant and Other Swedish Folktales, retold and illustrated by Ulf Lofgren, translated from the Swedish by Sheila LaFarge. William Collins and World Publishing Company, New York and Cleveland, 1978.

The Toothwitch by Nurit Karlin. Knopf/Pantheon, New York, 1973.

Jack and the Beanstalk by Joseph Jacobs. English Collection of Fairy Tales.

10
Our World

> ## THE WORRY BUNDLES
> ### Adapted from an Old Jewish Folktale

About the Story

This is a story about a woodcutter who thought he had all the worries in the world. He felt that he had more troubles than he could bear. On his way to work he met an old woman who told him she could help him. She took him to a large cave full of sacks. She told him that these were the worry bundles of the villagers. Some were very small and some were very large. She told him to look into all the bundles and to exchange his own bundle of worries for any of the other bundles. He was told to "Choose wisely!" The woodcutter was overjoyed and felt he finally had a chance to make his life easier. He spent a great deal of time examining the worry bundles of all the villagers. At the end of the day the old woman returned and the woodcutter was ready to leave with his very own worry bundle. He realized that everyone in the village had worries and he was no worse off than anyone else. Before he left, the old woman told him not to forget his blessing bundle, for everyone also has a blessing bundle. He looked into the bundle and found all his blessings, such as his family and his chickens and other animals. For all the things that were a worry, he found a good side. He went home feeling good. Sometimes he complained a little, but he was never miserable again.

Key Concepts and Themes and/or Universal Ideas

The key idea is that everyone has worries and that one person's worries are no better or worse than anyone else's. What seems to be worrisome or problematic for one person may not be for another person. Sometimes another person's problems may seem much worse than our own. Everyone also has blessings or things they can be thankful for. This story translates for very young children into things that worry us or that we are afraid of, for most times our worries are fears.

201

It also points out that no matter how many worries or fears we have, we also have blessings like our family, pets, and friends. The activities will focus on worries or fears and things that we feel lucky to have or to have experienced.

Suggested Companion(s)

a bundle of some sort

Preparation

Ask the children if there is something they worry about like getting lost or not having friends. Tell them that being worried is like being afraid something bad might happen.

Preparation for Visualization

Tell the Children:

Before we hear the story, we are going to take an imaginary trip. Close your eyes and imagine it is your birthday tomorrow. You begin to think of all the fun things that will happen and what a special day it will be. You think about how the other boys and girls will sing happy birthday and the special treat your mom will bring and you might even get some presents, too. But, all of a sudden you begin to worry. What if no one remembers? And no one sings happy birthday? If mom burns the cupcakes? The day is all over and there was no celebration? No one even said HAPPY BIRTHDAY? You fall asleep with your birthday worries. Zzzzzzzzzzzzzz. The next morning you wake up and you tip toe down to breakfast and SURPRISE! There is a big birthday sign on the wall and Mom and Dad and baby brother are all wearing birthday hats. Happy Birthday! Your Mom has made your favorite breakfast and when you get to school all the boys and girls sing you happy birthday. They have all made you cards, and guess who brings the cupcakes at treat time? What a great day. You see you really didn't have to worry after all. Now open your eyes and listen to a story about a man who had many worries.

Listen to the Story (Tape 2, Side A)

Follow-up Discussion Questions

1. What was the woodcutter's problem?
2. What was he worried about? What are worries? What are blessings?
3. Why do you think he worried so much?

4. What do you worry about? What are you afraid of?
5. What were the woodcutter's blessings?
6. How did he feel at the end of the story?
7. What are your blessings? What do you feel lucky about?
8. What would you put in your worry bundle?
9. What would you put in your blessing bundle?

ACTIVITY ONE: WORRIES, WORRIES, WORRIES

Objectives

—To develop oral communication skills
—To develop ability to make comparisons
—To develop ability to deal with fears

Introduction

This is an opportunity to deal with fears and worries. The children can talk, write, and draw about them. They can see that other children worry about the same things and that when we talk about our fears and worries they don't seem so bad. Sometimes they even go away.

Materials

a large piece of brown poster paper

a bulletin board

small brown bags and small white or colored bags for each child (about the size of sandwich bags)

markers or other drawing materials

writing materials

5″ × 7″ index cards or paper

Not a Worry in the World by Marcia Williams

Procedure

1. Cut out a huge piece of brown paper in the shape of a big sack or bundle and staple it to the bulletin board. Put a piece of yarn around the top and put the words "WORRY BUNDLE" on the paper bundle.
2. Talk with the children about what worries them. Use the following list to help them.

Worry list: I am worried about

meeting large dogs
the dark
that my mother or father will get sick
that I will get sick
that I will not have any friends
that the school bus will miss my stop
that no one will remember my birthday
that my younger brother or sister will break my toys
that my new teacher won't like me
the neighborhood bully
that there are secrets
that I don't run fast enough
that I am too small or too tall

and so forth.

3. Give each child a brown bag and have them decorate the bag with worry, sad, or afraid colors.
4. Help them to write one of their worries on a card and put it in their bag.
5. Hang all the bags on the worry bundle on the bulletin board.

6. This part of the activity may work better with primary age children. Have the children pick a bag that is not their own. Help them to read the worry on the card. Ask them to tell if this new worry was something they worry about and why. Ask them if they would like to exchange their first worry for this one.

7. Help the children write or tell a story about their worries.

8. Have the children draw a picture about what worries them.

9. Take the cards out of their bags and hang them with their pictures.

Language Development

1. Read the story *Not a Worry in the World* and ask the children if they have any of the same worries that are described. Ask them if they ever worry if monsters will get them. Have them draw the monster and tell all the rotten things the monster does.

2. *For older children*: The Woodcutter did not have a name in the story. Some people complain how miserable and worried they are all the time. What could we call them? The Miserable Family, The Worried Family, The Moaners, The Complainers or whatever the class comes up with. Have the children name each member of the family such as Moaning Mama, Fearful Father, Crying Charley, Sad Sister, and so on. Draw a picture of the family. Show them worried or sad.

3. Ask the children to talk about what they were afraid of when they were little and how they are not afraid of that anymore and why.

4. Talk about what they think adults like the teacher, mommies, daddies, the fireman, the policeman, the mailman, and the baker, worry about.

Extension

Have the children talk about children from other countries and what they may be worried about. Read or tell them stories about children's problems and discuss the children's worries or fears and compare them to the children in the class.

ACTIVITY TWO: BLESSINGS, BLESSINGS, BLESSINGS

Objectives

- To develop oral communication skills
- To develop ability to make comparisons
- To develop ability to deal with fears

Introduction

This activity focuses on blessings or good things that we have or feel good about. Why do we think we are lucky? What is good about our family, friends, schools, talents, pets, and the toys we have?

Materials

a large piece of brown poster paper

a bulletin board

small brown bags and small white or colored bags for each child (about the size of sandwich bags)

markers or other drawing materials

writing materials

5″ × 7″ index cards or paper

Procedure

1. Talk with the children about their blessings, why they think they are lucky.

   I feel lucky because:

   I have a nice mom.
   I have a nice dad.
   I have nice brothers, sisters, or both.
   I have the best dog who loves me.
   I have the most cuddly pussycat.
   I have a grandma who helps me read.
   I have a grandpa who plays with me.
   I have a best friend to play with.
   I am good at ____

   and so forth.

2. Create a blessings bag for the bulletin board like the worry bundle.
3. Give the children a white bag and have them decorate it with lucky colors.
4. Help the children write one thing that they feel lucky about on a card and put it into the bag. Put the bags on the blessing bag on the board.

5. This part of the activity may work better with primary age children. Have the children pick a bag that is not their own. Help them read the blessings on the card. Ask them to tell if this new blessing was something that they would like to have or already have. Ask them if they would like to get rid of their first blessing for this one.

6. Help the children write or tell a story about their blessings or their lucky things.

7. Have the children draw a picture about their lucky things or blessings.

8. Take the cards out of their bags and hang them with their pictures.

Language Development

1. The children can talk about why the teacher, their moms, their dads, their grandparents, might be lucky. Do they think they are a blessing for their mom or dad? Do they think their brother or sister is lucky to have them?

2. Have the children tell what makes other children feel lucky.

3. Have the children sit in a circle and have one child in the center at a time. The children around the circle will tell the child in the center what they like about them or why they think they are lucky or what is special about them. This becomes part of the child's blessings.

Extension

Have them create a picture of themselves with all the things that make them feel good around them.

STORY SUMMARY

I.   Introduction of setting and characters
    A. Woodcutter lived on the edge of the forest.
       1. He was miserable.
         a. The house was noisy and crowded.
         b. The baby cried.
         c. The dogs and cats fought.
         d. The chickens left feathers everywhere.
         e. The children were always fighting.
         f. His wife was sick.
         g. His mother-in-law came for a visit and sat on his rocking chair by the fire. (err-ee)
    B. One cold winter's day
       1. Cold air blew through the cracks in the house, the baby was crying, etc. (repeat complaints)
       2. And his son had grown out of his shoes, and his mother-in-law decided to stay!
       3. He picked up his ax and went into the forest.

II. In the forest
    A. An old woman was coming toward him.
       1. He had never seen her before (he knew everyone in village).
       2. She was as old as the hills.
       3. She had white hair and wore a heavy woolen scarf.
       4. She had a wrinkled face and twinkling blue eyes.
       5. She spoke to him, "I have heard that you think you have more worries than anyone else."
       6. She beckons him into the forest. He follows.
    B. They go into a cave.
       1. The path looks different (he knew every path in the forest).
       2. They come to a cave and the old woman disappears inside.
       3. He goes in, too.
       4. The cave is dark, dank, with sacks made of spider webs covering the floor. She says, "These are the worry bundles of all the villages, yours is over there by the entrance." She tells him to stay all day and exchange his bundle for any of the others but to choose wisely.
       5. The old woman leaves.

C. Alone in the cave

   1. He runs over to a small bundle, but rejects it because it is a terrible worry, just one, but it weighs a lot.

   2. Goes over to one of the large bundles, but it has too many worries.

D. Old woman returns

   1. The woodcutter is waiting for her, sitting in front of the cave holding his own worry bundle in his arms.

   2. She notices his wise decision, then takes him into another part of the cave.

      a. It looks like the sun lives here.

      b. There are bundles made of spun gold.

      c. Old woman tells him that these are the blessing bundles of everyone in the village. She points out his.

      d. He looks at his blessing bundle.

      e. There's the baby. She cries all the time, but isn't she a beauty.

      f. My chickens, feathers everywhere but what would I do without eggs for breakfast?

      g. My dogs and cats. They fight but they snuggle with him by the fire.

      h. My oldest son, he's growing but soon he'll be able to help me in the forest.

      i. My mother-in-law, she sits in my chair by the fire, but she's cooking for the family.

   3. He thanks the old woman and leaves.

III. A happier man

A. Walks back home

   1. Realizes that he's not so burdened.

   2. He still complains a little.

   3. Never again is he MISERABLE.

TURTLE TRICKS SPIDER
Adapted from an Old African Folktale

The Story

The two characters in this old African story from Ghana are a very tricky Spider and a friendly old Turtle. Now what you must know is that Spider was very VERY greedy and loved to trick other animals out of their food. He very rarely cooked for himself. But this day was different, he had been cooking all afternoon. His wife and sons were away visiting relatives and he planned to feast all night.

He set out his dinner on his kitchen table—a big pot of fish stew, a platter of chicken and vegetables and rice, fried plantain, and beancakes—m-m-m-m. His mouth watered just looking at all that delicious food. *[Exaggerate mouthwatering.]*

He sat down at the table, filled his plate, lifted the fork to his mouth . . . *[Use gestures to show the hand with fork.]* and there came a knock at the door.

KNOCK! KNOCK! KNOCK! *[Have audience knock.]*

"Oh no," thought Spider. "Not now! I don't want to share my food. I'll ignore the knocking."

KNOCK! KNOCK! KNOCK! *[Audience knocks again.]*

"Oh, all right—here I come!"

Spider walked over to the door, opened it up and there was Turtle, friendly Old Turtle, who was dusty and hot, hungry and tired.

[Use a deep, funny turtle voice each time Turtle speaks.] "Oh, Spider. I'm so glad you are home," said Turtle. "I lost my way and I'm hot, tired, and hungry. May I come in and rest?"

Now it is widely known in Ghana that hospitality is very important *[explain that hospitality means that you are very nice to people who come to visit]* , so Spider knew that he had to invite Turtle in. So he said, "Come on in, Turtle!" He tried to hide his delicious dinner from Turtle, but he couldn't.

"Oh, Spider," said Turtle.

210

"You have fish stew, one of my favorite foods, for dinner!" *[Look excited.]*

So what could Spider say?

"Would you like to stay for dinner?" (Please say no, Turtle, thought Spider.)

"I'd love to!" said Turtle feeling very excited.

Spider ran back to his bedroom and came back with a towel over one of his legs. *[Gesture to show towel.]*

"Here, Turtle, take this towel. At my house, in order to eat at the table you must be clean. Look at you, Turtle, you are dusty from head to toe. Go to the river and bathe. Then, you can join me for dinner."

[Say it once and have the audience join in a second time.]

> "Turtle dear, go and get clean.
> You are the dirtiest Turtle I've ever seen."

Turtle hurried, as fast as an old turtle could go, down to the river, jumped in—bathed himself and hurried back. *[Walk like Turtle—do it funny and fast.]*

Meantime Spider had been eating as fast as he could. *[Use gestures to shove food in.]* This greedy spider did not want to share his food with Turtle. He looked up and . . . there was Turtle!

"Oh, Turtle, you do move fast for an old turtle. But look at your feet. They are still dirty." *[Look at your feet.]*

[Say it once and have audience join in a second time.]

> "Turtle dear, you cannot eat,
> At *my* house with dirty feet!"

"Aw-w-w," said Turtle. "Do I have to go back to the river? Aw-w. Please, Spider."

"I'm afraid so," said Spider with a smile.

As soon as Turtle left, he ate as quickly as he could *[gesture Spider eating and Turtle moving fast]* , stuffing in the food so Turtle wouldn't get any. Meanwhile, Turtle hurried to the river, washed his feet and walked back on his toes as quickly as he could.

"Oh there you are . . . a speedy little turtle—my, my, Turtle, your toes are still dirty. You cannot eat at my house with dirty toes." *[Look at toes.]*

[Say once, then have audience join in:]

> "Turtle, dear, everyone knows,
> You can't eat with dirty toes."

"Aw-w," said Turtle, looking at his toes. "Aw-w-w, please, Spider, let me have some fish stew. It's almost gone."

"Sorry, Turtle, to the river!" said Spider.

Turtle hurried to the river, washed his toes and carefully walked back on the grass. When he got back his toes were clean. *[Gesture Turtle hurrying again and walking on his toes.]*

"Look Spider! Clean toes!" said Turtle

But so were the plates in front of Spider. He had eaten every single morsel. . . . Poor Turtle.

And that is only the beginning of the story.

One day when Spider was looking for someone to trick, he got lost. It was hot and Spider hadn't eaten ALL day—he was VERY HUNGRY.

Whom should he see on the road, but . . . *[Let the audience guess . . . Turtle]* Turtle.

"Hello, Turtle. Do you live near here?" asked Spider.

"Oh, yes, there's my house right over there. *[Gesture to show location.]* You look hot and tired, come join me. I'm on my way home for dinner. I'm having chicken stew."

"I'd love to!" shouted Spider. "Oh, goodie, dinner at Turtle's!" he thought.

Spider began to dance around and sing. *[Sing twice and children can join in.]*

"Chicken Stew
Oh chicken stew
I love my
Chicken stew!"

When they got to Turtle's house, Turtle went inside and brought out a tray with a big pot of chicken stew and a bowl of rice.

"Follow me, Spider," said Turtle.

"Where are we going?" asked Spider.

"To the lake! In my family, we eat at the bottom of the lake. Come with me," said Turtle. He led the way along the path to the lake.

"Wait for me! Turtle, did you say you eat *in* the water?"

Turtle jumped into the lake and bloop, bloop, bloop, bloop, bloop *[voice goes from high to low]* went down to the bottom. *[Gesture jumping in water and going down, down, down, down.]* He set out two plates and started to eat.

"Wait!" shouted Spider. "Wait for me! Here I come. Turtle!" Bloop, bloop, bloop, bloop, bloop. *[Use a voice that starts high and gets lower and lower.]* But his body went back up and floated on top! *[Gesture going down and back up.]*

"Oh no, what can I do? Turtle is eating without me," he cried.

"I know," said Spider, "I'll hold onto a rock, that will weigh me down and I'll be able to eat with Turtle."

Spider found a rock to hold in his two front legs and shouted, "Here I come, Turtle!"

Bloop, bloop, bloop, bloop, bloop. *[Gesture going down.]*

"Hello, Turtle, could you pass some of the chicken stew to me?" said Spider.

"Oh, Spider, you cannot eat at my table with a dirty rock. Put it down, please."

"But, . . . but I can't," said Spider. He put down the rock and bloop, bloop, bloop. *[Use a voice that starts low and gets higher and higher. Gesture going up, up, up!]*

Poor Spider. He watched as Turtle ate all the chicken stew and rice, and he couldn't do a thing about it. Poor Spider!

Now that is the end of my story.

Key Concepts and Themes and/or Universal Ideas

This story illustrates what can happen when we play tricks on others. Sometimes tricks will be played on us in return. Spider is a famous trickster from the Ashanti culture in Ghana. There are many spider stories that can be shared with your students. Most cultures have tricksters who come in different forms. In some Southwest Native American cultures the coyote is a famous trickster. In American folklore, Jack is the trickster in the Jack tales. One example is Jack and the story of the Beanstalk. Remember how he tricked the giant? The trickster's purpose in most instances is to trick someone in order to get something that he wants without working for it. In this story Spider tricks Turtle so that he does not have to share what he has and Turtle does the same to Spider to teach him a lesson. The activities show what it feels like to be tricked and how it isn't very nice to trick others. The children will also share different traditions or rules they have in their homes and in school related to meal times. The second activity will take off on the idea of an underwater fantasy with Turtle.

Suggested Companion(s)

a turtle and a spider (if you can, get a real turtle and a real spider to keep in the classroom)

Preparation

Has someone ever tricked you? How did they do it? How did you feel?

Preparation for Visualization

Tell the Children:

Before we hear the story, we are going to take an imaginary trip. Close your eyes. A friend comes to your house to play and brings along a bag of jelly beans. She shows you the jelly beans and they are all different wonderful colors. You love to eat jelly beans. You ask your friend, "Will you share your jelly beans with me?" and your friend says, "Sure, but could you get me a glass of water first?" So, being a good host or hostess, you get your friend a glass of water. When you come back you notice that half the jelly beans have been eaten. Your friend thanks you for the water and says that he or she will share the jelly beans with you but would like you to get out some of your games first so that you can play together. So you go and get your games. Your friend picks out the game that he or she would like to play. You notice that more jelly beans have disappeared. Your friend tells you that after you put the other games away, you can have some jelly beans while you play the game together. You put the other games away and come back ready to play a game and have some jelly beans. You set up the game and are ready to play and you wait for your friend to give you some jelly beans. Your friend says, "Oh my! I didn't realize it, but I finished all the jelly beans. Sorry!" How did you feel? Your friend tricked you. Now open your eyes and I'm going to tell you a story about how the Turtle tricked Spider.

Listen to the Story

Follow-up Discussion Questions

1. Did you like the story?
2. How did you feel when Spider tricked Turtle so that he didn't have to share his food?
3. Do you think Turtle taught Spider a lesson?
4. What would you do if you were Spider and had all that wonderful food to eat?
5. What if you were Spider, could you figure out a way to eat under water with Turtle?
6. Is it kind to trick other people? Why or why not?
7. What could happen to you and to the person you try to trick?
8. At what time of year do we say, "Trick or Treat"? What kinds of tricks can you do on Halloween that really do no harm to anyone?

ACTIVITY ONE: TRICK OR TREAT AND THE WAYS WE EAT

Objectives

—To develop the ability to compare and contrast
—To develop oral communication skills
—To develop creative thinking skills

Introduction

The students will share stories about the ways they may have been tricked by someone or how they have tricked someone. They can tell stories about Halloween when they go out and play "trick or treat." Start by having the children sit in a circle and share their stories. The experiences are related to eating behavior and some fun activities with food. This activity has two parts.

Materials

> writing materials
>
> peanut butter and jelly sandwiches
>
> food coloring
>
> marshmallows or any food that is accessible and can be changed with food coloring
>
> 12" × 18" colored and/or white construction paper
>
> markers or crayons
>
> writing materials
>
> scissors
>
> paste or glue

Procedure

Part One

1. Have the children sit in a circle and tell stories about how they have played tricks on others or how tricks have been played on them. Talk about Halloween and some of the tricks they have played on Halloween or tricks they know about. Talk about harmless tricks and ones that can cause problems for others.

2. Talk about how Spider insisted that Turtle be clean before he came to the table. He did this to keep Turtle occupied while he finished his delicious food. Ask the boys and girls if a brother or sister has ever done that to them. Talk about the rules of meal time. Have the children tell about the rules for meal time in their homes and write them on chart paper. Some of the rules might be:

   • Wash your hands before you eat.

   • Don't talk with your mouth full.

   • No dessert unless you eat your whole meal.

3. Talk about rules for eating in school, either lunch time or snack time. Some of the rules might be:

   • Wash your hands before you eat.

- Don't talk with your mouth full.
- Clean up your place when you are finished eating.
- Don't take food away from someone else.
- Use a knife and fork and spoon unless the food is supposed to be eaten with your fingers.
- Be careful not to spill your milk or juice.
- Wipe up your own spills.
- Help a friend clean up spills.
- Don't play with your food.

Have each child take one of the rules. If they can print, have them print the rule on the top of a 12″ × 18″ piece of colored or white construction paper and draw an illustration that fits the rule. Hang the finished pieces up around the room or in the halls.

Part Two

1. This part of the activity will give the children a chance to play a friendly trick on another class. Invite another class for lunch or for a special snack. If you choose lunch, talk about serving the lunch in a different order, such as the dessert first and the salad last. The menu could be marshmallow cupcakes or ice cream, peanut butter and jelly sandwiches, and a lettuce and cucumber salad for dessert with milk.

   The second part of the trick will be to use food coloring to change the color of the foods. For example, polka-dotted bread using light drops of food coloring, mixing yellow or green food coloring into vanilla ice cream or making yellow cupcakes with drops of blue and red food coloring mixed into the batter or changing the color of the marshmallows. You could also put green, blue, or red food coloring into the milk.

2. If this is more than you want to do, just plan a snack. Mix the food coloring into the milk and do the cupcakes, or make blue butter cookies or something that is similar and easy to change.

3. Have the children create an invitation or invitations to the other class. Have them put spiders and turtles all over the invitation and invite them for a special treat.

4. When the class comes in either you, you and the class, or the children will tell the visitors the "Turtle Tricks Spider" story. After the story have the children share the special treat with the humorous trick.

5. Have the children create placemats with Turtle and Spider. They can make repeated designs of Turtle and Spider all over the placemat or they can create a picture from the story. Encourage them to use the whole

space and remind them about the size relationship between Spider and Turtle. Spider is a big spider, but is still smaller than Turtle. Turtle is a small turtle. If possible, laminate the placemats and they can be reused.

6. You may want to have your children share their rules for eating with the other class.

7. After the sharing of the snack or lunch, read the children the book, *Sam's Sandwich* by David Pelham. This is a story about how Sam makes a sandwich for his sister and tricks her.

8. Discuss the experience with the children and how they felt about it. How did the children react to the unusual colored food?

Language Development

1. Read other stories about Anansi, the famous spider trickster from Ghana, and compare them to "Turtle Tricks Spider." Talk about the different kinds of tricks and how they are the same or different. Read other stories such as the Native American coyote stories or the Jack tales and compare and contrast the different kinds of tricks from the different cultures.

2. Have the children create a class story that is a sequel to the Turtle and Spider story. Have the children illustrate the story.

3. Create simple Spider and Turtle puppets, or use Spider and Turtle hand puppets if you have them, and have the children role play and recreate the story.

4. Have the children sit in a circle and say "If I was Spider, I would have . . ." and finish the sentence. Or "If I was Turtle, I would have . . ." and finish the sentence.

Extensions

1. The children can create a different set of rules for meal time; rules that they think would be fun such as, three desserts for each meal, being able to bring anyone to dinner they want, being able to decorate all their food, and so on.

2. Have the children create cut-paper spiders and turtles to decorate the table or the room. Create cut-paper coyotes and other famous tricksters and create a bulletin board called "Famous Tricksters from Folktales Around the World." If you have read several trickster stories to the children and they are beginning writers, have them write (or they can dictate) "My favorite trickster is . . . because . . ." Hang these up on the bulletin board.

ACTIVITY TWO: UNDERWATER FANTASY

Objectives

—To develop imagination
—To develop vocabulary
—To develop expressive language skills
—To develop problem-solving skills

Introduction

This activity will feature an underwater fantasy to encourage imaginative thinking and problem solving. The students will create an underwater environment focused on an underwater meal and celebration. The suggested materials are somewhat extensive. You can make this activity as elaborate or simple as you want depending on time, availability of materials, and students' age and ability levels.

Materials

colored construction paper ⎫
crepe paper streamers ⎪ If you do not have all the differ-
tissue paper ⎬ ent kinds of paper, use what
colored cellophane ⎭ you have.
string
drawing materials
writing materials
scissors
glue or paste
goldfish crackers or other "underwater" food
ocean or underwater sounds or music if available
tape or record player
old white sheet and/or pillow cases or muslin (whatever you can find)
fabric crayons

Procedure

1. Talk with the children about Turtle's dinner and what would happen if Spider could figure out a way to stay under water. He tried holding onto a rock so that he wouldn't float to the top, but it didn't work. What else

could he have done to keep the rock attached to him? What else could he have done to stay under water?

2. Once Spider has figured out a way to eat with Turtle, Turtle being the nice turtle that he is decides to have a celebration. He decides to invite all the underwater creatures. Have the children brainstorm all the underwater animals and creatures they can think of. Write them on the board or some chart paper or on individual strips of paper so that you can hang them around the room. Once the children have come up with all the ideas they can think of, get out some other resources and show them some other fish and underwater creatures. Tell the children that they are going to create an underwater celebration.

3. Have the children create the underwater creatures of their own choice in the best way they can depending on their ability level. Hang their creations around the room. Create blue bulletin boards and have the children cut out blue or white circles to create bubbles for the boards.

4. Use crepe paper to create seaweed and decorate the room.

5. Create a giant turtle and a giant spider. Cut them out and have the students paint them. You can cut them from craft paper making a top and a bottom for their bodies, stuff them and staple them and add the heads and legs. Have the children paint and decorate them.

6. Have them decorate a table and create a pot of chicken stew for Turtle and Spider. Look at some of the beautiful fabric designs and motifs from Ghana. After showing the students some of these designs, encourage them to use similar lines and shapes in their designs when they create a table cloth and placemats for the meal. Use simple cotton or muslin or old white sheets and fabric crayons.

7. Hang fish from the ceiling and talk about what might be found on the ocean floor. You and the children can also create cellophane and tissue paper fish and put them on the windows.

8. Have the children retell the story of Turtle and Spider using puppets or role play. Add other characters to the story. The other stories could be characters from the sea giving turtle advice about how to get rid of Spider and giving Spider advice on how to stay underwater.

Language Development

1. Have the children brainstorm all the different kinds of food that come from the water. Have them create a seafood menu that could be added to the underwater celebration.

2. In the story, Turtle and Spider do not have names. Have the children create names for Spider and Turtle and have a contest to see what would be the best names for them.

3. Create a sequel to the story. Now that you, Spider and Turtle have become friends, create another story called "Turtle and Spider Trick Goldfish" or whomever you wish.

4. Have the children create meals or recipes that they think Turtle and Spider would like to eat.

Extensions

1. Have the children make Spider and Turtle badges to wear and create Spider and Turtle relay races. The Spider teams have to move like spiders and the Turtle teams have to move like turtles.

2. Put on underwater music and have the children move as if they were a spider or turtle dancing underwater.

3. Students can experiment with the sounds of water by blowing into water with straws, creating bubbles; tapping a triangle musical instrument as you dip it in the water; dropping objects of different weights into the water. Let the students tape record their sounds. Use these sounds for their creative movement pieces. The following musical selections could enhance this activity:

   - "La Mer" by Claude Debussy
   - "Under the Sea" from *The Little Mermaid* by Alan Menken and Howard Ashman
   - "Underwater Waltz" from *Sounds of New Music* by Vladimir Ussachevsky
   - Folkways Recording, "The Twittering Machine" by Gunther Schuller

OUR WORLD: ADDITIONAL STORIES

 The Legend of the Bluebonnet, an old tale of Texas retold and illustrated by Tomie De Paola. G.P. Putnam's Sons, New York, 1983

This is a Comanche Indian legend about the origin of the bluebonnet flower which is found in Texas in the spring. It is a story of an orphaned girl named She-Who-Is-Alone whose courage and sacrifices save her people. She gives up her most prized possession, her warrior doll, to the great spirits as a sacrifice and rain finally comes to bring the land back to life.

Suggested Activities

The activities can include painting all different kinds of blue flowers, creating songs and dances to bring rain, and, if it is spring, planting flowers and watching them come up. The children can tell stories about their favorite dolls or toys and what would happen if they were asked to give them up for something that would help their family. The children can draw pictures of their favorite doll or toy and tell the teacher all about them as the teacher writes down the description. The teacher talks about rain from a scientific point of view. What makes rain? How is the rain important to us?

 Ming Lo Moves the Mountain, written and illustrated by Arnold Lobel. Scholastic Book Services, New York, 1982.

Ming Lo and his wife love their house, but they do not love the mountain next to the house. Ming Lo asks the help of the wiseman to move the mountain. After three ideas that do not work, the wiseman comes up with the perfect solution. Ming Lo and his wife believe that the mountain has moved.

Suggested Activities

The children will talk about what happened in the story and how the problem was solved. The teacher can present a similar problem that is appropriate to their environment and the children can brainstorm ideas on how to solve the problem. Someone can also play the role of the wiseman and can come up with solutions to the problem and the children can pick the solution they like best. The children can also act out the story. The teacher can create a simple paper mountain that fills the whole bulletin board and the children can imagine what might be on the other side. What could you see if the mountain were moved? The students can make up stories or descriptions and draw pictures of what they might see if the mountain were moved. This story is Chinese and the preceding one is Indian. The children should be shown a globe and told where the stories come from. Books with stories from other parts of the world should be available. Talk about mountains. Where are they located? What is the closest mountain range? What mountain stories can they tell?

Other Stories

Molly's Pilgrim by Barbara Cohen, illustrated by Michael Deraney. Lothrop Lee and Sheperd, New York, 1983.

The Village of Round and Square Houses, written and illustrated by Ann Grifalconi. Little Brown, Boston, 1986.

If I Were in Charge of the World and Other Worries, written by Judith Viorst and illustrated by Lynne Cherry. Atheneum, New York, 1981.

Not a Worry in the World by Marcia Williams. Crown Publishers, Inc., New York, 1990.

Sam's Sandwich by David Pelham. Dutton Children's Books, New Mexico, 1991.

 A Story A Story: An African Tale by Gail E. Haley. MacMillan, New York, 1970.

 Tikki, Tikki Tembo by Arlene Mosel. Henry Holt and Co., New York, 1968.

The Jack Tales, Folk Tales from the Southern Appalachians, collected and retold by Richard Chase. Houghton Mifflin Co., New York, Boston, 1943, 1971.

11
Friendship

THE LION AND THE MOUSE
Adapted from Aesop's Fables

About the Story

"The Lion and the Mouse" is about a mouse who helps a lion in spite of the lion's disbelief. The mouse was wandering through the jungle and found herself on top of a sleeping lion. When the lion woke up and discovered the mouse, he reached for the mouse and was about to eat her. The mouse pleaded for her life as she tried to convince the lion that someday she would save the lion's life if the lion would set her free. The lion found this to be very funny; and because he was so amused, he let the mouse go. After many months, when the mouse found the lion tangled in a hunter's trap, she proceeded to gnaw the ropes that held the lion and set him free. The lion was surprised and grateful and realized that the mouse was a good friend.

Key Concepts and Themes and/or Universal Ideas

Even the humblest of friends may be of great help. The story illustrates that no matter who we are, how big or beautiful, how small or plain, we have something to offer our friends. We all have different talents and we can offer help or friendship in ways we may not be aware of. The lion was big and strong and could roar very loud. He thought he could do anything and that he did not have to be afraid of anything. He thought the little mouse was useless except for something to eat. When the mouse offered to be his friend, he thought it was the silliest idea; but the mouse turned out to be a real friend when she kept her word and she saved him.

Suggested Companion(s)

a small stuffed or cut-paper mouse and a large stuffed or cut-paper lion

Preparation

Prior to hearing the story, talk about friends. Ask the students, "Who is your best friend? Is he/she big, little, fun, sad, funny? Can he/she play games, do tricks, ride a bike, read? What can he/she do that you can't do? How can you help each other?"

Preparation for Visualization

Tell the Children:

Before we hear the story, we are going to take an imaginary trip. Close your eyes. See a little mouse as she is happily skipping along through the jungle. Picture the mouse as she moves among the plants and trees. Feel the warm, damp air as she moves among the leaves of the plants and on the cool earth. Suddenly she feels the warm furry body of the lion under her feet. She is suddenly being pulled through the furry mane of the lion and finds herself in the lion's paw, nose to nose with the lion. How does she feel? Is she frightened? What is she going to say to the lion as she looks at his big teeth and large tongue and down his throat? Now open your eyes and I'm going to tell you a story.

Listen to the Story (Tape 2, Side A)

Follow-up Discussion Questions

1. What did you see?
2. What stands out most in your mind?
3. Did you think the mouse was smart or brave or a good friend?
4. Why was the mouse a good friend?
5. What was your favorite part of the story?
6. Who is your best friend? How do you help each other?
7. Do you have a pet? How can your pet help you?
8. Can you think of some way that someone smaller than you can help you?

ACTIVITY ONE: A HELPING HAND

Objective

—To identify the many ways we can help each other

Introduction

This activity has two parts. Part One is a drawing activity where the children will use the enclosed Picture Frame worksheet to create a picture of themselves and their friend posing together as if they were in a photograph.

Part Two is a writing and art activity. The children will create an outline of their hand, cut it out and write on it something they might do to help a friend, parent, or sibling.

Materials

Picture Frame worksheet
wax or oil crayons or markers
paper for hand drawings
scissors

Procedure

1. After talking with the children about their best friend, what they look like, what they do together, and how they help each other, the children will draw a picture of themselves and their friend together on the Picture Frame worksheet. If you want the children to make a larger drawing, have them create their picture-frame design on the border.

2. After the children have created the portraits, have them draw around their hand on a piece of paper and give their best friend the hand, symbolizing a gift of help. If the children are too young to write, write the gift on the hand and have them decorate the hand. Some of the gifts might be: I am going to help you tie your shoes, read, build a castle, and so on.

3. Continue the helping hand activity. Have the children outline their hands and write the different things they might do to help their parent or parents, sibling, or other friends. Compare young and old to small and large. Ask them how a very young and small person can help a larger and older person like an older brother or sister, a parent or grandparent. Write a note home asking how family members help each other. Have children bring back stories to share. Maybe they can also bring back pictures.

4. Have the children select another child's name out of a bag and have them make a helping hand for a classmate. Encourage them to give a gift of help that can be done in the classroom. Give the children a chance to follow through on their gifts. Give them time to help each other.

5. The children can take home the other hands at the same time and have them share with the class what their friends and parents and siblings thought of their gift. Have the children tell about how they helped each other.

Language Development

1. Have the children keep a weekly journal where they draw a picture once a week and write about or dictate what they have done to help another person. You can enlarge the concept to include how we help the environment, our pets, or our neighbors.
2. A second part can include people who help us like community helpers or people in the school who help us like the librarian, the nurse, and so on. You can make a class list of all the ways school personnel help the children.
3. Children can tell stories about, "The Day the Librarian (Nurse, etc.) Helped Me."

Extensions

1. During circle time have each child sit in the center of the circle and have the other children tell about something that is special about that child.
2. Talk about other friends and what makes them special: grandparents, brothers, sisters, the policeman, fireman, doctor, nurse, teacher, and so forth.
3. Create a class book about special friends and what they can do.
4. Use the lesson as an opportunity for the students to come up with a list of opposites, small-large, tall-short, and so on. Then they can illustrate one of the word pairs.

ACTIVITY TWO: UNUSUAL COMBINATIONS

Objectives

—To create unique and unusual combinations of ideas
—To develop imagination and creativity
—To develop expressive language skills
—To develop students' ability to identify and list attributes of specific animals

Introduction

The purpose of the activity is for the children to identify attributes and unique characteristics of two animals selected at random and then talk about how the animals could help each other in specific situations. For older children take a group of animal pictures and put them in two stacks. Turn over a picture from each stack. For example, you may turn over a snake and a horse. How could the snake help the horse or vice versa? The horse could carry the snake a long distance on his back. The snake could rattle or hiss and warn the horse that enemies are coming. The snake can wiggle into places the horse can't fit and get things for the horse such as the apple that rolled under the fence. Try to give the children an opportunity to come up with the situations; but if that is too difficult, you might have to present them with the situation. For example, if they pick a duck and a kitten. What if the kitten was separated from his family? How could the duck help the kitten? Maybe the duck could carry the kitten in her bill.

The animals should be selected at random to force the children to be creative and find ways the animals could help each other. This activity is also a way you can teach the children about the special attributes of different animals. The students can also act out or make up a story about the horse and the snake or any other pair of animals that come up.

Materials

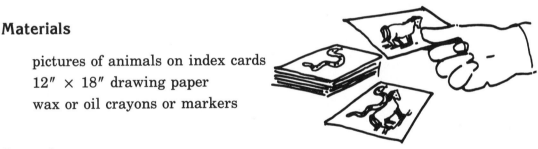

    pictures of animals on index cards
    12″ × 18″ drawing paper
    wax or oil crayons or markers

Procedure

1. Have the children find pictures of animals and cut them out and glue them on index cards. If you don't want to take the time, prepare the cards yourself.

2. Work with small groups or the whole class. Have one child pick one animal from each stack of pictures and show them to the group. Have the child describe the attributes of the animals: their looks, sounds, special talents, and abilities. All of the children can help.

3. After they have described the animals, present a specific situation or ask the children to suggest a situation where one of the two animals might need some help. Ask the students to suggest how one animal could possibly help the other. Encourage them to be imaginative and creative. Remind them of how the little mouse helped the big, ferocious lion.

Language Development

1. Have the children sit in a circle and create a story about the two animals they randomly selected from the two stacks. Give each child a chance to add to the story as they go around the circle. Another way to do this is to use the book *An Animal Shuffle* by Richard Heffer and Martin Stephen Moskof to create a story. (This book comes with one of the three commercially produced decks of cards that children can use to create stories.)

2. Use the activity to create conversations between animals. What would the horse say to the monkey as the monkey came to the farm? If the elephant found a puppy in the jungle, what would the elephant say to the puppy? The children can role play each animal and act out a simple conversation.

Extensions

1. Talk with the children about how we can take care of our pets and other animals. Have someone come in from the Animal Protection Society or the Humane Society to talk with children about pets and how to care for them. Remind the children that pets are their friends.

2. Have the children create a class list or recipe for the characteristics of a best friend or "Friendship is . . ."

STORY SUMMARY

I. Introduction to the setting and characters

    A. In the forest lived a lion

        1. The magnificent Lion, king of the beasts, was greatly admired.

        2. He had a special place to sleep.

        3. He enjoyed eating mice.
Song:
> I am a MIGHTY LION.
> L-I-O-N.
> I like to eat a little mouse,
> Every now and then.

        4. Adventuresome mouse sees Lion, climbs on his back, and slides down his tail.

        5. Lion wakes up and sings: I am a MIGHTY LION.

        6. She pleads with him not to eat her; she says she'll be his friend.

        7. He's so amused, he sets her free.

II. Lion is trapped.

    A. Hunters in the forest

        1. Watch Lion and decide to set a trap

        2. Set the trap

    B. Lion steps into the trap.

        1. Lion steps on the rope that brings the trap down on him. He ROARS.

        2. The other animals cannot help him.

    C. Along comes Mouse.

        1. She hears lion's roar and sings:
> I am a little mouse,
> M-O-U-S-E.
> I'll go and help the lion,
> For he was kind to me.

        2. She comes running and sees the trap.

        3. She calls her friends, the mice in the forest.

        4. The mice chew the ropes, until LION is FREE!

III. Lion and Mouse are friends
    A. Lion roars.
        1. Other mice and animals run away.
        2. Adventuresome mouse hides under his tail.
            a. She appears and Lion thanks her.
            b. Since then they have been the best of friends.

Activity One, Procedure #1

WOMBAT STEW
By Marcia K. Vaughan

The Story

[NOTE: Teach the children the WOMBAT STEW verse and perhaps movement, so they can join in each time. Also teach RIGHTO, IN THEY GO!]

One day, on the bands of a billabong, a very clever dingo caught a wombat. . . . and decided to make . . .

> WOMBAT STEW,
> WOMBAT STEW,
> GOOEY, BREWY,
> YUMMY, CHEWY,
> WOMBAT STEW!

Platypus came rambling up the bank. "Good day, Dingo," he said, snapping his bill. "What is all that water for?" "I'm brewing up a gooey, chewy stew with that fat wombat," replied Dingo, with a toothy grin. *[Perhaps a special voice for Dingo.]*

"If you ask me," said Platypus, "the best thing for a gooey stew is mud. Big blops of billabong mud." "Blops of mud?" Dingo laughed. "What a good idea. Righto, in they go!"

So Platypus scooped up big blops of mud with his tail and tipped them into the billycan. Around the bubbling billy, Dingo danced and sang. *[Have children join in]* :

> WOMBAT STEW,
> WOMBAT STEW,
> GOOEY, BREWY,
> YUMMY, CHEWY,
> WOMBAT STEW!

Waltzing out from the shade of the ironbarks came Emu. She arched her graceful neck over the brew. *[Be fun to actually waltz.]* "Oh ho, Dingo," she fluttered. "What have we here?"

"Gooey, chewy wombat stew," boasted Dingo.

"If only it were a bit more chewy," she sighed. "But don't worry. A few feathers will set it right."

"Feathers?" Dingo smiled. "That would be chewy! Righto, in they go!" So into the gooey brew Emu dropped her finest feathers. Around and around the bubbling billy, Dingo danced and sang . . .

> WOMBAT STEW,
> WOMBAT STEW,
> CRUNCHY, MUNCHY,
> FOR MY LUNCHY,
> WOMBAT STEW!

Old Blue Tongue the Lizard came sliding off his sun-soaked stone. "Sssilly Dingo," he hissed. "There are no fliesss in this ssstew. Can't be wombat ssstew without crunchy fliess in it." And he stuck out his bright blue tongue. "There's a lot to be said for flies," agreed Dingo, rubbing his paws together. "Righto, in they go!"

So Lizard snapped one hundred flies from the air with his long tongue and flipped them into the gooey, chewy stew. Around and around and around the bubbling billy, Dingo danced and sang . . .

> WOMBAT STEW,
> WOMBAT STEW,
> CRUNCHY, MUNCHY,
> FOR MY LUNCHY,
> WOMBAT STEW!

Up through the red dust popped Echidna. "Wait a bit. Not so fast," he bristled, shaking the red dust from his quills. "Now, I've been listening to all this advice—and, take it from me, for a munchy stew you need slugs and bugs and creepy crawlies."

Dingo wagged his tail. "Why, I should have thought of that. Righto, in they go!" So Echidna dug up all sorts of creepy crawlies and dropped them into the gooey, chewy, crunchy stew. *[Your wiggling fingers can be creepy crawlies.]*

The very clever Dingo stirred and stirred, all the while singing . . . *[let children stir, too].*

> WOMBAT STEW,
> WOMBAT STEW,
> HOT AND SPICY,
> OH SO NICEY,
> WOMBAT STEW!

Just then the sleepy-eyed Koala climbed down the scribbly gumtree. "Look here," he yawned, "any bush cook knows you can't make a spicy stew without gumnuts." *[Speak S-L-O-W-L-Y.]*

"Leave it to Koala to think of gumnuts," Dingo laughed and licked his whiskers. "Righto, in they go!" And into the gooey, chewy, crunchy, munchy stew Koala shook lots and lots of gumnuts.

"Ah ha!" cried Dingo. "Now my stew is missing only one thing."

"What's that?" asked the animals.

"The fat wombat!"

"Wait!" "Stop!" "Hang on, Dingo! You can't put that wombat into the stew yet."

"Why not?"

"You haven't tasted it."

"Righto! I'll taste it!" And that very clever dingo bent over the billy and took a great big slurp of stew.

AAARGRUFFOOEE!!!!! "I'm poisoned!" he howled. *[Be very dramatic and funny.]* "You've all tricked me!"

And he dashed away deep into the bush, never again to sing . . .

> WOMBAT STEW,
> WOMBAT STEW,
> GOOEY, BREWY,
> YUMMY, CHEWY,
> WOMBAT STEW!

Key Concepts and Themes and/or Universal Ideas

Here is another story which illustrates how friends help each other. By being very clever, all the animals helped their friend the wombat escape from being a part of the stew. The emphasis is on collaboration (which appears in other stories such as "Grandpa's Turnip" and "The Brementown Musicians"). The activities will demonstrate how friends can collaborate to help each other get a job done. The story also introduces the children to animals that are found in Australia.

Suggested Companion(s)

a big stew pot

Preparation

What are some activities that you do together with your group of friends? Did you ever get together and bake cookies or paint a mural?

Preparation for Visualization

Tell the Children:

Before hearing the story close your eyes and pretend that you are walking down the street on your way home from school and you hear a kitty meowing almost as if it were crying. You look all around but you do not see the kitty. Its meowing gets louder and louder and all of a sudden you look up and see the kitty is stuck in the tree. You can't get it out by yourself, but it just so happens you are in front of your friend's house. So you run and knock on the door. Knock! Knock! Knock! and you can hear your friend running to the door. Your friend swings open the door and you tell him about the cat. You ask him if he has a ladder, but he says no. He tells you about another friend across the street who might have one. So the two of you look both ways, to the right and to the left; and when there are no cars coming, you run to your other friend's house. Meanwhile the kitty is still meowing pathetically. Your other friend says his ladder is not tall enough, but he has heard that the fire department will come and use their ladder to help the kitty. So you go into the house and call the fire department and they come and help the kitty down from the tree. You and your friends are very happy and thank the firemen. Can you guess who the kitty belonged to? Now open your eyes and listen to a story about how some animal friends in Australia got together and helped a friend.

Listen to the Story

Follow-up Discussion Questions

1. Before the story ended, could you guess what the animals were doing to help the Wombat?

2. Do you think the Wombat knew what was happening?

3. Have you ever cooked something special like soup, stew, pizza or cookies with your friends? How did it come out?

4. Have you ever heard of any of the animals in the story?

ACTIVITY ONE: AUSTRALIAN ANIMAL FRIENDS

Objectives

   —To develop sequencing skills
   —To develop oral communication skills
   —To develop ability to collaborate with others

Introduction

This activity is not only a collaborative effort but it helps the children to become familiar with some animals from Australia. The boys and girls are going to put on a puppet show to recreate the story. Emphasize how they are to work together and create the story. The puppets will be simple paper bag puppets. The children will help each other to create a mural as the backdrop for the puppet show.

Materials

   small paper bags that fit over the children's hands
   glue or paste
   tempera paint, brushes, water containers, and big Kraft or poster paper
   scissors
   Animal worksheets
   markers or crayons
   12″ × 18″ construction paper

Procedure

Part One

Ask the children if they have ever seen a wombat. Ask them to create their own version of whatever they think a wombat looks like. Hang up all the wombats.

Part Two

1. Animal worksheets are provided so the children can become familiar with what these animals look like. You can reproduce them if you want

to make more than one set. If the children are old enough and can cut, have them cut out the animals. Otherwise they have to be cut for them. If you can find pictures of the animals in reference books, bring them into the classroom.

2. Have the children color the animals.

3. The children can paste the animals on the front of the bag.

4. Ask the children to tell you in what order the animals appear in the story and to get them in the right order.

5. There are several things you can do to include more children in the puppet show:

    a. Make several sets and have more than one show.

    b. Have the children create another story that is similar. Just use different animals.

    c. Find out about more Australian animals and add them to the story.

6. Have the children tell the story in their own words. Coach them along. The whole class can sing the verse.

7. The children can work in a group and create a mural of the banks of the billabong as the background for the puppet show.

8. Invite other classes to come and see your puppet show.

Language Development

1. Have the children make up other verses using their favorite foods. For example,

> PIZZA PIE
> PIZZA PIE,
> CRUNCHY,
> MUNCHY,
> FOR MY LUNCHY
> PIZZA PIE

> or

> PEANUT BUTTER
> PEANUT BUTTER
> WITH GOOEY JELLY,
> IN MY BELLY,
> PEANUT BUTTER

Encourage the children to help each other to create the verses.

2. Have the children sit in a circle and talk about what they put in the

wombat stew. Have the children talk about another kind of stew for another animal and have each tell what they think should be put into the stew. Have them tell why they think their suggestion would be a good addition. Have an imaginary or real pot in the center of the circle and as the children make their suggestions, have them go up and put them into the pot and stir the pot.

3. Have the children sit in a circle holding hands and go around the circle and ask the children to tell all the reasons they can think of why they need friends.

4. For older children, have them write a poem or a letter to their best friend telling them why they like them.

Extensions

1. Have the children make a paper chain and attach all of their chains together to make a friendship chain to decorate the room for the puppet show.

2. The children can think of all the fun activities they can do together with their friends.

3. Make a stew or soup in the class with all the children helping. Have the children work in groups to decorate their tables for their lunch. Cover each table with a large piece of paper and have the children use crayons to decorate it with all their favorite animals or all their favorite foods.

4. The children can make friendship stew. For example, the ingredients can include two cups of sharing, three cups of hugs, and so on. Each child can add something to the stew and you can write it on the board. You can have the recipe reproduced and the children can decorate the recipe. The children can also join hands in a friendship circle and dance as they sing the song from the story. Teach the children a friendship song. Write a friendship song.

ACTIVITY TWO: A FRIENDSHIP PICNIC

Objectives

–To develop oral communication skills
–To develop sequencing skills
–To develop organization skills

Introduction

This activity is intended to be a collaborative effort and fun for the children. Put the children into small groups of friends. Plan ahead so that you know which children are friends and usually play together. The groups should be anywhere from three to five children. The children are going to make a picnic lunch of peanut butter and jelly sandwiches, cookies, a piece of fruit, and something to drink. The lunch can take place on the classroom floor or out on the playground depending on your school area and the weather.

Materials

peanut butter and jelly

bread

juice or milk in individual containers

aluminum foil

blankets

boxes that can become picnic baskets

paper to create placemats

butter knives

Procedure

1. The first thing you will do is bring in some boxes that the children can decorate as a group. These will be the picnic baskets.

2. The children will then create a placemat for one of their friends in the group. These can be made as magazine collages, a design made of the letters from the friend's name and their name, pictures of themselves and their friends doing something together, or anything you or they want.

3. At a table, put one jar of peanut butter, one jar of jelly and a loaf of bread. Each child is to make a sandwich. Give them butter knives to spread the peanut butter. Give them separate pieces of aluminum foil and have them help each other wrap the sandwiches. Give them the cookies, juice or milk, and fruit, and have them pack their baskets including their placemats and napkins.

4. Give each group a blanket and let them find a spot where they want to sit. Tell them that after lunch they can tell each other stories about their favorite foods and their favorite places to eat or they can tell the group some other stories or fairytales that are their favorites.

Language Development

1. The children will work with you and write a group story about their peanut butter and jelly picnic. They will make pictures about the picnic and you will put them up around the story. Older children will write individual stories.

2. The class will create an imaginary sandwich that an animal such as a dinosaur or other creature might like to eat.

3. The children will try to come up with reasons to convince the Dingo not to cook the Wombat. Encourage divergent thinking, the more imaginative the better.

Extensions

1. The students will pantomime cooking something or eating a particular kind of food. The other children will try and guess what they are doing.
2. Have the class make a friendship alphabet book. Each letter can be about different kinds of friends, why they are friends, things that friends can do together.

Echidna

Wombat

Activity One, Procedure, Part Two #1

Emu

Old Blue Tongued Lizard

Activity One, Procedure, Part Two #1

Koala

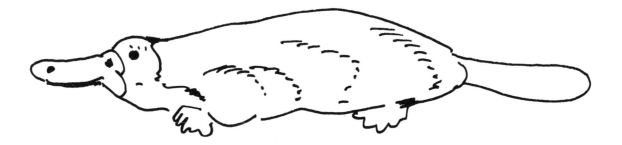

Platypus

Dingo

Activity One, Procedure, Part Two #1

FRIENDSHIP: ADDITIONAL STORIES

 Frog and Toad: The Lost Button by Arnold Lobel. Harper and Row, New York, 1976.

Frog and Toad are best friends. Frog always helps Toad when he has problems. In this story Toad loses a button to his jacket. Frog leads an exhaustive search uncovering many buttons but not the lost one. Toad sadly goes home. To his surprise, it is at home that he finds his button. Toad thanks his good friend Frog and he sews all of the many buttons they found together on his jacket and gives the jacket to Frog.

Suggested Activities

The children should be encouraged to tell stories about their best friend, imaginary or real. They can be asked to talk about things they have done together or how they have helped each other. The teacher can give the children pre-cut paper jackets or rectangles of muslin or cotton with a slit in the center like a poncho. Give the children crayons that work on cloth, buttons, ribbons, yarn, scrap cloth, and glue, and have them decorate a jacket for their best friend or a friend in their class. Have them create a card for their friend. Simple Frog and Toad puppets can be made and the children can make up their own Frog and Toad stories. Have the children bring a button to school that has a story behind it. Have the children tell the stories.

 Tico and His Golden Wings by Leo Lionni. Pinwheel Books, Mamaroneck, New York, 1964.

Tico is born without wings, but he's not unhappy because his friends supply him with everything he needs. One night his recurring dream comes true; the wishing bird gives him golden wings and he takes flight! In the morning his jealous friends turn against him. He ends up giving his golden feathers away to those people that need them and to his surprise there are black shiny feathers underneath. Tico learns a lot about sharing and friendship.

Suggested Activities

Have the children talk about giving something of their own to someone else who may need it more than they do. Cut out large golden feathers, one for each child. Have the child write what they can bring for a homeless person on the feather and take it home. If they can't write, do it for them. The children can bring in clothing and food and toys and these can be brought to centers for the homeless.

 A Special Trade by Sally Wittman, illustrations by Sally Gundersheimer. Harper & Row, New York, 1978.

Old Bartholomew, Nelly's elderly neighbor, would spend warm and loving times with her. When Bartholomew grew old and sick, Nelly spent warm and loving times with him.

Suggested Activities

Have the children talk about their favorite stories. Ask them to select a story that they think a grandparent or older adult friend would like. Invite some grandparents and older adults to class and have the children tell them stories. Adopt some senior adults that the children can do special things for.

Other Stories

Crictor by Tomi Ungerer. Scholastic Book Services, Harper & Row, Toronto, 1958.

Good Dog Carl by Alexandra Day. Green Tiger Press, New Jersey, 1985.

Mice Are Rather Nice, poems selected by Vardine Moore. Atheneum, New York, 1981.

12

Places to Live

> ### THE THREE PIGS
> ### Adapted from an Old English Folktale

About the Story

This is the well-known story of the three little pigs and their encounter with The Big Bad Wolf. To refresh your memory, the mother pig sent off her pigs to make their way in the world. The three pigs tearfully said farewell and went out into the world, each going his separate way. The first little pig built a house of straw, the second a house of sticks, and the third a house of bricks. The first and second pigs were anxious to be free to play so they used the first materials they came across, straw and sticks. The wolf came along and blew their houses down and got the little pigs. The third pig was wise and took his time. He built his house of bricks, waiting to play until his work was done. The wolf could not blow the third pig's house down, and while trying to come down the chimney, he landed in a pot of boiling water and became dinner for the third little pig.

Key Concepts and Themes and/or Universal Ideas

The theme or main idea of the story is that we should get our work done and do it well before we take time to have fun. If we do not give the task our best effort, the outcome may be disastrous. This is the primary message of the story. There are some other lessons to be learned related to animal architecture and places to live.

Suggested Companion(s)

> pictures of different kinds of houses
> stuffed pigs or pig pictures

Preparation

Ask the children if their mother had ever told them to do something and they had rushed through the job because they wanted to play. What happened? For example, were they asked to clean their room and didn't finish the job? What happened? Did their Mom ask them to wash their hands before dinner and they rushed and their hands were still dirty? What happened? Did their Mom make them wash their hands again?

Preparation for Visualization

Tell the Children:

> Before we hear the story we are going to go on an imaginary trip. Close your eyes and imagine you are in your house and your mother is reading you your favorite story. You are all snuggled up. It is a wonderful story, but suddenly you hear the wind blowing. You hear the trees and the leaves and the windows creaking. You know that you are safe with your family because your house is very strong. The wind is making a whrrrring sound and leaves and papers are flying around but your house is strong and snug and warm. You and your Mom peek out the window and watch the wind blowing by. Everything begins to get quiet and you get to hear the rest of your story. You feel safe and snug because you know your house is very strong and sturdy and will keep you safe from bad weather and strangers. Now open your eyes and I'm going to tell you a story.

Listen to the Story (Tape 2, Side B)

Follow-up Discussion Questions

1. Did you like the story?
2. What was your favorite part?
3. Do you think the first two pigs were very smart? Why?
4. Why do you think the third pig was smart?
5. The first two pigs were in a big hurry to play. Their houses were not very strong because they were in too much of a hurry to play. What happened to the first two little pigs?
6. Why was the third pig's house so strong?
7. What kind of house would you have built?
8. Discuss how the children have to finish their work in the classroom before they can play and how this relates to what happened with the pigs. What are the consequences if we do not finish our work before we play?

This does not always have to be the case. Sometimes play can be part of work, but the story relates to the concept of "work before play."

ACTIVITY ONE: THE HOUSE THAT WE BUILT

Objectives

-To develop organization skills
-To develop fine and gross motor skills
-To develop spatial relationships

Introduction

This activity provides an opportunity for students to construct a place to play in and to experiment with different materials. For this activity you need to bring some large sheets or pieces of cloth into the classroom and some large cardboard boxes. The students will create some simple structures.

Materials

large sheets
the tables in your classroom or a card table
boxes large enough for children to crawl into
crayons or markers that will work well on cloth or boxes
House Parts worksheet
construction paper
scissors
paste or glue

Procedure

Part One

1. Compare the three houses and the different components of each house.
2. Talk about the parts of their houses or apartments and some decoration or landscaping (i.e., windows, doors, bricks, wood, stairs, chimney, porch, bushes, trees, etc.).
3. Give the children the House Parts worksheets and one of the following sizes of construction paper (9″ × 18″ for apartment buildings, 9″ × 12″ plus a triangle for the roof for a two-story house, and 8″ × 12″ for a ranch style house). The different shapes can be cut on the paper cutter and the

children can pick the piece of paper they want after you tell them what each one represents. If this is too cumbersome, give each child a 12″ by 18″ piece of construction paper and have them draw an outline and the details of where they live.

4. Give them the worksheet and have them cut out the parts and glue them onto the appropriate places on their house. If their cutting skills are too poor, cut the rectangles with each part on the paper cutter and give them to each child. If they have some cutting skills, have them cut out the rectangles or the shape of each object themselves.

5. Once the children have pasted down their house parts in the appropriate places, have them add any decoration they want with crayons or markers.

6. After they have completed their house, have them tell the group about their own houses or tell it to you or an aide who can write it down. If they are old enough to do some simple writing, have them write about their house.

7. Display their work.

Part Two

1. Talk about what fun it would be to build a place to play. When their work is finished they can go into this place and play or read or whatever is appropriate for your classroom.

2. Show them how they can throw the sheet over the table and create an environment.

3. Have the children decorate the outside of the sheet or box adding windows, plants, designs, whatever they like. You might want to cut out holes for windows.

Language Development

1. Write words on separate pieces of paper that describe the various parts of the classroom. Put tape on the words and have the children go around and label the room.
2. For older children, create a bulletin board or large mural and have the children draw a big straw house, a big stick house, and a big brick house along with three pigs and the wolf. With your help, have them label the parts of the picture with the appropriate words.
3. Create a class story and have another animal play the role of the wolf. Talk about how the story would be different.
4. Read the book *The True Story of the Three Little Pigs* by A. Wolf as told to Jon Scieszka (Viking Kestral, 1989). Have the children compare the two stories.

Extensions

1. Have the children act out the story.
2. Have the children create pig helpers—helpers that could have come and helped the first two pigs build stronger houses. For example, pig carpenter, pig bricklayer, pig architect. Introduce helpers that are involved with building houses. Have them come and talk to the children. Have the children draw pig helpers and tell what they can do. If they have some writing skills, have them write about them.
3. Pre-cut some geometric shapes and have the children use the shapes by gluing them onto colored construction paper to create some fancy pig houses for the pigs.

ACTIVITY TWO: ANIMAL ARCHITECTURE

Objectives

—To develop organizational skills
—To develop fine and gross motor skills
—To develop students' understanding of animal architecture

Introduction

The children will talk about animal architecture, the different kinds of shelters that animals create. The children will be provided with a list of animals, their picture, and a picture of their shelter and its name. The children will try to match the shelter with the appropriate animal.

Materials

Animal Architecture worksheet
drawing materials
blocks
assorted boxes and containers
glue or paste
construction paper
scissors

Procedure

1. Talk with the children about different places that animals live and who built these places. Did the farmer build them? Did another person build them? Did the animals build them?

2. Ask them where the following animals live and who built their shelter?

   —a bird builds a nest

   —a bee builds a hive

   —a caterpillar/butterfly builds a cocoon

   —a spider weaves a web

   —a mole digs a hole

   —an ant creates a hill

   —a chimpanzee builds a sleeping platform

   —a beaver builds a mound

   (Resource: "Animal Architects" from *World Explorers*, National Geographic Society, 1987).

3. Give the children the Animal Architecture worksheet and have them match the animals by number and letter. You can also cut the sheets and have them do the matching with the appropriate structure.

Language Development

1. Ask the children to tell the class about any of the structures that they have actually seen, such as a bird nest or beehive or spider web, and if they ever saw the animal building it.

2. Ask an architect to come to the class and talk to the children.

3. Ask the children to make up a story about another animal and how he built his house and what happened when someone tried to blow it down.

Possible animals might be zebras, cows, or giraffes. Tell them to use their imaginations. Ask them to illustrate their stories.

Extensions

1. For kindergarten and preschool children, ask them to use blocks and to create the best or strongest house they can. (Shoe boxes, milk containers, tin cans, and other containers can also be used.)
2. Older children can use the assorted materials mentioned above and create the fanciest pig house they can think of.
3. Children can design the fanciest or most exciting house for their dog or cat or another pet. Talk about the kinds of places where farm animals live, like barns or pens. Ask the children to create a beautiful barn or pen for the farm animals.
4. *For older children*: Ask them to interview the animal and ask them what kind of house they want. One child plays the architect and the other, the animal.

STORY SUMMARY

I.   Introduction of characters and setting

    A. Mother Pig sends her three pigs out into the world.

       1. Mother Pig tells her pigs to gather their belongings and seek their fortune.

       2. Pigs go into their rooms and gather their belongings into sacks.

       3. Pigs say goodbye to Mother Pig.

    B. Pigs walk together into the woods.

       1. The smallest pig took the road to the right.

       2. The middle pig took the road to the left.

       3. The biggest and wisest pig took the middle road.

II. The three pigs build houses.

    A. Let's follow the smallest pig.

       1. He met up with a man selling straw.

          a. "Oh, Mr. Man, could I have some of your straw? I need to build myself a house in the forest."

          b. He smiled and sang,

            "Oh yes, oh yes, oh yes indeed.

            Take all the straw that you need."

          c. He took the straw and quickly built himself a house.

          d. He had time to play.

          e. He had time to make soup.

       2. The Big Bad Wolf blows the house down.

          a. There came a knock.

          b. "Little pig, little pig, let me come in."

          c. The pig answered, "Not by the hairs of your chinny, chin, chin."

          d. "Then I'll huff and I'll puff and I'll blow your house in."

          e. He huffed and he puffed and he blew the house in, and he got the first little pig.

    B. Now, let's follow the middle-sized pig who took the road to the left.

       1. He met a woman selling sticks.

          a. "Oh, excuse me, do you think I could have some of those sticks? I need to build myself a house in the forest."

          b. She said,

            "Yes, oh yes, oh yes indeed.

            Take all the sticks you need."

    c. He built himself a house of sticks.
       (He took longer than first pig.)

    d. He didn't have time to play.

    e. He had time to eat his favorite cereal CREAM OF CORN.

2. The Big Bad Wolf blows the house down.

    a. There came a knock at the door.

    b. "Little pig, little pig, let me come in."

    c. The pig answered, "Not by the hairs of your chinny, chin, chin."

    d. "Then I'll huff and I'll puff and I'll blow your house in!"

    e. He huffed and he puffed and he blew the house in, and he got the second little pig.

C. Now, let's follow along with the biggest and the wisest pig.

1. He met a man selling bricks.

    a. "Oh, Mr. Man, may I have some of your bricks? I need to build myself a house in the forest."

    b. He answered,
       "Oh yes, oh yes, oh yes indeed.
       Take all the bricks that you need!"

2. He built himself a brick house in the forest.

    a. He didn't have time to play or eat.

    b. He worked all day, all night, and all the next day.

    c. He built a house with:

    two windows

    a chimney

    painted his door bright red

    and planted seeds in the garden

    d. Then he rested.

3. The wolf came but couldn't blow his house down.

    a. Then came a knock

    b. "Little pig," etc.

    c. "Not by the hairs," etc.

    d. "Then I'll huff," etc.

4. He huffed and he puffed and he huffed some more, but, he couldn't blow the house down.

5. At night, the wolf came back.

6. He climbed up the side of the house and jumped on the roof.

    a. He made noise.

      b. The pig saw him on the roof.

  7. The pig made a fire in the chimney.

      a. Filled his big, black pot.

      b. Put it over the fire.

      c. Water began to boil.

  8. Wolf counted one-two-three and jumped.

      a. Landed in pot of water.

      b. Pig put on lid. End of wolf.

III. Conclusion.

As far as I know, the pig lived happily ever after in his snug brick house and he had wolf stew for dinner for one full week.

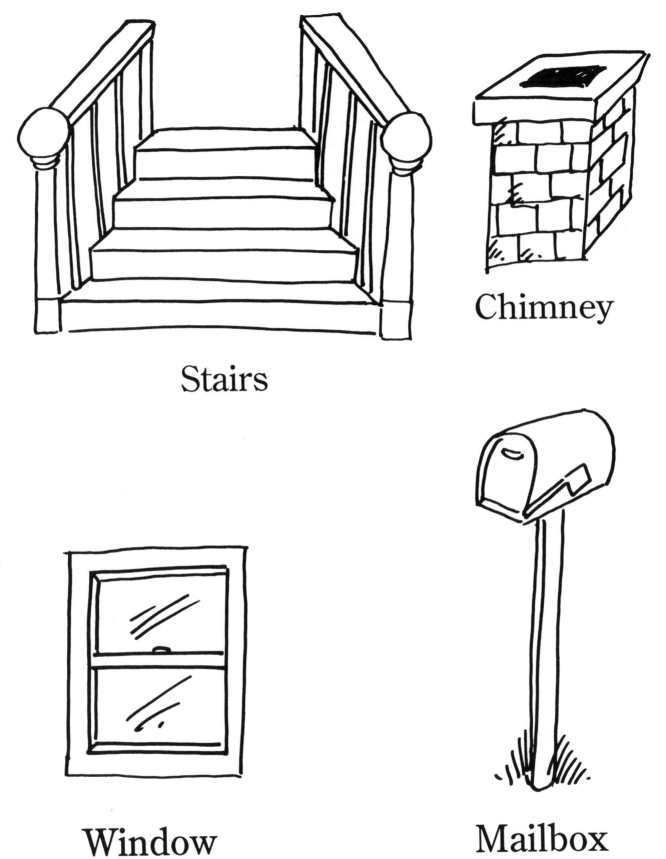

Stairs

Chimney

Window

Mailbox

Activity One, Procedure, Part One #3

Porch

Activity One, Procedure, Part One #3

Bushes

Door

Window

WELCOME

Door Mat

Activity One, Procedure, Part One #3

a beaver

an ant

a bee

a chimpanzee

a bird

a mole

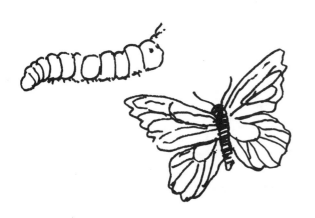

a caterpillar/butterfly

a spider

Activity Two, Procedure #3

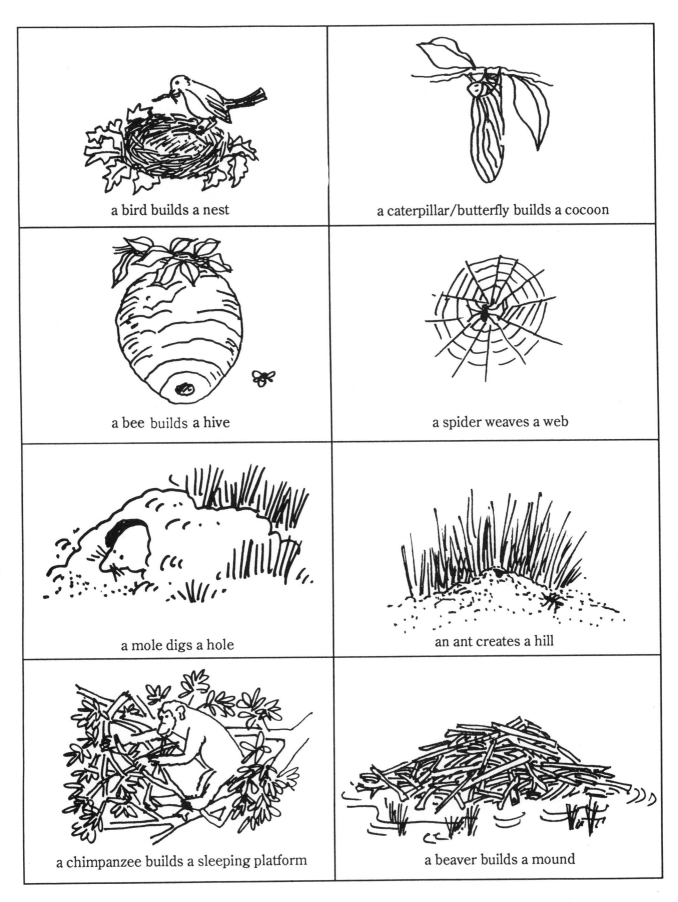

a bird builds a nest

a caterpillar/butterfly builds a cocoon

a bee builds a hive

a spider weaves a web

a mole digs a hole

an ant creates a hill

a chimpanzee builds a sleeping platform

a beaver builds a mound

Activity Two, Procedure #3

THE CITY MOUSE AND THE COUNTRY MOUSE
Adapted from Aesop's Fables

The Story

Slick was a city mouse. *[You can snap your fingers like a cool mouse.]* He loved noise, bright lights, big houses, fancy food and excitement. Every night he would feast on cheeses, steak, lobster, cakes, and jellies . . . whatever he wanted. He LOVED the good life.

But one morning Slick woke up with a stomach ache *[O-O-OH]* from too much rich food, a headache *[A-H-H]* from too much loud music, and his feet hurt *[OUCH!]* from too much dancing and prancing. *[Demonstrate by touching stomach and head, and sit down and hold feet.]*

"I need a rest," he said. "I'll go and visit Clem, my country cousin!"

Clem invited him often. He'd say,

"Come and visit the country. It will be a nice restful vacation for you. There's plenty of fresh air, delicious food, and wide open spaces."

So Slick, the city mouse, packed his suitcase full of clothes for days and nights in the country. And off he went. *[Snaps again to show him traveling. Children snap with you if they can.]* When he arrived, Clem greeted him *[welcoming gesture]*,

"Welcome to my home."

Slick looked around and realized that his country cousin lived in a field. Clem said,

"I know you're not used to the wide open spaces, but you can see that I live under the blue skies, with the sun shining down and the soothing sounds of the insects and birds. City Cousin, you have come a long way, you must be tired and hungry. There's plenty of delicious, fresh food to eat. Come, let's eat!" *[said with excitement]*

He served barley corn, roots, beans, and a few peas; and for dessert he proudly presented two fresh stalks of wheat on a bed of mushrooms. Clem ate with a hearty appetite, but Slick just picked at his food. He couldn't believe how dull it was, and how boring country life could be.

[Song sung to the tune of "Hush Little Baby, Don't You Cry." Sing twice so children can join in.]

> Country Mouse, O Country Mouse
> You live in a very simple house.
> Your food is very plain, I see.
> This dull life is NOT FOR ME.

The next day he said,

"Thank you for your kind hospitality, Clem, but one day in the country is enough for me. *[Begin snapping his fingers. Audience join in!]* I'm ready to go back to my exciting life in the city. Why don't you come with me . . . see where I live, and taste my food? Experience the city life for yourself."

"I don't think so, Slick," said Clem. "My life here may be boring and dull to you, but I like it. It suits me just fine."

"But in the city *[cool snapping again]*," said Slick, "every day is a party! There are wonderful exciting things to eat, you get to live in a HUGE house with three floors and twenty-five rooms! Come with me, you'll never want to return to your life in the fields, eating barley corn and peas."

"All right, all right, I'll go," said Clem. "I AM curious about the city."

They set out that very day for Slick's home in the city. Clem traveled light, taking only the clothes on his back. Slick led the way, with his unopened suitcase slung over his shoulder.

The bright lights and the traffic in the city frightened Clem. He stayed close to Slick and kept asking *[said with nervous voice]*,

"Are we there yet?" And Slick would say, "Not yet!"

Finally they arrived! They crept into the house. Clem followed Slick into the dining room, where there were the remains of a fine feast. There were turkey, meats, cheese, iced cakes, breads, and sweets of many shapes and kinds! Clem could not believe his eyes.

"WOW!" *[said with great excitement]* he shouted. "You were right, this is great."

But before Clem could decide what to eat, the kitchen door swung open and two kitchen helpers came out. Light flooded the table.

"Follow me, quickly!" yelled Slick. He jumped off the table and ran into his little mouse hole. Clem quickly followed him. His eyes were wide with fright, and his heart was beating fast in his little mouse body.

"Whew!" he said. "That was close!"

"Don't worry about them," said Slick. "They're gone now. Come back to the table. Let's eat!"

The two mice climbed up on the table again and began to eat.

[Show pleasure.] "Yum-m-m, this is good," said Clem, licking his paws. He was eating the icing off a big hunk of chocolate cake.

BUT, the door opened again and out came two huge, barking dogs.

"Ruff! Ruff!"

"Run!" *[great emotion]* cried Slick. "Back to the hole, QUICK!"

Slick and Clem ran as fast as they could. One dog almost got Clem's tail as he disappeared into the hole.

"That was scary!" *[with conviction]* said Clem.

"I'm going home."

[Tune of "Hush Little Baby, Don't You Cry." Sing twice so audience can join in.]

> City Mouse, O City Mouse
> You live in a very fancy house.
> Your food is very elegant, I see.
> But living in fear is NOT FOR ME.

"Your food, my dear cousin, is much more exciting than mine, but I'm too tired and too scared to enjoy it. I'm going home to my simple life in the country, where I can eat barley corn and peas in peace."

He said goodbye to his city cousin and went home. As far as I know, they are both happy now . . . Clem in the country and Slick in the city.

Key Concepts and Themes and/or Universal Ideas

The underlying theme or concept is that we have a tendency to be comfortable with what we are familiar with and know best and we sometimes pre-judge or reject something or someone new or different without taking the opportunity to become more familiar with the place or the individual. In this story we are involved with places to live.

Suggested Companion(s)

two mice—one dressed as a country mouse, the other as a city mouse
a city scene and a country scene

Preparation

Prior to hearing the story, ask the children if they have ever been to the country or city depending on where you live. Did they like their visit? What did they like? What was new to them? What were the things that they did not like or that frightened them? For younger children, you may want to ask them if they have ever been to a town or farm or place that is different from where they live.

Preparation for Visualization

Tell the Children:

[If you live in the country, use the following guide. If you live in the city, use the second guide. If you live in the suburbs, use either one.]

I Before we hear the story, we are going to take an imaginary trip. Close your eyes. Pretend you are a little mouse with a suitcase who gets off the train in the middle of the city. Picture the mouse as he runs between the feet of all the people as they rush about. Feel how crowded the little mouse feels as he is pushed and shoved by the crowds and all the other little mice as they rush about. Smell all the smells of the city: gasoline, hot dogs, freshly baked cakes. Hear the screeching cars, the barking dogs, the meowing cats, the street musicians, and the laughing people. What an exciting place! Now open your eyes and I'm going to tell you a story.

II Before we hear the story, we are going to take an imaginary trip. Close your eyes. Pretend you are the little mouse with a suitcase who gets off the train in the middle of a small town. Picture the mouse as he looks around, sees the hills and mountains, hears the birds chirping and sees a few people going to work and doing their business. As you start out for the farm, you see lots of trees, wheat fields, cows, pigs, and chickens. Hear the crickets chirping, cows mooing, pigs squealing, and birds singing. Besides these nature sounds you don't hear very much. As you reach the farm, you smell freshly baked cornbread and soup. What a peaceful place. Now open your eyes and I'm going to tell you a story.

Listen to the Story

Follow-up Discussion Questions

1. What did you see?
2. What stands out most in your mind?
3. Which place did you like best?
4. Where would you like to be?
5. Did you see the country?
6. What did you see?
7. Did you see the city?
8. What did you see?
9. Where do you live?
10. Is it like the city or the country?
11. What do you like best?
12. If you could go to the city (country), would you like it?
13. Why do you think the country mouse didn't like the city?
14. Why do you think the city mouse didn't like the country?
15. Do you think that if the mouse had stayed longer in the city (country), he would have liked it? Explain.

ACTIVITY ONE: BEST OF ALL WORLDS

Objectives

—To be able to compare and contrast
—To analyze the elements of two different environments
—To be able to see the best of both worlds
—To develop classification skills
—To identify geometric shapes

Introduction

Show children pictures of the country and the city. Talk about what one might find in a busy city and what one might find on a quiet farm. Bring in many magazines with city pictures and country or farm pictures. For this age, you might focus on what one might find on a farm. The children are going to make a large class collage of all the things they like about the city and the country in one picture. The idea is that one is not better than the other; but that they are different and each has its advantages.

The activity can be done in two ways. The better for the younger children would be to cut out magazine pictures of the country and city and have the children paste them on to the collage. The second way for children who are older is to have them draw some objects and use pre-cut paper to make others to create a city-country environment.

Materials

City/Country Mouse Sort worksheet

magazines

glue

drawing materials

12″ × 18″ construction paper

pre-cut geometric shapes (large squares, triangles, rectangles, circles)

scissors

large mural paper

pictures of different kinds of architecture (optional)

Procedure

1. In preparation for the following activities use the City/Country Mouse Sort worksheet with the children. Reproduce one sheet for each child or one for every two children if you want them to work in teams. If they work in teams, one child can be the country mouse and find his own pictures, and the other can be the city mouse and find her own pictures. Cut the worksheet on the paper cutter along the lines and give each child a set. If the children can cut well enough, have them cut out their own rectangles. Each rectangle has something that one would find in the country or city. Have them fold a piece of construction paper in half and glue the country pictures on one side and the city pictures on the other side. Have them talk about their choices.

2. Ask the children to tell a story about a place they have visited. Ask them if it was most like the city or the country. Ask them what they liked best about the place. Ask them if they would like to live there or just visit. Put up two large pieces of chart paper that can be saved and referred to. Write City at the top of one and Country or Farm on the top of the other. As the children tell what they liked best about their places, write their choices on the appropriate sheet. After several children have told their stories, ask the children what other things they could add to each sheet that they might find in the country or city. Add them to the list.

3. Put up the mural paper. Tear or cut country and city pictures from a magazine or calendars. Hold up each picture and ask the students to tell

you what side of the mural it would go. Paste the pictures on to the mural paper. Do it throughout the discussion. Do not wait until the end.

4. *For older children:* Tell them they are going to create a place to live that will be the best of the city and the country. Mark some streets on the mural paper and a few lines that indicate some hills or streams just to get them started. On one day, have them take the pre-cut shapes and glue them on another paper to create skyscrapers, small houses, farm houses, and barns. They can also make museums and shopping malls, and so on. They can then take drawing materials and add details. You might want to bring in pictures of different kinds of architecture. After the buildings are created, they can put them on the mural.

5. At another time they can draw country and city animals and put them on the mural. They can add cars, trains, airplanes, flowers, and trees as well as people fishing and playing baseball. Have them make the people from smaller pre-cut geometric shapes with details added with drawing materials.

6. Have the children create their own country mouse and city mouse with geometric shapes. Give them oval shapes of different sizes, a variety of small triangles and yarn for tails and whiskers. For younger children it will be necessary to guide them through the creation of the mouse one step at a time. Use red and yellow paper for the country mouse and purple and gray paper for the city mouse. Children can use crayons or markers to add details to the mice. Older children can create their mouse in any way they want by pasting the shapes on another piece of paper. Have them use drawing materials to dress the mice according to whether they live in the country or the city. They might have a farmer mouse and a business person mouse. Have them cut out all the mice and put them on the mural.

7. Have them create a new name for their city/country environment and tell why it would be fun to live there.

Language Development

1. For older children, have the children use the words from the lists and write "Why I would like to live in (the country or city)."

2. For younger children, have them think of sounds of the city and sounds of the country. Pretend they are sitting on a farm or in the center of the city. Refer to the pictures for help.

3. The children can create a family of mice with different jobs: farm jobs and city jobs. Have the children tell about what the person would do on the job.

4. As a class have the children make up a city song or poem, and a country song or poem on why someone should come to visit each place.

5. Have the children think of all the words they can about the country or city that start with the letter C.

Extensions

1. Bring in environment tapes with city sounds and country sounds and let the children guess what they are.

2. Make some typical country food with the children such as cornbread or homemade butter or jam.

3. Bring music about the country or city and play it for the children. Have them do some creative movement and move like farm animals or cars on the highways.

ACTIVITY TWO: THE BEST PLACE FOR ME

Objectives

—To be able to compare and contrast

—To analyze the elements of two different environments

Introduction

The country mouse and the city mouse are very fond of their own environments. Each thinks it is the better place to live. Most children believe that their house is the best place to live because it is what they know best. However, given the opportunity, they could always think of ways to make it even better.

This activity encourages the students to analyze and think about their own hometown and what they like about it. They are to draw a picture of their own house on one side of the paper and then add all the things they would like to make it even better on the other side.

Materials

18″ × 24″ drawing paper

drawing materials

two large triangles per student

glue or tape

an architect

Procedure

1. Ask the children why they thought each mouse liked its environment so well. Why did the country mouse like the country so much? Why did the city mouse like the city so much? Why didn't the country mouse like the city? Why didn't the city mouse like the country?

2. Ask the children if they like their own house and why they like it. Ask them what is special about their house or apartment building.

3. Bring in an architect and have him or her talk to the children about what makes a house special. Have them bring illustrations and models. Encourage the children to ask the architect many questions.

4. Give each child a piece of 18″ × 24″ drawing paper and some drawing materials. Fold the paper in half so that each side is 12″ × 18″. The children can draw their own house on one side of the paper including all of the things that they think are special.

5. On the opposite side of the paper have them draw their house and add all of the things that they would like that would make it even more special. Brainstorm with the children. If you can add anything to your house to make it more fun, what would you add?

6. Hang up the children's pictures and have them talk about their houses and why they like them.

Language Development

1. Have the children write a class letter or individual letters to the architect thanking him or her for coming and describing what they liked about the presentation.

2. Make a class alphabet book called "Places to Live" or "Houses." Children can create places to live for other people, for animals, or for other countries or cities. For example, create a dog house, a cat house, a house for a bat, etc. How about a place for a country mouse or a city mouse? The children can label their houses and write one sentence about each place on their own or with your help.

3. For older kids, how about a "I love my neighborhood campaign" where all the students create posters about what is neat about their neighborhood?

Extensions

1. Create a story in the round. Have the children sit in a circle and you start the story. The story is about how you came to visit the country cousin or city cousin or both and they took you around their town to show it off. Each child adds to the story by telling about a place the cousin told them

to see. If the children need help, put cut or drawn pictures on cards and give each child a card. The card will show what the child should tell about.

2. Have children use blocks or boxes and create a farm or a city. Use all the resources in the room.

3. Have the students listen to short excerpts from samples of music inspired by different environments. Some examples are:

Symphony No. 6	Ludwig van Beethoven
"An American in Paris"	George Gershwin
"Beautiful Noise"	Neil Diamond
"Nocturnes"	Claude Debussy
"City Kids"	Spyro Gyra
Recordings of different sound effects	

Activity One, Procedure #1

PLACES TO LIVE: ADDITIONAL STORIES

 "The Fisherman and His Wife," any version of this German folktale collected by Jacob and Wilhelm, the Brothers Grimm.

This is the story of a poor fisherman and his greedy wife. When he catches a magic fish, she insists that they wish for more and more and more. With each wish they live in a bigger and more spectacular house and have a higher station in life. But alas, she just gets too greedy and they end up back in their poor little house again.

Suggested Activities

Talk about what happens when we get greedy. What does greedy mean? If we have enough candy for the whole class, but some people take more than their share leaving some people without candy, then we can call the candy grabbers "greedy." Have the children act out the story. Then have someone become the fish. Each child can have three wishes; but no one can wish for anything that money can buy. For example, they can wish for love, kindness, good friends, and so on. Create a big simple house on the bulletin board. Have the children brainstorm all the things we need in order to live and those we would like to have. Have them draw them or make them out of cut paper and put them in the house. What happens when the house gets too full? Have the children write a list of wishes. Have the children draw a picture of the most wonderful, not necessarily the biggest, house.

 Make Way for Ducklings by Robert McCloskey. Viking Press, Puffin Books, New York, 1941.

This is a story of a family of ducks who are looking for a place to live. They walk through the city of Boston and in the parks trying to find the perfect place.

Suggested Activities

Read or tell the story to the children. Have the children act out the story and add details about what they see along the way. Take them for a walk around the school pretending they are the ducklings looking for a perfect place to live. Children can create a picture of the perfect pond to live in and show where it might be. It could be in a park they know in the city or somewhere in the country.

Other Stories

 Mousekin's Golden House by Edna Miller. Prentice-Hall, New York, 1964.

The Quilt Story by Tony Johnston and Tomie de Paola. G. P. Putnam's Sons, New York, 1985.

 The Biggest House in the World by Leo Lionni. Pantheon, New York, 1973.

A House for Hermit Crab by Eric Carle. Picture Book Studio, New York, 1987.

The House that Jack Built by Rodney Peppe. Delacorte, 1985.

A House Is a House for Me by Mary Ann Hoberman. Viking Penguin, New York, 1978.

13

Earth, Wind, Sun, Moon, and Stars

> **WHY THE SUN AND MOON LIVE IN THE SKY**
> **Adapted from an Old African Folktale**

About the Story

This is a story about two friends, the Sun and the Moon. The Sun and the Moon lived together and were also friends with Water. They wanted Water to visit them; but when they asked him, he said that there was not enough room in their house. So Sun and Moon built an addition to their house so that there would be room for Water to visit. They made a wonderful dinner and invited Water. When Water got there, he wanted to know if his family could come in. The Sun and the Moon said sure; and Water's family came in and filled the house. Before they knew what was happening, Water also wanted to bring his friends in. Water, his family and friends moved Sun and Moon right up out of their house, until they were up in the sky. They gave their house to Water, and Water and Earth stayed together while Sun and Moon stayed in the sky.

Key Concepts and Themes and/or Universal Ideas

This folktale explains how the Sun and the Moon came to be a part of the sky and how water became such a large part of the Earth. As in some of the other stories in this resource kit and in hundreds and hundreds of other folktales and myths, the story is one people's way of explaining one of the mysteries of the universe. The children should be encouraged to be creative and think of different explanations for the existence of natural phenomena.

275

Suggested Companion(s)

a globe and a picture of the Sun and the Moon

Preparation

Have you ever wondered how the Sun and the Moon stay up in the sky?

Preparation for Visualization

Tell the Children:

Before we hear the story, we are going to take an imaginary trip. Close your eyes. It is summer time and you have gone swimming. As you swim around under the Water you come across two fish. They look like they are good friends and they are having a chat. "Gurgle, gurgle, gurgle, did you know how the Sun and the Moon got into the sky?" The other fish says, "I heard from Willie Whale that they used to live down here." Fish number one says "Really? I didn't know that." You hide behind a rock and listen because you want to know, too. The Water is warm and feels really good; and with your snorkeling mask you are getting all the air you need, so you hang around a bit longer. And along comes Charlie Crab. Charlie asks the fish, "What are you talking about?" and they ask him, "Do you know why the Sun and the Moon are in the sky?" Charlie says, "I heard that . . ." Just then a big boat comes by and the Water rocks and rolls and you float away and don't hear Charlie's answer. Now open your eyes and I'm going to tell you the story of "Why the Sun and the Moon Live in the Sky."

Listen to the Story (Tape 2, Side B)

Follow-up Discussion Questions

1. Did you ever wonder how the Sun and the Moon got into the sky?
2. Did you like the story?
3. Would it be fun if the underwater creatures came to visit you?

ACTIVITY ONE: WHY?

Objectives

—To develop imagination.
—To develop oral communication skills

—To develop creativity

—To develop fine motor skills

—To develop visual expression

Introduction

This activity encourages students to use their imagination and explore the reasons for the existence of natural phenomena as they relate to their world. The students should be encouraged to use their imagination and come up with their own ideas for stories. They will also explore the visual images created by the story and create their own interpretations.

Materials

drawing materials

colored construction paper

writing materials

large kraft paper (blue if you have it)

Procedure

1. To start the activity, have the children sit in a circle and get two big balls. Give two children the balls and tell them one is the Sun and one is the Moon. Ask them how they would keep the Sun and the Moon in the sky. Have them pass them one at a time to other children and let the other children come up with some ideas. Encourage them to use their imaginations. Anything goes. For example, they might say, "With scotch tape," or "The clouds move under them when they seem to be slipping and keeping them from falling down," or "They are held up with an invisible net," or whatever.

2. After they run out of ideas, ask them some of the following questions and tell them to use their imaginations and come up with some explanations:

   • How does the Sun stay hot?

   • Why is the sky blue?

   • Where do the stars come from?

   • Who polishes the stars at night?

   • How did the clouds get so cottony?

   • Where does snow come from?

   • Where does lightning come from?

   • How is thunder made?

   • How does the Earth move?

Encourage the older children to create stories to answer these questions. The younger children can brainstorm and come up with some ideas. Encourage them to use their imagination.

3. For a science activity, provide some simple scientific explanations for these problems.

Language Development

1. Create a group story for one of the questions such as, "How the Sun stays up in the sky." Have the children come up with different ideas and create their own story. The class can act out the story or write the story or do both. You need to coach them and encourage them. Ask questions. Is it held up with sun tape, by elves, by the stars, by invisible strings? Have the children brainstorm ideas and create the class story. Illustrate the story.

2. Have the children brainstorm all the words they can think of that could describe the sun and the moon. Put a big sun and a smaller moon on the bulletin board with all the words around it.

3. Talk about how generous Sun and Moon were by having everyone come to their house until there was no more room for them. Ask the children about when family and friends come to stay over and they have to give up their room or when the house is so crowded there is hardly any room for them. Ask them if their family ever had a party when every room in the house was so full of people that there was hardly any room for them. Ask them how it felt.

Extensions

1. Use a large piece of blue kraft paper or cover a bulletin board with blue paper. Put a simple outline of a huge house on the paper with a piece of brown yarn or a marker. Keep it simple. Talk with the children about what the house might have looked like with all the underwater creatures in it. Listen to the story again. Tell them to close their eyes and use their imagination. Have the children create all kinds of fish and underwater life to go into the house. Have them draw them and cut them out, or make them out of cut paper, or paint them. Use whatever method is easiest for your children or use a combination of all three. Children can also cut fish out of newspapers or magazines. Make a fish stencil. Have them outline the stencil on the newspaper or magazine page and cut it out. Your fish will have many different textures. Try to combine different materials for this activity and fill the whole house. Have one child make a large Sun head and another child make a large Moon head and put them on top of the house as they are floating into the sky.

2. Show the children the globe and talk about how much Water covers the globe. Talk about what it would be like to live in a house boat or on the Water. Talk about some of the fun things they do in the Water such as fishing, swimming, or boating.

ACTIVITY TWO: MOONLIGHT FANTASY

Objectives

- —To develop imagination
- —To develop creativity
- —To develop gross motor skills
- —To develop the ability to compare and contrast

Introduction

The purpose of the activity is to encourage the students to use their imagination about what goes on at night among the plants and animals while they are asleep. They need to be reminded that although the Sun and the Moon live in the sky, they send us light and warmth. The children will role play and create Moonlight dances.

Materials

tapes or records and a tape recorder or record player

a spotlight, lamp, or flashlight

writing materials

black or gray construction paper

oil crayons or regular crayons or tempera paint

Procedure

1. Ask the children what happens at night, when the sun is asleep and the moon is watching over us. Ask them if the sun is really asleep. Does the sun ever sleep? If the sun is not asleep, where is it while we are sleeping at night? What are the animals doing, what are the flowers doing? What happens in the moonlight? Who comes out at night? Do the fairies come out and dance? What do the animals do?

2. Read to the children *The Goodnight Circle*. Talk about the moths, the tiny gray mice, the owl, the spring peepers, the opossum, the beavers, the gray-green pickerel, the Water snakes, and the raccoon and what they do at night. What do you think they talk about?

3. Darken the room and create a circle. Try to have one light on the circle. Use a flashlight, a spotlight, a tracklight, or whatever you can create. You might have the children prepare in the dark and when a group is ready use a flashlight to project some light on them. Ask the children what the owls might be saying to each other at night. Have two children role play the owls. "What are the raccoons saying to their babies?" Have the children role play the raccoons.

4. Have the children talk about imaginary creatures like the moonlight fairies and how they dance from flower to flower and visit all the animals, and how, maybe, they even look in on them while they are asleep. Ask what a moonlight fairy might look like. Play some fairy music and have the children pretend they are moonlight fairies and move to the music. Coach them as they move. Encourage them to get down near the flowers and to visit the animals. Have some children be animals and flowers, while the moonlight fairies move around them. Maybe the moonlight fairies sprinkle moondust on them and that becomes the dew in the morning. Encourage them to use their imaginations.

5. After this experience, have the children create an illustration of the moonlight fairies visiting the animals at night. Give them black paper and oil crayons or gray paper and regular crayons. Younger children can just paint a picture of what they think a moonlight fairy would look like.

6. For older children, have them write about "The night I woke up and found a moonlight fairy in my room." For younger children, create a group story on the same topic.

Language Development

1. With the older children, brainstorm about all the imaginary creatures that may come out at night. Have them write stories about them or just write a description. If they do not have writing skills, do it as a group and write the description on chart paper. Have them create illustrations to match the descriptions.

2. There are many other stories about the Sun and the Moon; for example, *Goodnight Moon, The Angry Moon* and many others. Tell or read them the stories and have the children compare and contrast them to this one.

Extensions

1. Have the children create simple puppets of Sun and Moon with paper plates and sticks. Have the children create conversations between Sun and Moon. Have the children use pre-cut yellow, red, orange, and purple construction paper for the sun and pre-cut whites and grays for the moon. You might give them several kinds of white paper for the moon, empha-

sizing the different textures such as napkins, paper towels, wallpaper, toilet paper, construction paper, or tissue paper.

2. Brainstorm all of the gifts we receive from the sun, such as how it helps things grow and gives us warmth. Talk about pollution and what we need to do to avoid air pollution and protect the gifts of the sun.

3. Create a song to greet the sun and/or a song to say goodnight to the sun and welcome the moon. Use a globe to show the children all the water in the world. Have the children write or tell stories about the sun and the moon and what it is like to be in the sky. What do they see? Can they see us every day? If there were a man in the moon, what would he say? If they were a woman or child in the moon, would they say something different?

4. Some excellent music to enhance movement for this experience:

   • *The Planets* by Gustav Holst
   • "Amazon Rain Forest" by Lori Diefenbacher, from *Nature Sings*
   • "Thumbelina" by Raffi, *Rise and Shine*
   • "Animalia" by The Banana Slug String Band, from *Adventures on the Air Cycle*
   • "Fantasy in Space" by Otto Leuning, *Sounds of New Music*, Folkways
   • *A Voyage Through His Greatest Hits*, Tomita Electronic music transcriptions of *The Planets, Pictures at an Exhibition*, "Pacific 231," *Firebird Suite*

5. Children can improvise "fairy music" on water glasses, triangles, xylophones, metallophones, or wind chimes.

STORY SUMMARY

I. Introduction

   A. Long ago Sun and Moon lived on the Earth.

      1. Everyday Sun would visit Water.

         a. Sun loved to visit Water.

         b. "Why don't you visit me?"

            1. "I'm too big," said Water.

            2. I'll build a second story to my house.

            3. I'll send a message through Wind, "Come and visit, come and visit."

II. Sun rushed home to Moon to build a bigger house.

   A. Asked Moon to help make house bigger.

      1. Moon agreed.

      2. Rat-a-tat-tat-tat-tat-tat

      3. They added bedrooms, another bathroom, a large playroom, a nice-size den.

   B. Sun suggested a feast for Water.

      1. They cooked and baked.

      2. Put out turkey, mashed potatoes, string beans, muffins, chocolate cookies, and lemonade.

      3. They sent the message, "Come and visit, come and visit," with Wind.

III. Water's visit

   A. Water bubbled over and knocked.

      1. Sun opened door, "Come on in."

      2. Water flowed in—bubbled, splashed, gurgled—filled first floor—had a wonderful time.

      3. Sun and Moon moved to second floor.

   B. Water's children flowed in:

      1. Fish, turtle, seahorse, octopus, whale, shark, and other sea animals flowed in.

         a. Fish in bathroom, turtle on waterbed, seahorse looked out window, octopus loved playroom (eight toys at once), whale got stuck, shark gave him a push.

         b. They filled up second floor.

         c. Sun and Moon moved up to roof.

    2. "Water, are you enjoying yourself?" asked Sun.

    3. "Yes, but can my friends come in?" asked Water.

C. Water's friends flowed in.

    1. In came shells, seaweed, rocks, pebbles, and bubbles.

    2. They flowed up the stairs, out the windows, up to the tree tops.

    3. Sun and Moon moved up to the sky.

D. Sun and Moon decide to stay in sky.

    1. They loved it so much in the sky that they gave Water the Earth.

GRANDMOTHER SPIDER SEWS THE WORLD TOGETHER
By Elizabeth Ellis

The Story

The Hopi Indians have lived in the desert in what they call the Blessed Way for many, many years. They tell wonderful stories that help people like you and like me understand the earth and its animals and people. The Hopi grandfathers tell us this story.

Our world is made up of two parts, the sky world and the earth world. I'll show you. Hold your hands together like this. Wiggle your fingers for the earth world. This is where man, women and children live. Now stop wiggling the earth world and start shaking the sky world. The sky world is where the spirits live.

One night, while the Hopis slept, the two worlds drifted apart. *[Use your hands to demonstrate. Listeners can do it with you.]* The sky world went up, up, up into the heavens. And when the men, women and children woke up, they began to cry.

"Our sky world is gone! What are we going to do?"

All the animals and the people met around the council fire. This is the Indian way to discuss and solve problems. Now what you must know is that at this time, the animals could speak and the people listened.

"What are we going to do?" asked a young Hopi boy.

Bear stood up and said *[use a deep bear voice, pound on your chest like Tarzan for added effect]* ,

"Do not worry, I

285

am the biggest and most powerful of all the animals here. I will hold the worlds together."

Bear dipped his paws into honey and could not resist a lick—m-m-m. He walked up to the highest mountain, climbed to the top and reached up and grabbed the sky world. *[Demonstrate with gestures.]* He brought it down to the earth and held it together with sticky honey.

"Look, I did it!"

Bear was so proud of himself, but he couldn't hold the worlds together, forever, and he got very, very HUNGRY. So he took a lick of the honey and whoosh, the sky world moved back into the heavens. *[Demonstrate with gestures.]* Bear decided that even the strongest animal couldn't HOLD the world together.

Back to the council fire. This time Coyote stood up and said,

"Bear, you may be big and powerful, but I am the cleverest of animals. I am COYOTEE-E-E. *[Have the listeners repeat, "Coyoteee."]* I will trick the sky world into coming back to the earth, just watch."

Coyote mixed a big vat of brown paint, gave all the people paint brushes and said *[gesture—pretend to throw paint brushes out to the audience so they can paint but make it clear that they cannot touch each other]* ,

"When I give the signal, everyone dip your brushes into the brown paint and paint the grass brown, the flowers brown, the bushes brown. It will look as if the earth is dying. Then, the sky world will look down and think that the whole earth is dying, and they will drift back down."

So Coyote gave the signal, and all the Hopis painted *[gesture painting with the audience painting, too]* the grass, the flowers, the trees, the bushes. The sky world looked down and saw that the earth was dying. Should they come back to the earth? But, just at that moment something happened. It does not rain very often in the desert, but it began to rain. *[Make sound of rain with hands on knees.]* It washed away all of the brown paint, and the sky world stayed up in the heavens.

Coyote decided that it was foolish to keep the worlds together with a trick.

The Hopi people were very sad. The efforts of Bear and Coyote had failed. Many men, women and children had ideas, but every one of them failed, too. They were just ready to give up when they heard a tiny, creaky voice coming from the tall grass.

"Let a woman spider do her work," the voice said. *[Use an old lady voice, with old body gestures to accompany it.]* It was Grandmother Spider!

They laughed at teeny, tiny Grandmother Spider, almost hidden in the tall grass. Powerful bear, clever Coyote and all of the Hopi people were not able to bring the worlds together. How could a teeny, tiny old spider do it?

"Stop laughing and follow me," she said.

They followed Grandmother Spider to the edge of the world and watched as she began to do what she does best. From deep in her heart, she began to spin her silkened thread. She pulled and she pulled and she pulled until she felt it was long enough to reach the sky world. She threw it up to the heavens. *[Use gestures. Pull out silken thread from your mouth and throw it up to heavens.]* But it fell short, and came back down. She was not ready to give up, she spun again and again and AGAIN. On her fourth try, the thread was very long for she had knotted all the pieces together. She threw it up into the sky world and this time it stuck! Everyone cheered!

Then she began her long journey from this world to that one. When she got there, she rested. *[Use your hand, your fingers representing her legs.]* She continued spinning and resting and spinning and resting until she had sewn the two worlds TOGETHER. *[Use hands again.]*

The grandfathers tell us that she didn't stop there, she continued sewing. She sewed the river in its course, the mountain in its place. It's very important to remember this and never to kill Grandmother Spider or damage any of her work. For it was Grandmother Spider's work that holds the worlds together.

(Elizabeth Ellis of Dallas, Texas, adapted the traditional character of Grandmother Spider to create this story. This story has been adopted for young children from Elizabeth Ellis's original version.)

Key Concepts and Themes and/or Universal Ideas

This is another story that tries to explain the ways of the Earth, its people and its animals and how they all get along together. Spiders are very important in both Native American and African folklore. One main idea of the story is that it is not always the biggest or the most clever creatures that have all the answers. Sometimes someone who is small but very old and wise can solve the most difficult of problems. We should not laugh at someone else's suggestion for it may be the best idea. You also may want to remind the children of how each animal got a chance to try to solve the problem and that there are many ways to solve a problem. The children need to be reminded that if one solution does not work, they should try again and that they should remember to seek help from others.

Suggested Companion(s)

a spider and its undisturbed spider web outdoors or a picture of one

a spider puppet

a photograph of the Hopi mesa showing the sky and the earth coming together

Preparation

Ask the children if they ever think about where the sky begins and the Earth ends. Ask the children if they know what a *mesa* is. A mesa is a high plateau with steep sides. It looks like a large hill that is flat on the top with sides that go almost straight up and down. Show the children a picture if you can and tell them that many Hopis live on a mesa in Arizona. Show them the Hopi reservation on the map.

Preparation for Visualization

Tell the Children:

Before hearing the story close your eyes and pretend that you are standing on a mesa and a cloud comes along. You think to yourself what a soft and fluffy cloud this is. It would be fun to crawl up into it and take a nap. So you crawl up into the cloud and it folds gently around your body feeling cuddly and cozy like a big, damp quilt. You look at the beautiful blue sky around you and slowly close your eyes and begin to fall asleep. As you are sleeping and dreaming about the beautiful Earth with all your wonderful animal friends and the great forests and the giant cactus, the cloud just floats along. You sleep for a very long time. When you awaken, you stretch your arms and open your eyes and nestle up into the cloud and you begin to look over the side. The mesa is very far away. You cry and cry. What are you going to do? How are you going to get back? All of a sudden you see a spider coming down along side of you. You tell the spider your problem and the spider says, "Well, maybe I can help you." You begin to laugh, saying, "How can you help me?" and the spider says, "Don't you laugh at me. Won't you feel silly when I solve your problem?" So you wait and see what the spider is going to do to bring you back to the mesa. Now open your eyes and listen to a story about a very wise old grandmother spider.

Listen to the Story

Follow-up Discussion Questions

1. What did you think of the story?
2. Why do you think the Bear's idea did not work?
3. What was wrong with Coyote's idea?

4. What did you think when they laughed at Grandmother Spider?

5. Do you have a grandmother? Is she very wise? Tell us about some of the things she can do.

6. Have you ever seen a spider web? What do spiders do with their webs?

7. Do spiders catch things to eat, like flies, in their webs?

ACTIVITY ONE: CLEVER SPIDERS IN THE SKY

Objectives

—To develop creative thinking skills

—To develop fluency of ideas

—To develop oral communication skills

—To develop fine motor skills

—To develop the ability to follow directions

—To develop ability to think of rhyming words

Introduction

The students are going to brainstorm different ideas for ways that spiders can use their webs and spinning ability to help people and animals. These do not have to be realistic. They can be fanciful and imaginative. They are going to create their own spider, a spider poem, and a weaving.

Materials

black paper cut into circles or ovals and long black strips

9″ × 12″ black paper and strips of color paper for a paper weaving

the Spider Poem worksheet

writing materials

drawing materials

paste or glue

white crayons or Cray-Pas®

scrap materials, buttons, ribbons, white cotton, odds and ends

Procedure

1. Tell the children about Little Miss Muffet who sat on her tuffet and ask them if she should have been afraid of the spider. Ask the children to think of all the different things that spiders could weave and all the different ways they could use their webs to help animals and people. Tell

them to think of as many ideas as possible so that they can convince Miss Muffet not to be afraid of spiders and show her how valuable they are. Save the ideas for the poems.

2. Have the children cut out or give them pre-cut black circles and have them paste or glue the long strips of black paper on the circle to create spider legs. Give each child four long strips that can be pasted across the spider's body and come down on each side to form two legs each. Give the children white crayons and scrap materials to decorate the spider. If the children are older, you might suggest they try to make the spider look like a wise old grandmother.

3. After the children have created the spiders, go back to their original ideas and as a class create several two-line poems (couplets) about the spiders. Have them try to think of rhyming words and make the poems rhyme if they can. For example:

> Spiders aren't big and tall,
> But spiders can help us all.

4. After there are several poems on the board or on chart paper, have the children pick the one they like best and write it on their Spider Poem worksheet. If they need help, write it with them. Display their spiders and their poems on the wall or bulletin board.

5. Tell the children they are going to learn how to weave like spiders. First and second graders can prepare the paper themselves. Younger children will need help or you can have it pre-cut. Fold a 9″ × 12″ piece of black paper in half and cut strips on the fold to about 1 inch from the end of the paper. Open the paper and show the children how to take the colored strips and weave them under and over the black strips. Remember to show them how to alternate each strip. Display their weavings with their spiders and their poems.

Language Development

1. Have the children create a group story about another way that Grandmother Spider used her skills to help someone with her weaving.

2. Tell or read children other spider stories from Native American folklore and from the Ashanti in Africa where Anansi the spider originated.

3. Have the children tell a story about older people or grandmothers who can sew.

Extensions

1. Have the children do an illustration of the story. Encourage them to make the sky come to the earth and to use the whole space for their illustration.

2. Have the children create a dance of the spiders as they celebrate Grandmother Spider's accomplishments.

ACTIVITY TWO: EARTHLY ANIMAL HELPERS

Objectives

—To develop oral communication skills
—To develop fine motor skills
—To develop sequencing skills
—To develop imagination

Introduction

Talk to the children about why animals are important in the world. Besides being fun to look at and to have for pets they are an important part of the world. Focus on some of the simpler concepts about how animals help us. You may talk about the fact that we eat animals and that some people feel that we should protect them and respect them, not eat them. Tell them that these people usually only eat vegetables, whole grains and rice, nuts, and beans. They also eat dairy products because the milk, cheese, and butter can come from the animals without hurting them. Some of the same people believe that we should not wear leather or fur clothing because in order to make the clothes or shoes the animal has to die. Ask the children what they think about this idea. You may also want to talk about the meaning of endangered species and why it is important to protect these animals. The children need to know that animals are an important part of our environment, and that we need to care for them and respect them as our friends, not something we can destroy without thought. The children need to know that traditionally Native Americans have great respect for animals and the natural environment and that they perceive the animals as their brothers and sisters.

The activities will focus on some of the things that we get from animals. Depending on their age, the children will create the animals and, as a group or as individuals, create stories about them.

Materials

writing materials
markers or crayons
18″ × 24″ drawing paper or manila paper
scrap materials
paste and glue
small paper bags for puppets

Procedure

1. Talk with the children about the different animals that help us. Here is a list to start with: bees, horses, dogs, cats, sheep, cows, and beavers. Ask the children what these animals give us. The bees make honey, horses carry us, dogs and cats are our friends, sheep give us wool, cows give us milk, and beavers build dams. Ask them if they can think of any others. Show them pictures of other animals and ask them what they might do.

2. Have the children sit in a circle and tell a story in a round. Tell them just as in the story about Grandmother Spider, they are going to create a story about how other animals are smart and helpful. You can start the story like this,

    > Once upon a time there was nothing sweet to eat and people became very bored with their food, so the bees had an idea.

    For younger children just have them sit around you and volunteer ideas and help you with the story.

3. Try this with the different animals. For the younger children, have them draw a picture for one of the stories. For the older children, have them fold their paper into four parts and draw four parts of the story showing what the animal can do. Have them use their picture and retell the story.

Language Development

1. Make a bulletin board with these animals on it. Have the children go home and bring in samples of wool, labels from milk products, labels from products that have honey. Put them on the board.

2. Have the children make paper bag puppets of the bear, the coyote and the spider; and have them reenact the story. Have the older children come up with other environmental problems that Grandmother Spider might solve and have them create a new story.

3. Talk about how in some families the grandmother is very important because she helps take care of the whole family and she holds the whole family together.

Extensions

1. Tell the children that the Sky and the Earth were so grateful to Grandmother Spider for holding them together that they gave her many gifts. What gifts do you think Grandmother Spider would like to receive from the Earth or the Sun? Have the children create gifts for Grandmother Spider.

2. The spiders need a home to dance in so the students can create a web by arranging themselves randomly in an open space. One student begins by holding a ball of yarn or string. She throws it to another "spider" across the space while holding on to her part of the web. This continues until all children have held a part of the web. Music can be played as the web is created. When the students have completed the web, they can move the web "up" and "down" to the music (side to side works well also). How did the shapes change as the web moved? Children can move the web to the music of Little Richard's "Itsy Bitsy Spider" from the recording *For Our Children* by Disney Productions. Continued experiences in movement could extend at another time to include moving like spiders. Discuss the qualities of a spider's movement as it creates a web, as it walks, as it begins to hide, and so on.

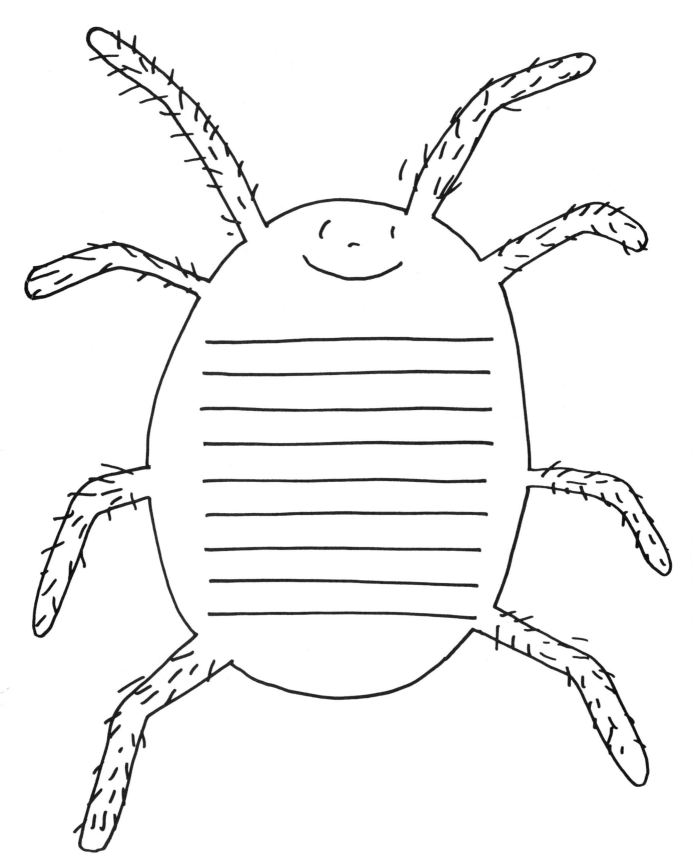

Activity One, Procedure #4

EARTH, WIND, SUN, MOON, AND STARS: ADDITIONAL STORIES

 Earth Namer, a California Indian myth retold by Margery Bernstein and Janet Kobrin, illustrated by Ed Heffernan. Charles Scribner and Sons, New York, 1974.

This is a children's version of a Maidu Indian legend about how Earth Namer made the world. In the beginning there was only water and turtle was the only living thing. Earth Namer came along and with his special magic he created and named everything in our world.

Suggested Activities

For young children put a huge circle on the bulletin board to represent the Earth. Have the children tell you all the things that they know come from the Earth. Write them on the circle. Have the children draw some of these things and add them to the Earth. For older children have them do the same thing but on their own circle, each child writing whatever words they can with your help. Give each child a rock, a personal piece of the Earth to take care of. Have them look at it carefully, describe it, make up a story about it, and give it a special name. Talk with the children about all the wonderful things that we get from the Earth. Have the children talk about and possibly write all the ways we can take care of the Earth because it gives us so much.

 "The Story of Stories," from *Legends of Earth, Air, Fire, and Water,* by Eric and Tessa Hadley, illustrations by Bryna Waldman. Cambridge University Press, Cambridge, 1985.

A young Indian hunter comes upon a large talking stone. "Shall I tell you stories?" the stone asks. The stone tells the stories of what happened a long time ago before man lived on the Earth. The young hunter tells the stories to his family. Everyday he listens to the stories and every evening he shares the stories around the fire. This is how the Seneca Indians gained knowledge of the world and passed it on to us.

Suggested Activities

This story provides another opportunity for the students to talk about what the Earth gives us. Talk about the Earth in relation to the five senses. What are the sounds of the earth? Think of the words that describe the sounds. What are water sounds, winter sounds, fire sounds, tornado sounds, animal sounds, and wind sounds? Can the children make up a song about the sounds of the Earth? Continue with the colors of the Earth, the smells of the Earth, and so on. For the colors, have the children create different plants and other parts of the Earth. Put them on the bulletin board inside one large Earth. Bring plants from the outside so children can smell the Earth. Have them brainstorm Earth words and put them on file cards so the children can use them for stories. One child can be the stone and tell the others a made-up story about the Earth. Have the children write a story by the stone about how trees came to be, how fish came to be, and how mountains came to be.

 The Northwind and Sun by La Fontaine, illustrations by Brian Wildsmith. Oxford Press, New York, 1987.

This is the well-known fable of the North Wind's challenge to the Sun. "See the man with his beautiful new cloak. We'll see which one of us can get him to take it off." The strength of the blustery wind does not work, but the gentle rays of the warm Sun cause the man to remove his cloak and clothes and swim the river.

Suggested Activities

Have the children name all the wonderful things the Sun does for us. Create a dance to the Sun. Have the children role play what it is like to wake up in the morning and feel the sun. How does it feel? How would it feel if you were a flower or a tree? Can the Sun hurt us? How? Have the children write thank-you letters to the Sun. Have the children create a picture of what flies through the air when the wind blows. Have them label all the objects in the picture. Have the children pretend the wind is blowing them across the room and create a wind dance. Some children can role play the wind blowing the others across the room.

Other Stories

Goodnight Moon by Margaret Wise Brown, illustrations by Clement Hurd. Harper and Row, New York, 1947, 1975.

The Goodnight Circle by Carolyn Lesser, illustrations by Lorinda Bryan Cauley. Harcourt Brace Jovanovich, Publishers, New York, 1987.

The Angry Moon retold by William Sleator, illustrations by Blair Lent. Little Brown, and Company, Boston, 1970.

The Star Cleaners Reunion by Cooper Edens. The Green Tiger Press, La Jolla, California, 1979.

 Spider Weaver from Little One Inch and Other Japanese Children's Favorite Stories by Florence Sadake. Charles E. Tuttle, Vermont, 1958.

Moongames by Frank Asch. Scholastic Inc., New York, 1984.

 Papa, Please Get the Moon for Me by Eric Carle. Scholastic Inc., New York, 1990.

14 Food

HAMBURGER, HAMBURGER ON A BUN
By Annette Harrison

About the Story

This is a story about a very nice little girl named Ruthie who only liked to eat hamburgers on a bun. She would eat different buns and would add ketchup; but she would not eat anything else. Her mother and father tried everything they could to encourage Ruthie to eat different foods; but she refused. Even her friends tried to encourage Ruthie to eat some different foods, but she refused. One beautiful fall day Dad decided to take the family apple picking and off they went to the orchards. Some of Ruthie's friends were there with their families and everyone was having a great time. Ruthie's Mom got an idea. As Ruthie opened her mouth very wide to tell her Mom how much fun she was having, Mom put an apple in Ruthie's mouth. In order for Ruthie to close her mouth she had to bite down on the apple. Ruthie was surprised because the apple was so good. After that Ruthie was willing to try the food in the picnic basket and she liked it all. After that day Ruthie ate everything but one kind of food. Guess what that was?

Key Concepts and Themes and/or Universal Ideas

The main idea is that we need to try different kinds of foods and should not reject any food without trying it. The story encourages children to be adventurous with food and to try everything. The activities will all focus on different foods and menus. Have some picnics with your children.

Suggested Companion(s)

a toy hamburger or a McDonalds bag with a hamburger container

Preparation

Ask the students if they have a favorite food. Ask them to tell what that food is. Ask them if they eat it often.

Preparation for Visualization

Tell the Children:

> Before we hear the story, we are going to take an imaginary trip. Close your eyes. Think very hard of your favorite foods. Are hamburgers your favorite foods? Chocolate chip cookies? Ice cream? Fried chicken? Watermelon? Spaghetti? Pizza? Can you smell them? Can you taste them? It is your birthday and your Mom has made all your favorite foods. Just lick your lips and imagine what it all tastes like. Take a taste of each one. Chew it slowly. Isn't it delicious? Don't eat too much and get a tummy ache. The party is over and you give your Mom a great big hug for making all of your favorite foods. Now open your eyes and I'm going to tell you a story about a little girl who loved hamburgers.

Listen to the Story (Tape 2, Side B)

Follow-Up Discussion Questions

1. What happened in the story?
2. Why do you think Ruthie didn't like anything but hamburgers?
3. What is your favorite food?
4. Do you want to eat it all the time?
5. Do you ever get tired of it?
6. What happens when your Mom asks you to try new foods?
7. Do you try them? If you don't want to, what happens?
8. Has anyone ever asked you to try something that you thought you wouldn't like and then you were surprised?
9. What would be your favorite dinner or lunch? If your Mom asked you what you would like for your favorite dinner or lunch, what would you tell her?
10. How do you think you could get Ruthie to like some new foods?

ACTIVITY ONE: A SPECIAL MEAL FOR RUTHIE

Objectives

—To develop language skills
—To develop planning and organization skills
—To develop the ability to compare and contrast
—To develop knowledge about healthful eating habits
—To develop classification skills

Introduction

This is an activity that allows the children to talk about different foods that they like and to explore some foods that they think Ruthie might like. The activity introduces the students to some simple menu planning with foods that could be part of a healthy diet. The children first select a menu for Ruthie, using the Menu Planner worksheet. You can then follow up the idea by making another one with the class. There are several other activities that involve the students with food in ways that might help to encourage Ruthie or any other child to try different foods. This activity has two parts, Menu Planning and a Food Magazine.

Materials

Menu Planner worksheet
food magazines
markers or crayons
empty boxes for sorting foods
grocery store learning center with play food
12″ × 18″ or 9″ × 12″ drawing paper
scissors
paste

Procedure

Part One

1. After the discussion talk with the children about planning a special meal for Ruthie that she would like. If the children are old enough, have them do the Menu Planner worksheet alone. If they are too young, give each child a separate sheet, go over each item as a group and then ask them to circle or mark one food item in each column that they think Ruthie would

like. For color association and identification, you may want the students to color in the appropriate colors for each food.

2. Once the children have made their selection and colored the food to be as appetizing as possible, select a child to be Ruthie. Select another child to convince Ruthie that the menu they planned is really delicious and that Ruthie would like it. If the children have cutting skills, have them cut out the foods they selected and paste them on a large circle to represent a plate. They can then present the meal to Ruthie as it might appear on a plate. Continue this activity until the children lose interest or do a few on different days. Always choose different children to play Ruthie. If the child refuses the new meal he (Ronald instead of Ruthie) or she will sing, "Hamburger, hamburger on a bun, the only food that is any fun."

Part Two

1. Bring in many food magazines. Go through the magazines with the children and have them pick out their favorite foods. Have them paste them on a paper plate. For older children, have them identify different foods and put the names on cards for the children. Leave room for the children to draw a picture of the food on the card if they choose. Children will keep their own favorite food card deck to use later in writing a story about their own favorite food.

2. Have the children tear out pictures of their favorite foods in order to make a class food magazine for Ruthie. Have them brainstorm different names for the book such as Ruthie's Food Fantasies, or Foods for Ruthie, or whatever comes up. Talk about the different food groups or different kinds of foods and make a 12″ × 18″ page for each group. For example: meats, fish, poultry, pasta, fruits, vegetables, breads, drinks, desserts, and so on.

3. After the children have torn out the foods of their choice, have them paste them on the appropriate page. Put the name and a picture sample on each page. Help them find the correct page. Have those children who can write, label the foods.

4. Have the children decorate a front and back cover and some inside pages for the book, such as a page dedicated to Ruthie or illustrated pages from the story. Put the magazine together.

5. The children can tell the story and share the food magazine with another class.

Language Development

1. Make another menu planner on big chart paper. Have the children fill in their favorite foods and then plan menus that they can take home to their family.

2. Set up a grocery store learning center and have the children buy food that they think Ruthie would like, and then prepare a meal and invite her for dinner.

3. Create a set of boxes that match the categories on the menu planner. Cut up the menu planner, mix up the items and have the students sort the pieces into the appropriate boxes. Add foods if you wish to extend the experience.

4. Create songs or sing different songs about food. Play the song "Food, Glorious Food" from the musical *Oliver* for the children.

Extensions

1. Create clay foods and have children create a meal out of clay. Display the different meals.

2. Have the children design placemats for their clay meals.

3. Take the children apple picking for a field trip.

4. Bring in a different food for them to taste every day for a week or have parents bring in their child's favorite food and have a food-tasting banquet.

5. Read or tell the story *Cloudy with a Chance of Meatballs* to the class. Talk about what it would be like to live in the town of Chewandswallow. Talk about what Ruthie would do if she lived in the town of Chewandswallow.

6. For older children, you can do an activity called "You Are What You Eat" and they can draw a picture of themselves out of their favorite foods. For example, pizza heads, chicken legs, spaghetti arms, chocolate chip cookies, ice cream, etc.

7. Create a restaurant learning center, complete with menus the children have made. Use file folders filled with magazine pictures of food to use for food. Children can put the pictures on paper plates and serve the food. Scrap pieces of paper stapled together can serve as waitress/waiter pads and paper money can also be used.

ACTIVITY TWO: MEALS FOR MONSTERS

Objectives

—To develop creative thinking skills
—To develop imaginative use of language

Introduction

This activity emphasizes the students' imaginative play with food planning and actual cooking. The first lesson encourages children to explore and think about healthy foods that provide well-balanced meals. This lesson allows them to be more playful.

Materials

muffin mix
mixing bowls
muffin tins (large)
spray oil
mixing spoons
fresh or frozen berries or other fruit that is cut into small pieces

Procedure

1. Brainstorm with the students about different kinds of monsters from the books they have read, stories they have heard ("The Loom Pa Pas" or "The Giant Caterpillar" from Chapter 9) or monsters they have made up. Tell them that monsters get very, very hungry and that they are going to plan monster menus and make something for monsters to eat. This cooking activity is fairly simple and allows the children to use some creativity.

2. Tell the students they are going to make Monster Muffins. Ask them what they think they might be. Show them the muffin tins and the mix and talk about the fruits. If possible, take a field trip to the grocery store to buy the ingredients.

3. Tell the children they are going to use the muffin mix and add whatever fruit they want to make delicious Monster Muffins. Buy fresh or frozen blueberries, strawberries, blackberries, or whatever other berries are available. You can also mash in bananas, finely cut-up apples, peaches. Let the children pick two fruits to mix into their muffins. Have the students work in teams of three or four, taking turns mixing the batter. Make sure to dry the fruit and don't let them put in too many fruits, otherwise the muffins won't hold together.

4. While the muffins are baking, brainstorm with the children and have them make up names for the muffins. For example, older children can try to make up names that start with the same letter, Mysterious Monster Muffins or Delicious Dessert for the Dangerous and Daring. Younger children may want to make up nonsense words for the muffins such as Moogoo Muffins or whatever comes to their minds.

5. Older children can create an ad to sell the muffins to monsters. The best way to do this would be as a class on chart paper. The children can draw their own versions of the muffins and then can be pasted to the large ad. They can all decorate the ad once you have recorded the words that they come up with.

6. Have the children tell you what they would tell the monster to convince him or her to eat the muffins. You or someone else may dress up and play the role of the monster.

7. Don't forget to serve the muffins to the children.

Language Development

1. Talk about different monsters or creatures from other stories. Ask the children what they think they might want to eat. Ask them to imagine some possible meals and to create a monster stew. Bring in a huge pot with a huge spoon. Have the students tell you what should be put into the stew such as toad tails, snails, frogs, flies, and made up foods like mashed moogies, or squashed squiggles, etc. Children can then draw a picture of the stew if you wish. Make up a song about the stew to get the monster's interest.

2. Have children make up monster hamburgers like "Dagwood" sandwiches. Cut out a huge bun and piece of hamburger and paste it on the bottom of a large piece of paper. Tell the children that they are going to try and create the world's largest hamburger. Have children tell you what to add to the hamburger. Have them tear or cut some of the ingredients out of paper and add details if they can. Otherwise help them with this part of the activity. Add each ingredient as they tell you and write the name of the ingredient next to it. Some suggestions might be lettuce, tomatoes, cucumbers, mushrooms, green peppers, olives, cheese, and so on.

3. Have the older children create a story in

the round about the monster who wouldn't eat and was losing all his powers and how they got him to eat.

Extensions

1. For older children, have them create their own restaurant that would serve monster food.
2. Have children create a monster pizza. Cut out a huge circle of paper for about every four children. Have them tear food pictures out of magazines to create monster pizzas. Have them tell the rest of the class about the pizzas.
3. Have the children create songs about monster food.
4. A pre-arranged tour to a fast food hamburger restaurant would be a fun field trip for the children. The children can try and figure out how many hamburgers monsters can eat, how many sodas they can drink, and so on.

STORY SUMMARY

I. Introduction

    A. Ruthie, who lived with her mother and father, was a wonderful child.

        1. She'd clean up her toys.

        2. She'd help Dad soap up, rinse and shine the car.

        3. She'd go right to bed.

        4. She'd help set table, share toys, etc.

    B. But, Ruthie had a problem.

        1. All she would eat was Hamburger on a Bun.

        2. If other food was put in front of her, she'd shake her head 'til her curls wiggled and jiggled and she'd sing: "Hamburger, Hamburger on a Bun, the only food that's any fun!"

II. A. Her parents worried.

        1. She wasn't eating chicken or fish.

        2. At least she ate ketchup with her hamburger.

        3. She changed her roll everyday.
           Monday–sesame, Tuesday–poppyseed, Wednesday–whole wheat, Thursday–sourdough, Friday–pumpernickel, Saturday–five grain, Sunday–a regular hamburger roll.

    B. Parents tried to solve the problem.

        1. Mother surprised her with seven-layer cake with chocolate icing.

           a. She shook her head until her curls wiggled and jiggled.

           b. And sang–refrain ("Hamburger, etc.").

        2. Parents tried every kind of food–same response.

        3. They invited Ruthie's friends over.

           a. Called them on the phone: Come on Sunday. Bring your favorite food.

           b. Friends came on Sunday and offered food.

           c. Every time, she sang "Hamburger, etc."

           d. She would not try any of the food.

III. Solving the problem

    A. Beautiful fall day

        1. Dad suggested apple picking.

           a. He packed up car.

    b. They took picnic lunch.

    c. They went off to Eckert's Orchard.

2. Picking apples

    a. Ruthie said, "Mom, this is FUN!"

    b. Mom asks her to repeat and pops an apple in her mouth.

    c. Ruthie tastes it, M-M-M-M.

    d. Dad says, "Ruthie, I'm glad you like apples, just wait until you taste the food in the picnic basket."

3. Ruthie tastes all the food in the picnic basket.

    a. Fried chicken, M-M-M, corn, M-M-M, pickles, M-M-M, etc.

4. From that day on, Ruthie tasted every thing that was put in front of her; but never again did she eat HAMBURGER ON A BUN!

Plan A Meal For Ruthie!

Fruits   Vegetables   Desserts   Drinks

Activity One, Procedure, Part One #1

THE WIDE MOUTH FROG
Adapted by Perrin Stifel from an Old American Folktale

The Story

Once there was a little Wide Mouth Frog. He lived with his family near a babbling brook. He was a curious little frog, always asking questions. One day he said to Mother Frog,

"Mama, what do other animals feed their babies?" *[Said with exaggerated wide mouth.]*

"That's a very good question, my little one, you are really growing up," said Mother Frog. "Why don't you go to the other mother animals and ask for yourself."

"That's a good idea, Mama," said the little Wide Mouth Frog. *[Use wide mouth each time he speaks.]*

Hippity-Hoppity-Hop-Hop-Hoo, Baby Frog has something to do! *[Use hands on knees to hop in rhythm with words.]*

So Baby Frog crossed the brook and followed the path into the forest. Soon he came to a small clearing. There was Mother Deer. He hopped up to her and said, "Mrs. Deer, what do you feed your babies?"

She answered, "Why, I feed my babies berries and leaves off the trees."

"That's very interesting!" said Baby Frog. "Berries and leaves. I'm a Wide Mouth Frog! Goodbye, Mrs. Deer, thank you!"

Hippity-Hoppity-Hop-Hop-Hoo! Baby Frog has something to do! *[Hands on knees to keep rhythm.]*

Baby Frog hopped away, getting deeper and deeper into the

forest, until he came to a cave. Inside the cave was Mrs. Bear playing with her baby cubs. He looked up at Mama Bear and asked, "Mrs. Bear, what do you feed your babies?"

Mrs. Bear answered, "My baby bears eat honey from the bees and fish from the stream." *[You can create a bear voice.]*

"Oh, that's very interesting! Honey and fish. I'm a Wide Mouth Frog! Thank you, Mrs. Bear. Goodbye!" said Little Frog.

Hippity-Hoppity-Hop-Hop-Hoo! Baby Frog has something to do.

Baby Frog hopped deeper and deeper and DEEPER into the forest. He came to a big river by the swamp. He stopped to play for a while and he sang *[Sung to the tune of "All Around the Mulberry Bush." Have the children join in.]* :

> Baby Deer eat berries and leaves,
> Berries and leaves, berries and leaves.
> Baby Deer eat berries and leaves
> All day long.
>
> Baby Bears eat honey and fish,
> Honey and fish, honey and fish.
> Baby Bears eat honey and fish
> All day long.

He looked up and he was staring into the eyes of Mother Alligator. *[Speak slowly for dramatic effect.]*

"Hello, Mrs. Alligator, I would like to know what you feed your babies," asked Little Frog.

"That's a very good question, little fellow. I feed my babies Wide Mouth Frogs." *[Gesture the alligator's mouth with arms attached at elbows, moving arms out and in.]*

"Wide Mouth Frogs? Oh!" *[exaggerate the smallness of your mouth and speak small and funny]* said Baby Frog making his mouth appear as small as possible. "If I find any Wide Mouth Frogs, I'll let you know! Bye bye!"

He hopped as fast as he could past the river, past the cave, through the forest and back to the babbling brook, where Mama Frog was waiting for him. *[Use hands on knees to hop, getting faster and faster.]* Now, the little Wide Mouth Frog was safe and happy. *[Have children join in singing.]*

> Alligators eat Wide Mouth Frogs,
> Wide Mouth Frogs, Wide Mouth Frogs.
> Alligators eat Wide Mouth Frogs
> ALL DAY LONG.

Key Concepts and Themes and/or Universal Ideas

The two important concepts in this story have to do with curiosity or finding things out for oneself and what animals eat. Students need to know that it is important to ask questions and to be curious. The boys and girls can also do a survey to find out what people like to eat and what other animals eat.

Suggested Companion(s)

a frog or a mother and baby animal of any kind

Preparation

Ask the children if they are curious. Ask them if they like to ask questions. What kinds of things do they want to know about?

Preparation for Visualization

Tell the Children:

Before hearing the story we are going to close our eyes and pretend that we are in the woods on a lovely day. The sun is shining and you are walking along looking at everything. The leaves and twigs are crunching under your feet. Crunch! Crunch! Crunch! The wind is gently blowing through the trees. All of a sudden a big bird swoops down past you, scoops something up from the ground and flys back up into the trees. You wonder what she is doing. Suddenly, you see the bird do it again and this time you see a huge worm hanging from her mouth. This time you see a nest in the tree and hear little chirps. Chirp! Chirp! Chirp! You see the big bird drop the worm into the little bird's mouth. You begin to wonder. Is it lunch time in the woods? You continue to walk along and you see a squirrel scurrying by. His tail almost brushes against your leg. As you watch the squirrel, you see him stop and hold some nuts in his paws and chomp away. He must be having lunch, too. Along comes a rabbit and you decide to follow him and see what he's having for lunch. You hope you don't have to follow him down a hole like *Alice in Wonderland*. Off you go hopping down the trail following the little rabbit. You can barely keep up and you are getting out of breath. Suddenly the rabbit crawls under some bushes and without even thinking you follow him. We can't even see you anymore. I wonder what you found? Now open your eyes and listen to a story about "The Wide Mouth Frog" who was also very curious.

Listen to the Story

Follow-up Discussion Questions

1. What did you think was going to happen to the frog when he met the alligator?
2. Do you think it is all right to be curious and ask questions?
3. Do you ask a lot of questions?
4. What kinds of things can you find out by asking questions?
5. Do you ever wonder what animals eat?
6. Do you have a pet? What does it eat?

ACTIVITY ONE: WHAT DO ANIMALS EAT?

Objectives

- —To encourage students to ask questions
- —To develop oral communication skills
- —To begin to introduce research skills to children
- —To develop classification skills

Introduction

The purpose of this activity is to encourage children to be curious and ask questions and to find out what kinds of foods animals eat. Bring in several books about animals to read to the children and for the children to look at.

Materials

animal books
writing materials
markers and drawing paper

Procedure

1. Review the story with the children. Ask them to tell you what deer eat, what bears eat, what alligators eat. Ask the children if they wonder what other animals eat.
2. Ask them to name an animal and then have the class guess what they think they eat. Use chart paper or the board and record the animal's name with guesses. Do this with several animals.

3. Then have the children sit around you and look through the books in order to find out what the animals actually eat. See how many of their guesses are correct. Depending on where you are located, you can also have someone from the zoo or a local farm or university come into the class to make a presentation.

4. For children who are capable of writing, have them draw a picture of the animals eating and write about them.

5. For younger children, have them use the stuffed animals in the class and have an animal picnic or feeding time at the zoo or on the farm.

6. If it is possible, take the children to the zoo during feeding time.

Language Development

1. Use the same list of animals. Put two categories on the board.

   • ANIMALS THAT EAT MEAT AND FISH
   • ANIMALS THAT ARE VEGETARIANS

   For older children, ask the children to tell you which column the animals will go under. Remind them that some animals will fit under both headings.

2. What would the animals do if no food came to the zoo? Have the children brainstorm ideas. Make up some group stories about some of the ideas.

Extensions

Ask the children, "What do you think a Wide Mouth Frog looks like?" Draw a picture of a Wide Mouth Frog. Put the children in groups and have them create a sequence of pictures to tell the story. Picture one would include the Wide Mouth Frog and his mom. Picture two would include the Wide Mouth Frog and the deer. Picture three would be the Wide Mouth Frog and the bear. Picture four would be the Wide Mouth Frog and the alligator. Ask them how picture four would be different from the first three. To extend the story, after the children have more information about what animals eat, ask the children whom else the Wide Mouth Frog might meet. Add some of these scenes to the story. Do as many as you want. After the pictures are completed, have the children use them to tell the story.

ACTIVITY TWO: A SURVEY

Objectives

—To encourage students to ask questions
—To develop oral communication skills
—To begin to introduce research skills to children
—To develop classification skills

Introduction

The purpose of this activity is to introduce the children to how to do a survey to find out what people might like to eat.

Materials

Food Survey worksheet

Procedure

1. Tell the children that if they were to open a new restaurant near the school, they would have to find out a few things. If you are working with older children, ask them what they might need to know. For younger children, tell them that they would have to find out what people like to eat. Ask them what they think kids like to eat.

2. Make a list such as pizza, hamburgers, hot dogs, ice cream, and peanut butter and jelly. Put the list on a piece of paper and make copies for each child or use the worksheet that is included with these materials. You can always add food to the worksheet list.

3. Have the children check off their favorite food and then those of the other children in the class. Show the children how to make a slash mark next to the name of the food when someone tells them their choice. If the children can handle it, have them take the survey home and find out what their family likes to eat.

4. Make arrangements with another teacher to have your children use the survey with her or his class.

5. Make a large replica of the survey on chart paper. Have the children come up and put their results on the chart. Help them if they can't count or write their numbers.

6. Based on the outcomes of the survey, discuss what foods would be served in the new restaurant.

7. Young children can play restaurant and create the new restaurant. Older children can create menus for the new restaurant and decorate them with pictures of the foods they are going to serve.

Language Development

1. Have the children create a bug menu for frogs. They can also create make-believe bugs and give them names. Display the illustrations as The Wide Mouth Frog Grocery Store.

2. Have the children create a story about how Wide Mouth Frogs escape alligators.

Extensions

1. Have the children use the stuffed animals in the classroom and do a survey to find out what they would like to eat.
2. The children can create an ad to sell their bugs to the Wide Mouth Frogs.

Food Survey

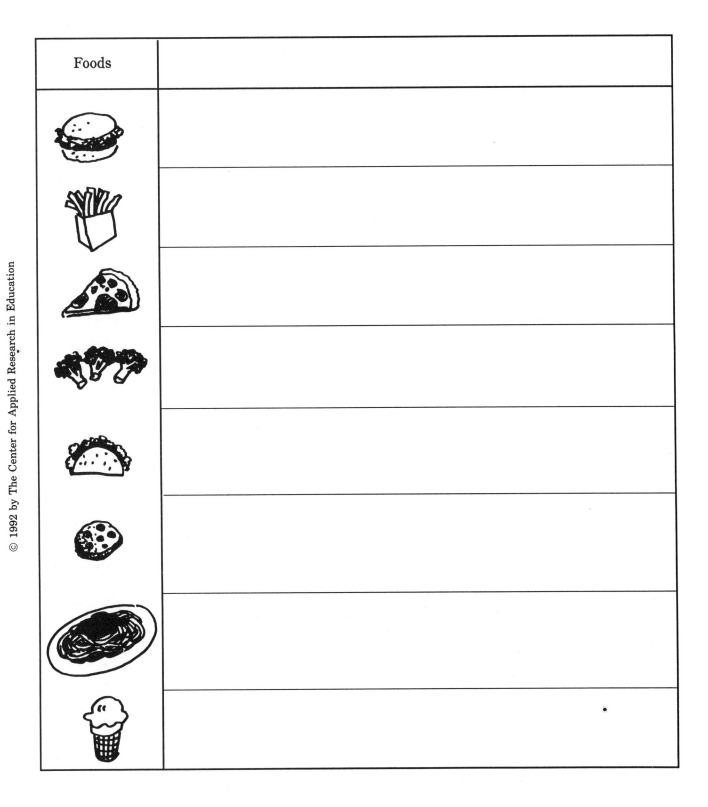

Foods	

Activity Two, Procedure #2

FOOD: ADDITIONAL STORIES

 Stone Soup written and illustrated by Marcia Brown. Scribners-Atheneum, New York, 1947.

Three soldiers come into a French village of peasants. The soldiers are hungry, but no one offers them food. The soldiers show them how to make stone soup and how to cooperate.

Suggested Activities

This is a favorite story. Children can tell their own stories about when they help their mothers, fathers, or grandmothers make their favorite foods. Write recipes for stews. Create recipes for seasonal soups, seasonal foods. Have the children dictate the recipes as a group. Have the children write new recipes for desserts and/or salads. Make a class recipe book for the children to take home. Have the children illustrate the book.

 The Little Red House, adapted by Annette Harrison from *A Dash of Seasoning,* a cassette tape.

A young boy sets out on an adventure to find "a little red house, without a door, with a star inside." He travels over the land, past the farm and up the hill. Much to his surprise, he discovers what he is looking for is a BIG, RED, JUICY APPLE!

Suggested Activities

List different attributes of foods and see if the children can guess which food is which; for example, cold, sweet and round. Sit in a circle and pass a food around and have each child add a new word to describe it. For example, an orange: round, juicy, hard outside, orange, soft inside, pulp, bumpy, seeds, and so on. Write down all the words. Have children talk about their favorite foods.

Other Stories

> *Cloudy with a Chance of Meatballs* written by Judi Barrett and illustrated by Ron Barrett. Atheneum, McClelland and Stewart, Ltd., Canada, 1978.

 Chicken Soup and Rice by Maurice Sendak. Scholastic Inc., New York, 1962.

> *Sam's Sandwich* by David Pelham. Dutton Children's Books, White Heat Ltd., New Mexico, 1990.

The Gingerbread Boy by Paul Galdone. The Seaburg Press, New York, 1975.

 The Doorbell Rang by Pat Hutchins. Greenwillow Books, New York, 1986.

Soup Should Be Seen, Not Heard by Beth Brainard and Sheila Behr. Dell Publishing Co., New York, 1988.

Bread and Jam for Frances by Russell Hoban. Scholastic Inc., New York, 1964.